WRITER:
Aron E. Coleite
PENCILERS:
Mark Brooks
& Clay Mann (Issue #95)
INKERS:
Jaime Mendoza
& Carlos Cuevas (Issue #95)
with Troy Hubbs (Issue #94)
ADDITIONAL ART (ISSUES #95-96):
Brandon Peterson

COLORS:
Edgar Delgado
LETTERS:
Comicraft's Albert Deschesne
COVER ARTIST:
Gabriele Dell'Otto
ASSISTANT EDITOR:
Lauren Sankovitch
EDITOR:
Bill Rosemann
SENIOR EDITOR:
Ralph Macchio

COLLECTION EDITOR:
Jennifer Grünwald
EDITORIAL ASSISTANT:
Alex Starbuck
ASSISTANT EDITORS:
Cory Levine & John Denning
EDITOR, SPECIAL PROJECTS:
Mark D. Beazley
SENIOR EDITOR,
SPECIAL PROJECTS:
Jeff Youngquist

SENIOR VICE
PRESIDENT OF SALES:
David Gabriel
PRODUCTION:
Jerry Kalinowski
VICE PRESIDENT OF CREATIVE:
Tom Marvelli

EDITOR IN CHIEF:
Joe Quesada
PUBLISHER:
Dan Buckley

PREVIOUSLY IN

PREVIOUSLY IN
ULTIMATE X-MEN

In the aftermath of the X-Men's vicious battle with Apocalypse and the crazed mutant's fiery demise at the hands of the Phoenix, Professor Xavier has gone to Muir Island to recuperate, while the mutants of Xavier's School regroup at the mansion. Former students have returned and several new faces are now trying to keep the Professor's dream alive.

The mystery of Jean Grey's possession by the Phoenix entity has only deepened as she has unexpectedly returned to the mansion after vanishing in the wake of Apocalypse's end.

The X-Men have gone back to basics. Danger Room sessions, training and softball games — trying to discover what it means to be a hero. But the closely guarded secret of one X-Man is soon to have catastrophic consequences for all of their lives.

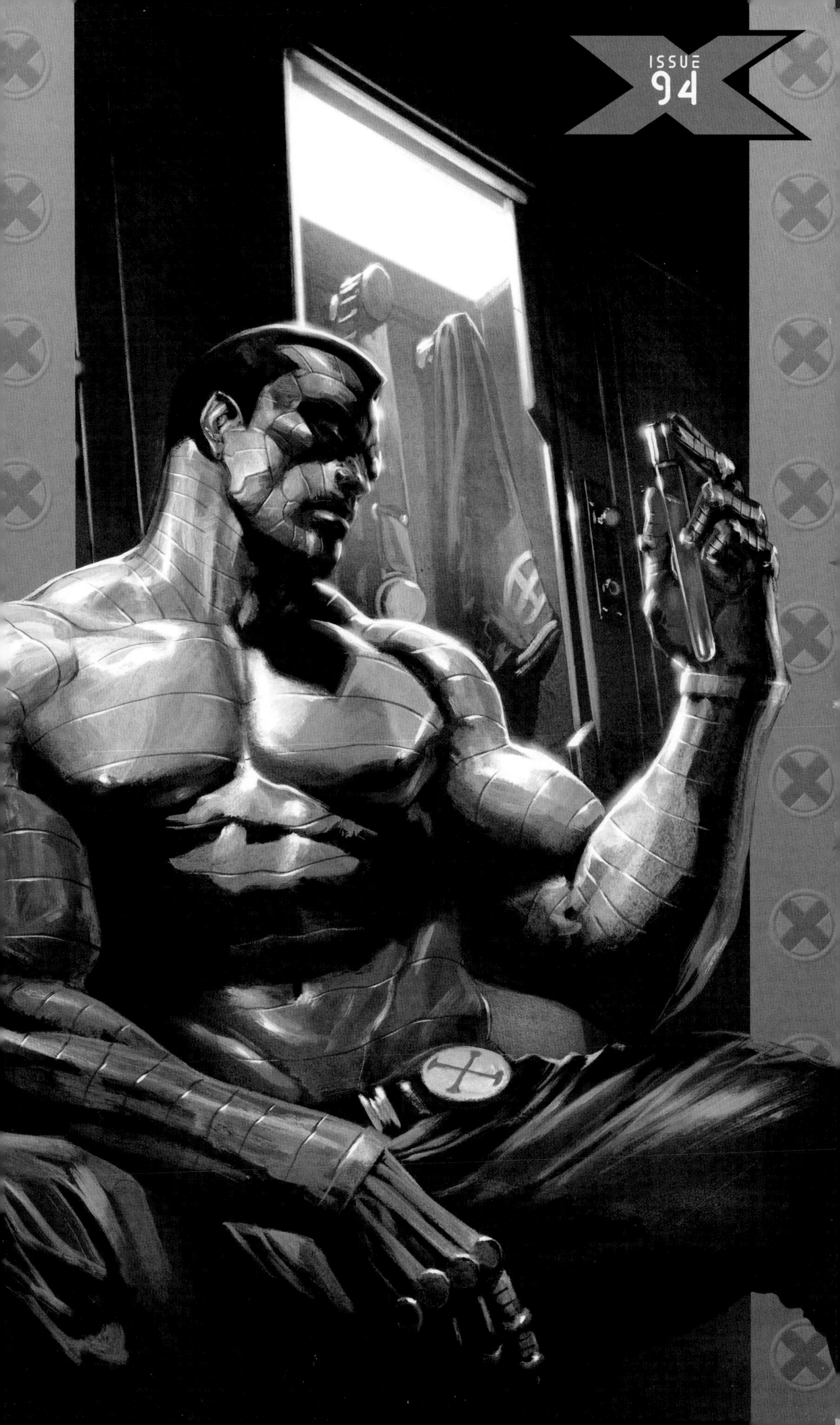
ISSUE
94

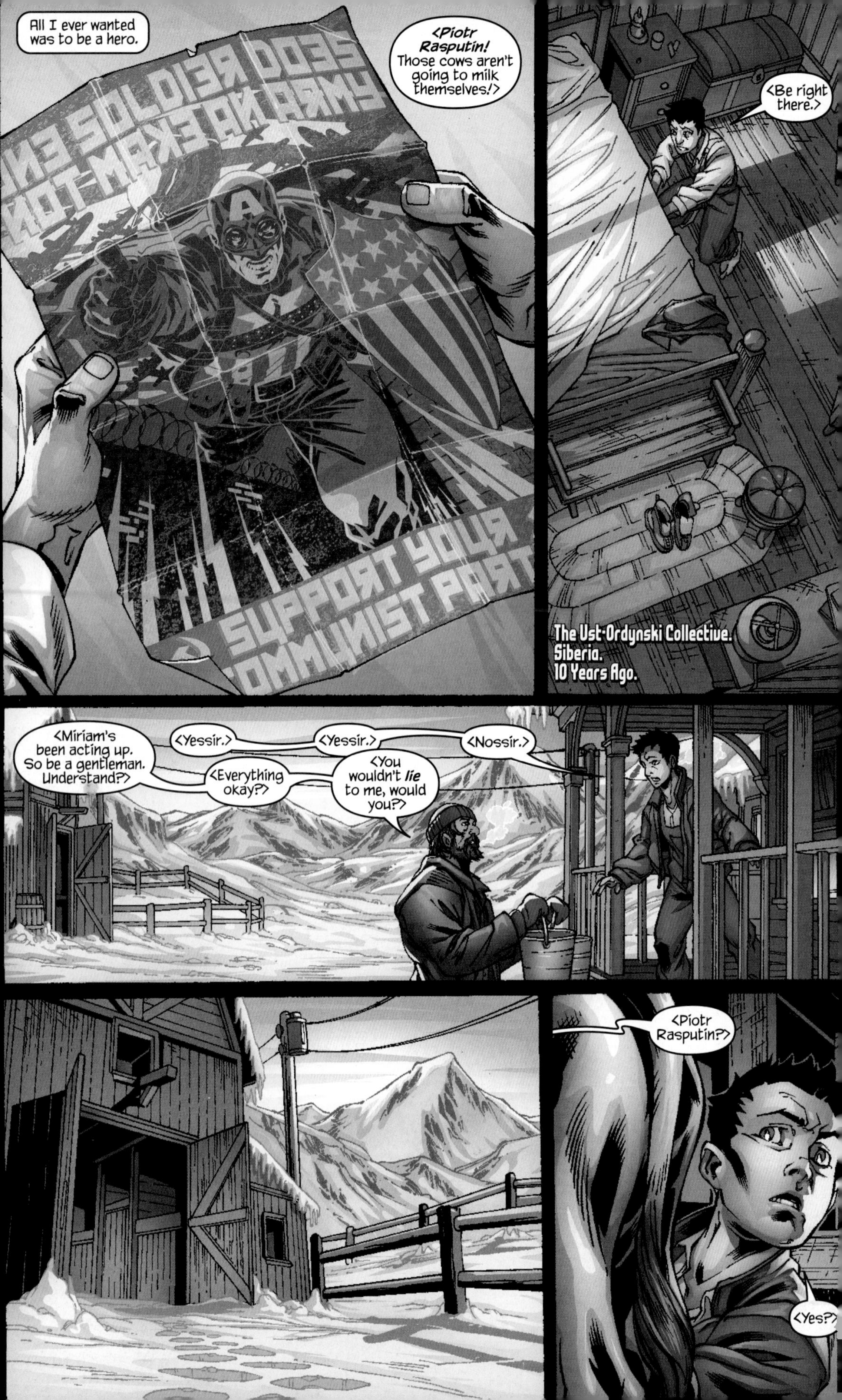
All I ever wanted was to be a hero.
<Piotr Rasputin! Those cows aren't going to milk themselves!>
SUPPORT YOUR COMMUNIST PART
<Be right there.>
The Ust-Ordynski Collective.
Siberia.
10 Years Ago.
<Miriam's been acting up. So be a gentleman. Understand?>
<Yessir.>
<Everything okay?>
<Yessir.>
<You wouldn't *lie* to me, would you?>
<Nossir.>
<Piotr Rasputin?>
<Yes?>

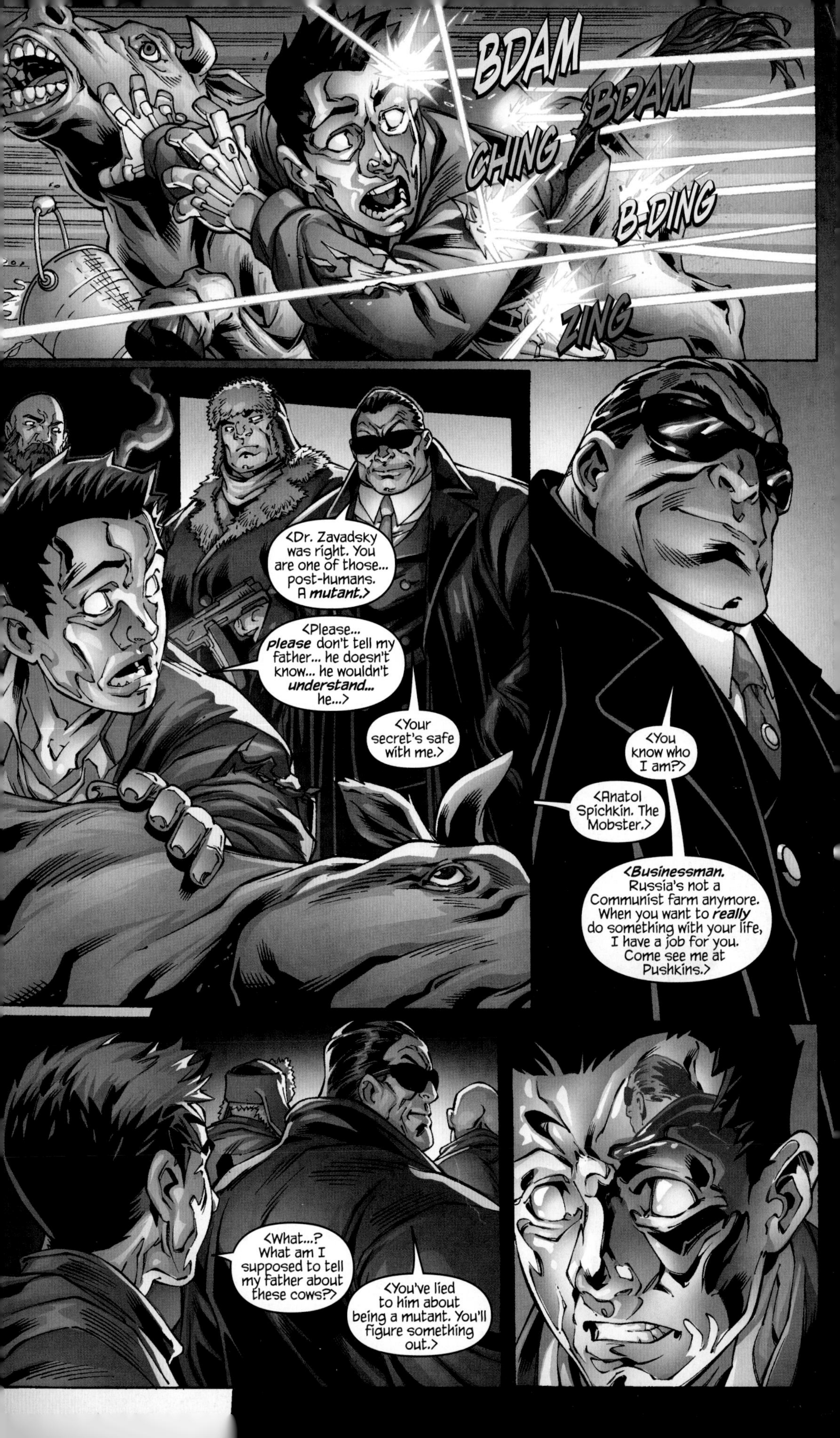
BDAM
BDAM
CHING
B-DING
ZING
<Dr. Zavadsky was right. You are one of those... post-humans. A *mutant.*>
<Please... *please* don't tell my father... he doesn't know... he wouldn't *understand...* he...>
<Your secret's safe with me.>
<You know who I am?>
<Anatol Spichkin. The Mobster.>
<*Businessman.* Russia's not a Communist farm anymore. When you want to *really* do something with your life, I have a job for you. Come see me at Pushkins.>
<What...? What am I supposed to tell my father about these cows?>
<You've lied to him about being a mutant. You'll figure something out.>

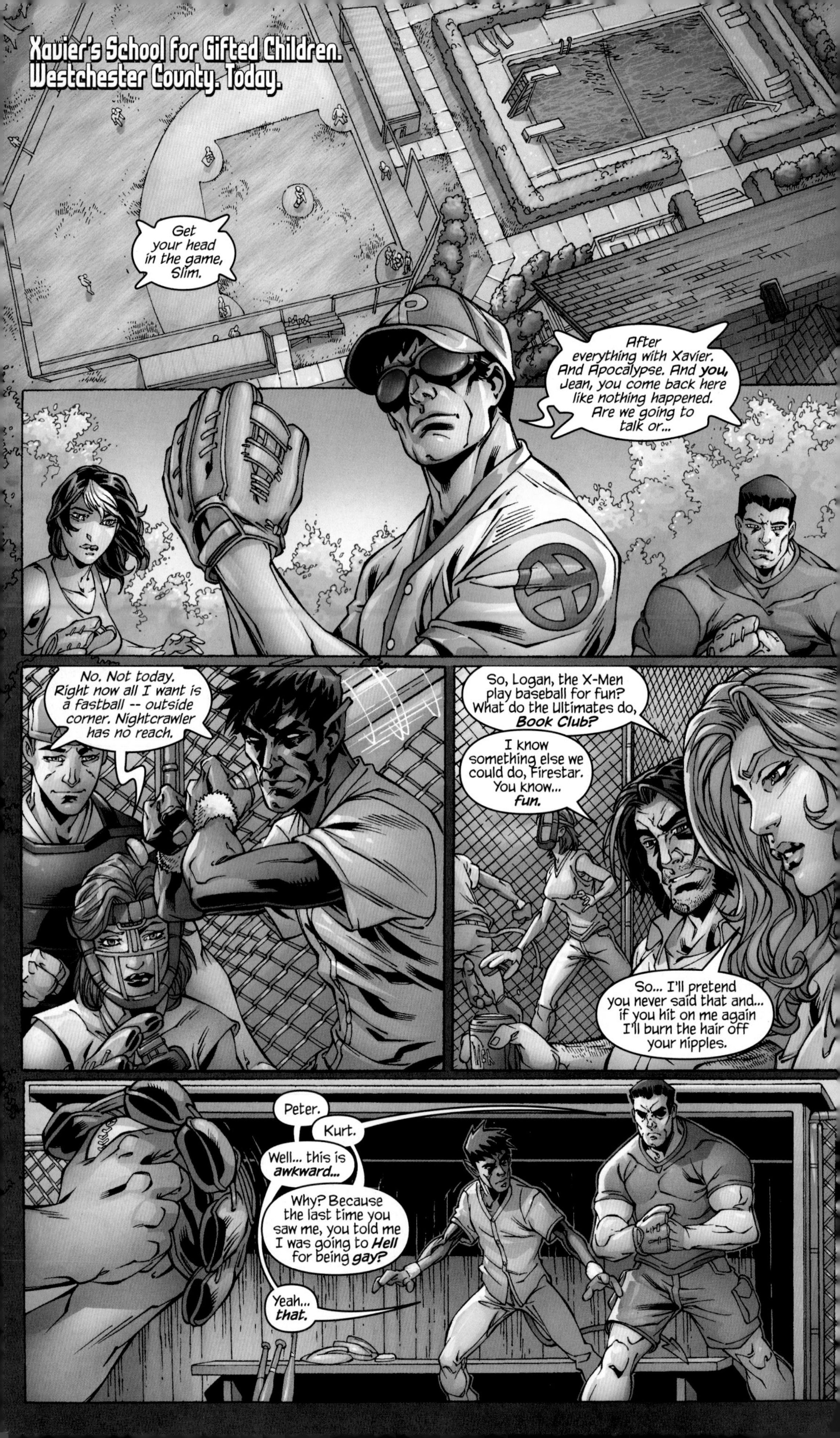
Xavier's School for Gifted Children.
Westchester County. Today.
Get your head in the game, Slim.
After everything with Xavier. And Apocalypse. And **you,** Jean, you come back here like nothing happened. Are we going to talk or...
No. Not today. Right now all I want is a fastball -- outside corner. Nightcrawler has no reach.
So, Logan, the X-Men play baseball for fun? What do the Ultimates do, ***Book Club?***
I know something else we could do, Firestar. You know... ***fun.***
So... I'll pretend you never said that and... if you hit on me again I'll burn the hair off your nipples.
Peter.
Kurt.
Well... this is ***awkward...***
Why? Because the last time you saw me, you told me I was going to ***Hell*** for being ***gay?***
Yeah... ***that.***

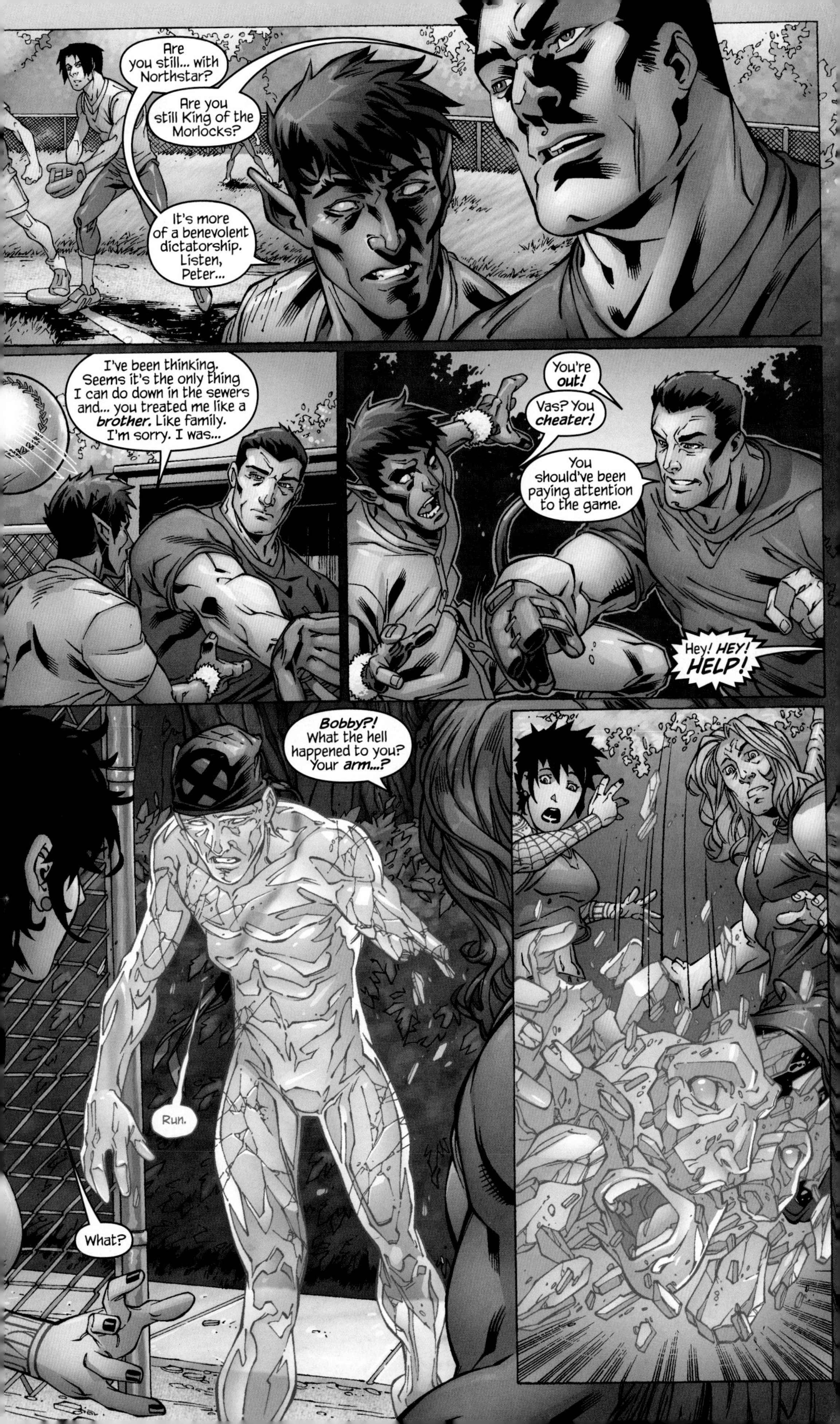
Are you still... with Northstar?
Are you still King of the Morlocks?
It's more of a benevolent dictatorship. Listen, Peter...
I've been thinking. Seems it's the only thing I can do down in the sewers and... you treated me like a *brother.* Like family. I'm sorry. I was...
You're *out!*
Vas? You *cheater!*
You should've been paying attention to the game.
Hey! *HEY! HELP!*
Bobby?! What the hell happened to you? Your *arm...?*
Run.
What?

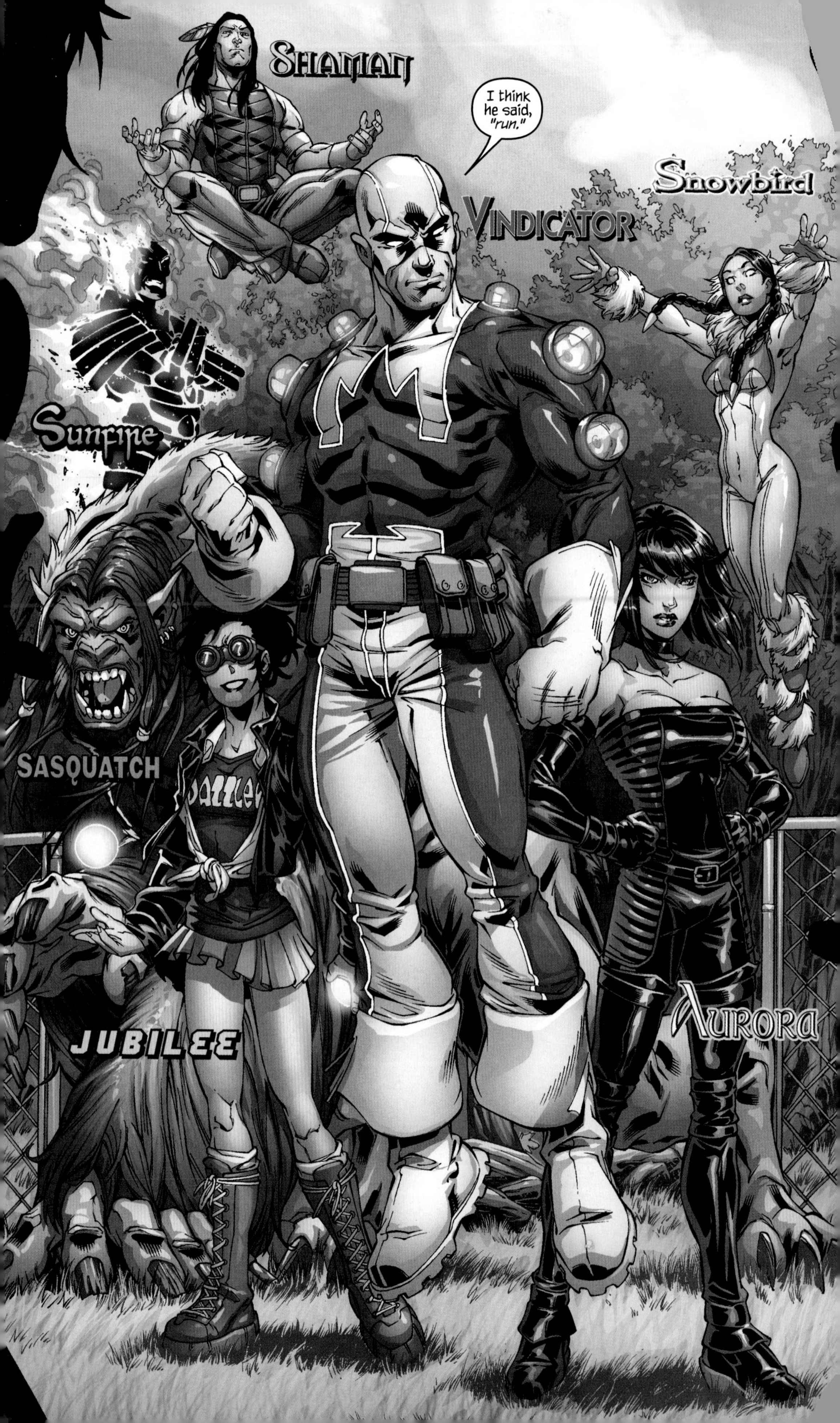
SHAMAN
I think he said, "run."
Snowbird
VINDICATOR
Sunfire
SASQUATCH
JUBILEE
AURORA

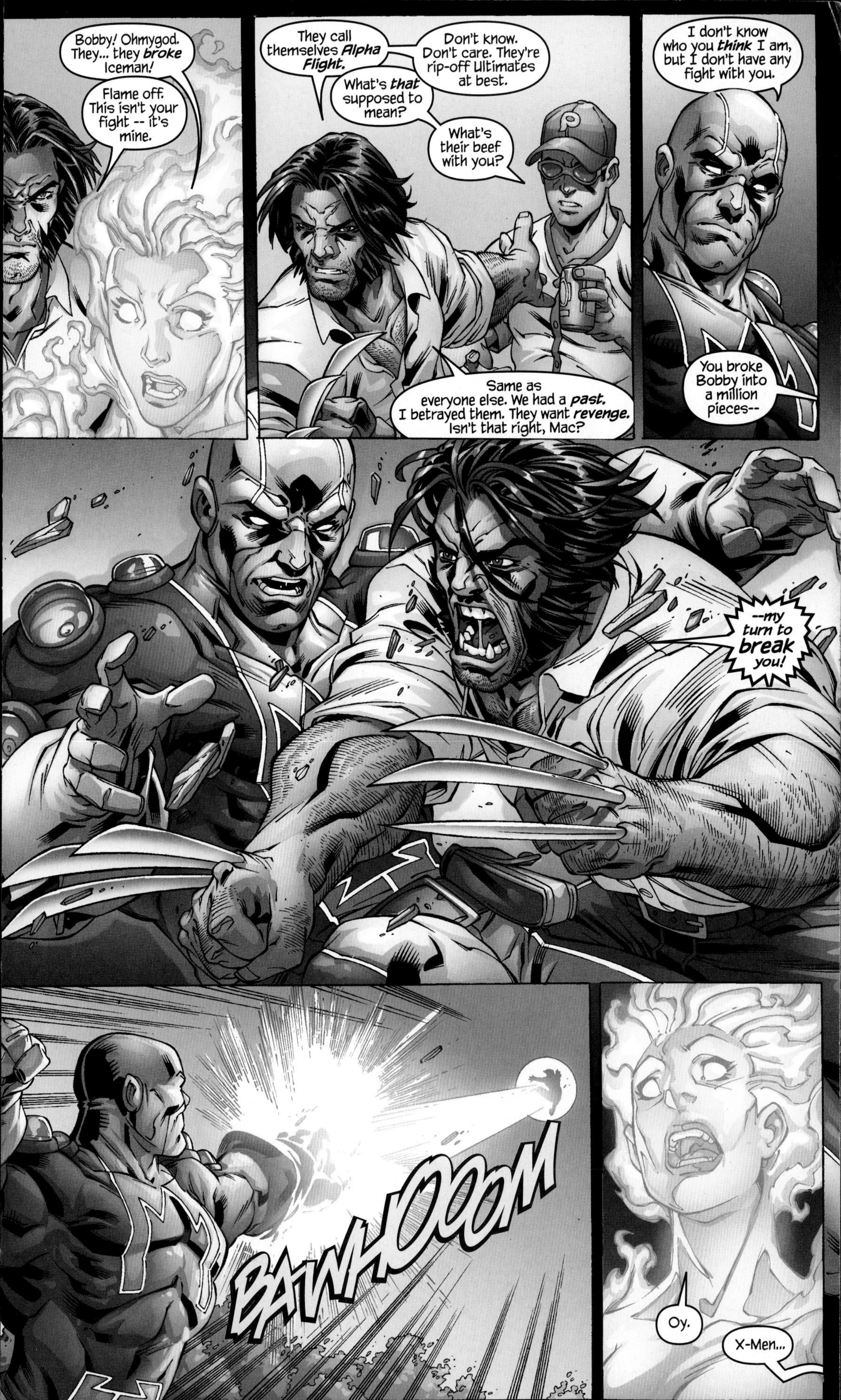

Bobby! Ohmygod. They... they *broke* Iceman!
Flame off. This isn't your fight -- it's mine.
They call themselves *Alpha Flight.*
Don't know. Don't care. They're rip-off Ultimates at best.
What's *that* supposed to mean?
What's their beef with you?
Same as everyone else. We had a *past.* I betrayed them. They want *revenge.* Isn't that right, Mac?
I don't know who you *think* I am, but I don't have any fight with you.
You broke Bobby into a million pieces--
--my turn to **break** you!
BAWHOOOOM
Oy.
X-Men...

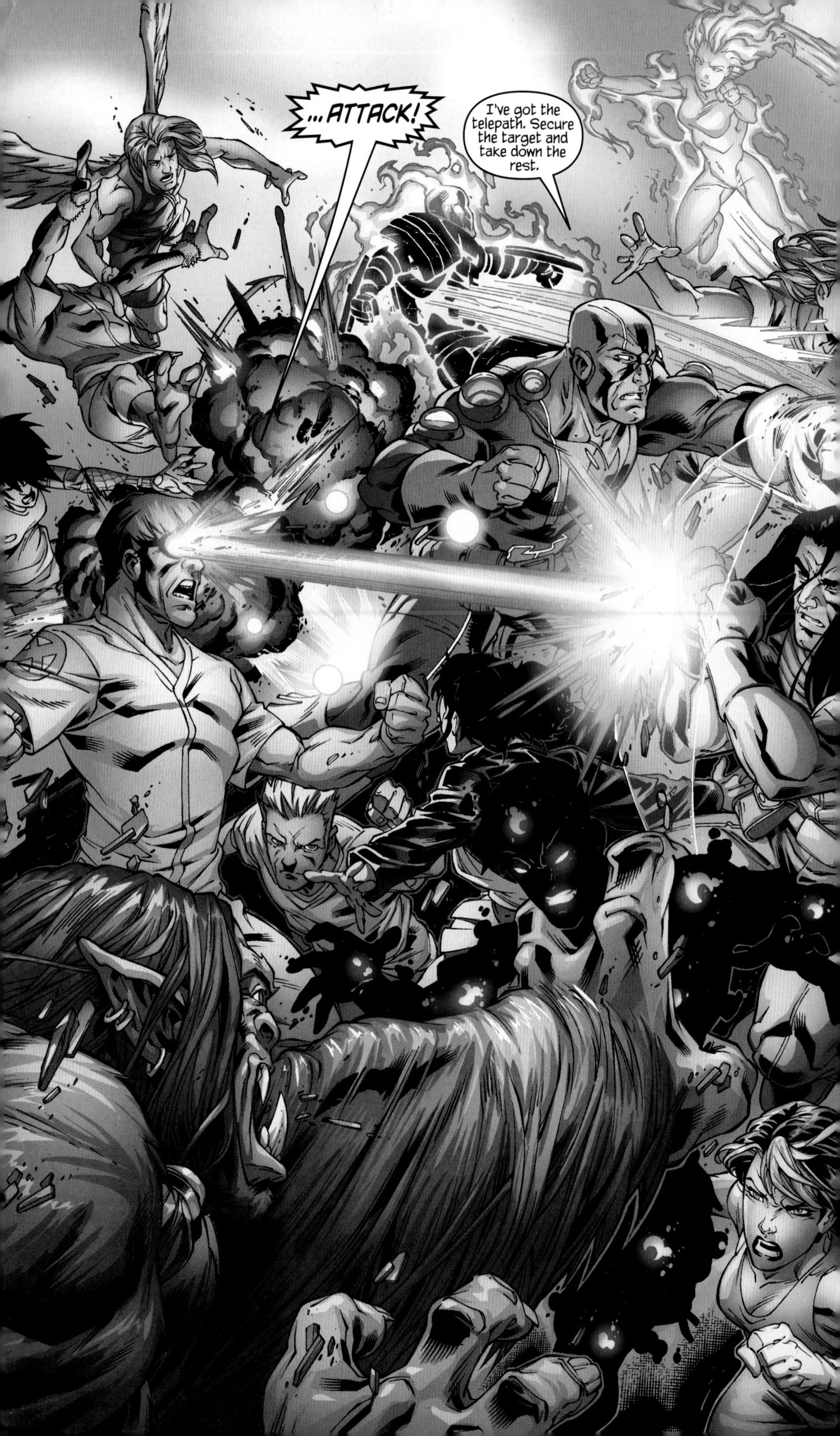
...ATTACK!
I've got the telepath. Secure the target and take down the rest.

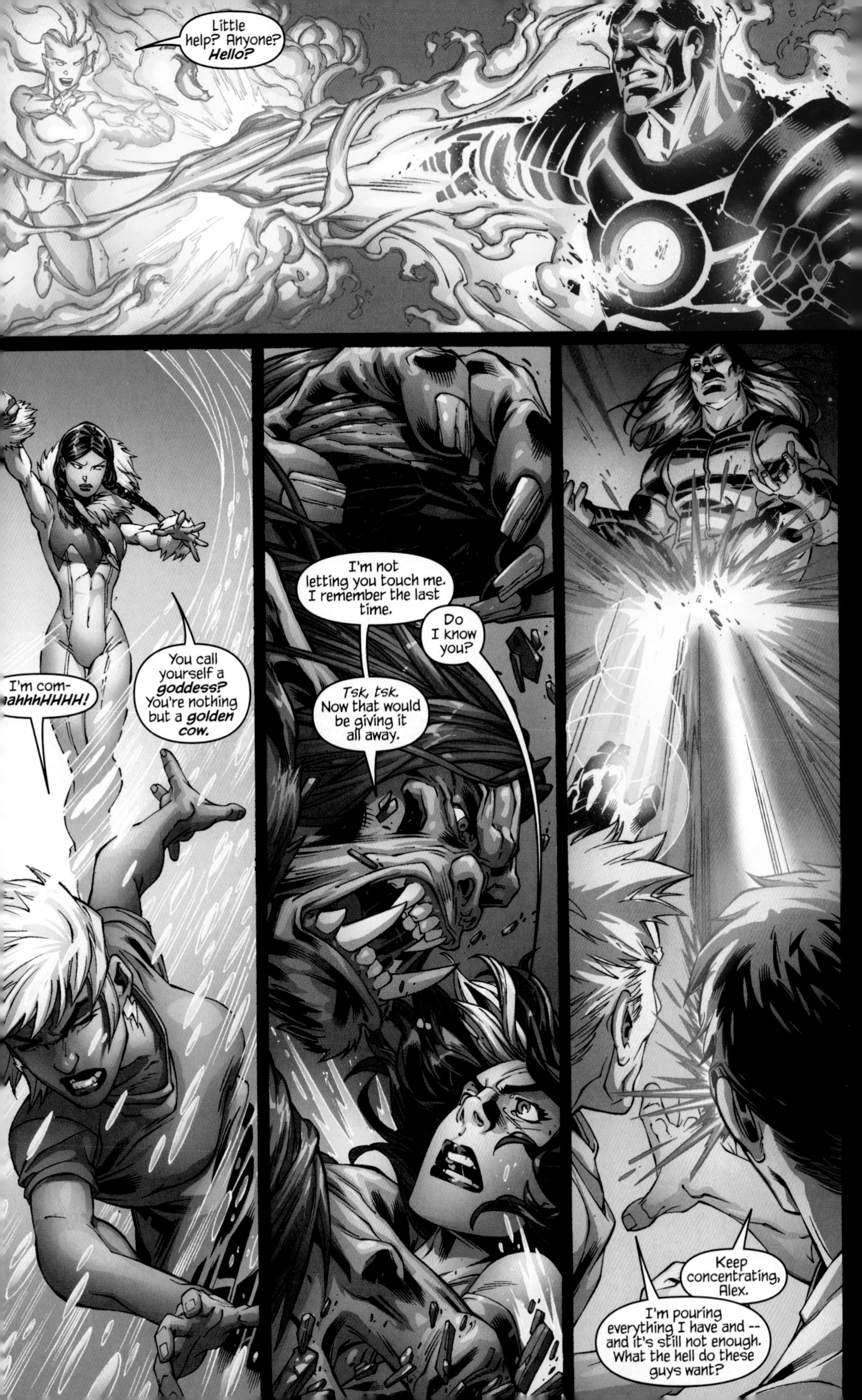

Little help? Anyone? *Hello?*
I'm com-ahhhhHHHH!
You call yourself a *goddess?* You're nothing but a *golden cow.*
I'm not letting you touch me. I remember the last time.
Do I know you?
Tsk, tsk. Now that would be *giving* it all away.
Keep concentrating, Alex.
I'm pouring everything I have and -- and it's still not enough. What the hell do these guys want?

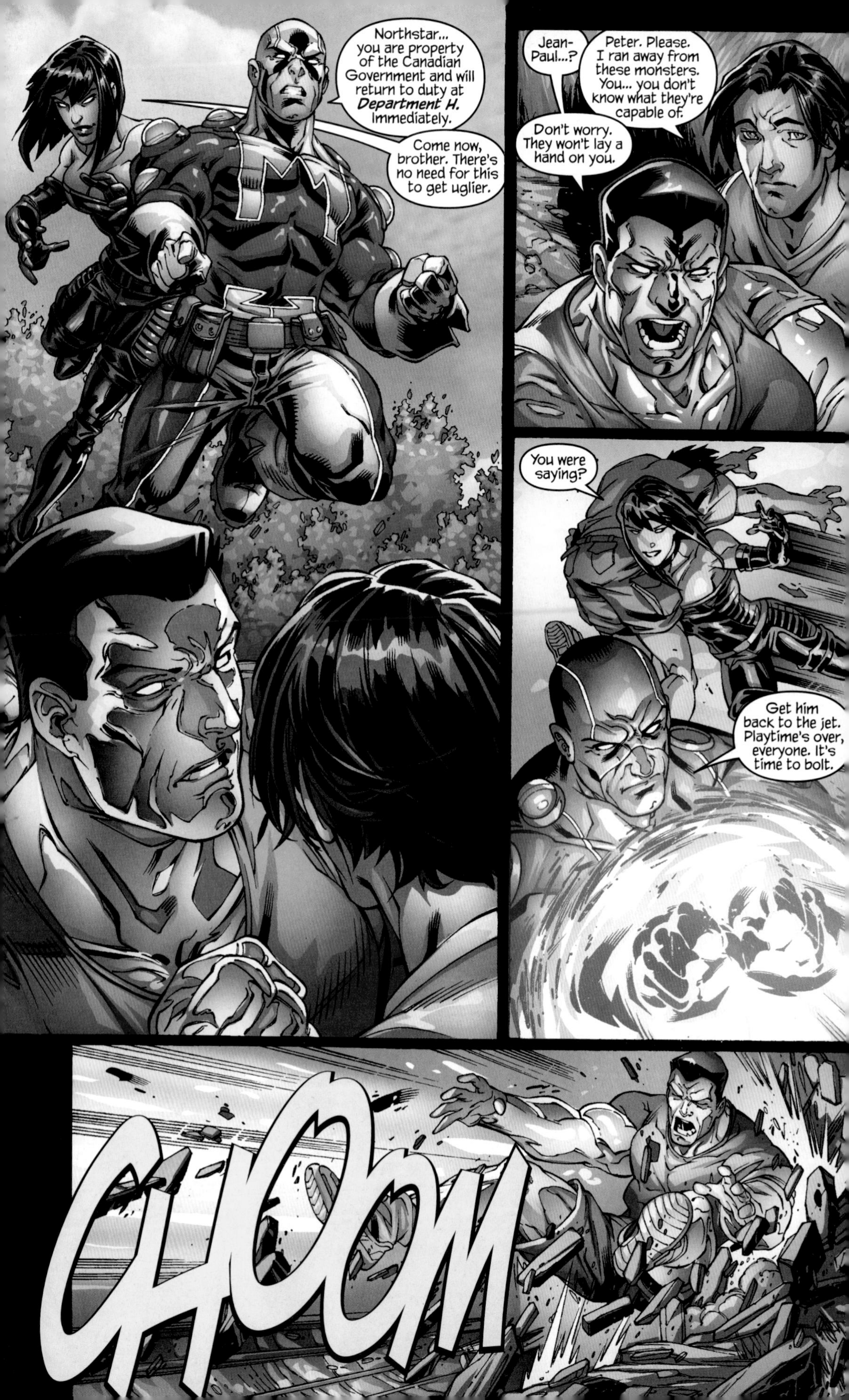
Northstar... you are property of the Canadian Government and will return to duty at *Department H.* Immediately.
Come now, brother. There's no need for this to get uglier.
Jean-Paul...?
Peter. Please. I ran away from these monsters. You... you don't know what they're capable of.
Don't worry. They won't lay a hand on you.
You were saying?
Get him back to the jet. Playtime's over, everyone. It's time to bolt.
CHOOM

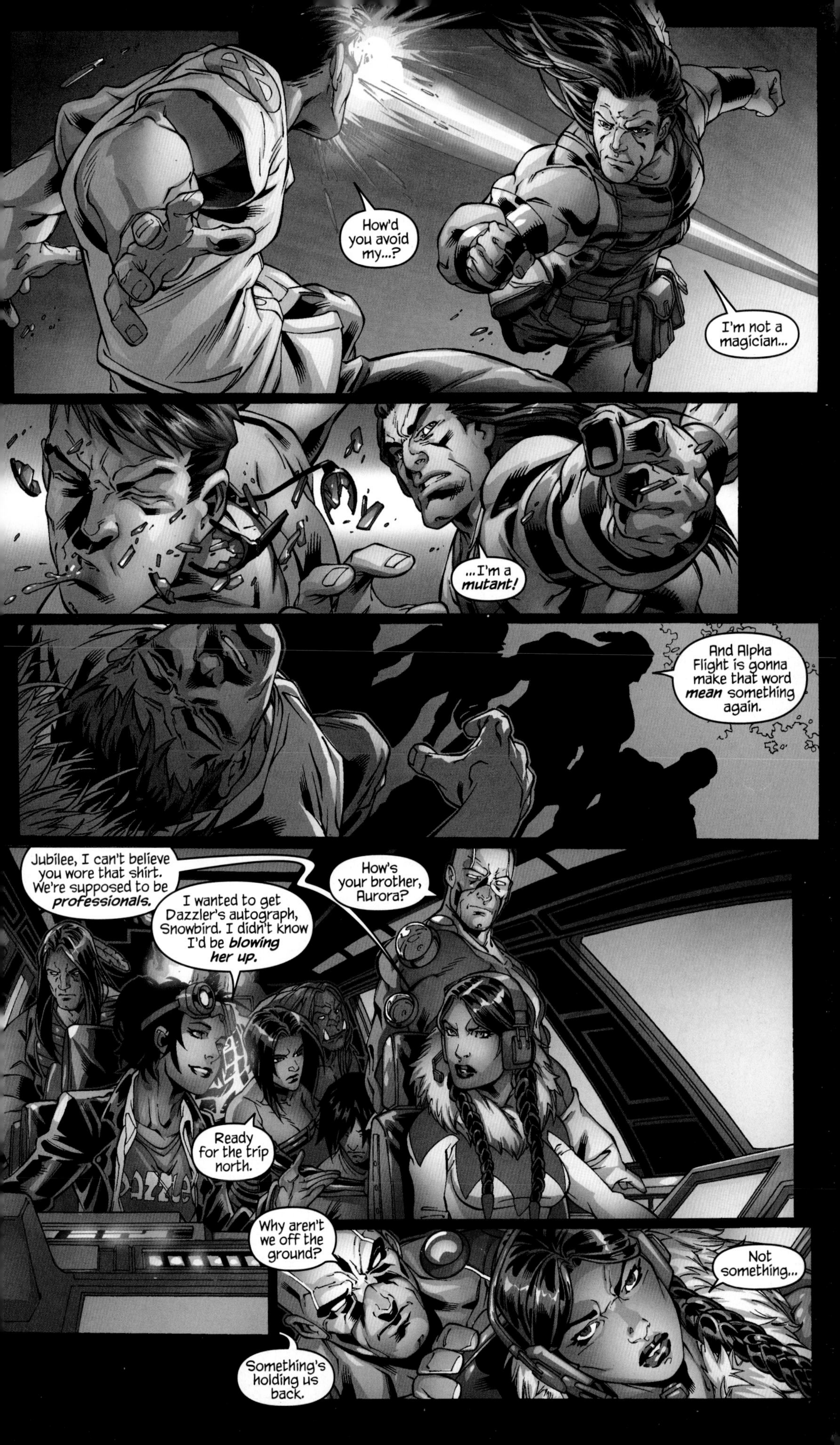
How'd you avoid my...?
I'm not a magician...
...I'm a *mutant!*
And Alpha Flight is gonna make that word *mean* something again.
Jubilee, I can't believe you wore that shirt. We're supposed to be *professionals.*
I wanted to get Dazzler's autograph, Snowbird. I didn't know I'd be *blowing her up.*
How's your brother, Aurora?
Ready for the trip north.
Dazzler
Why aren't we off the ground?
Not something...
Something's holding us back.

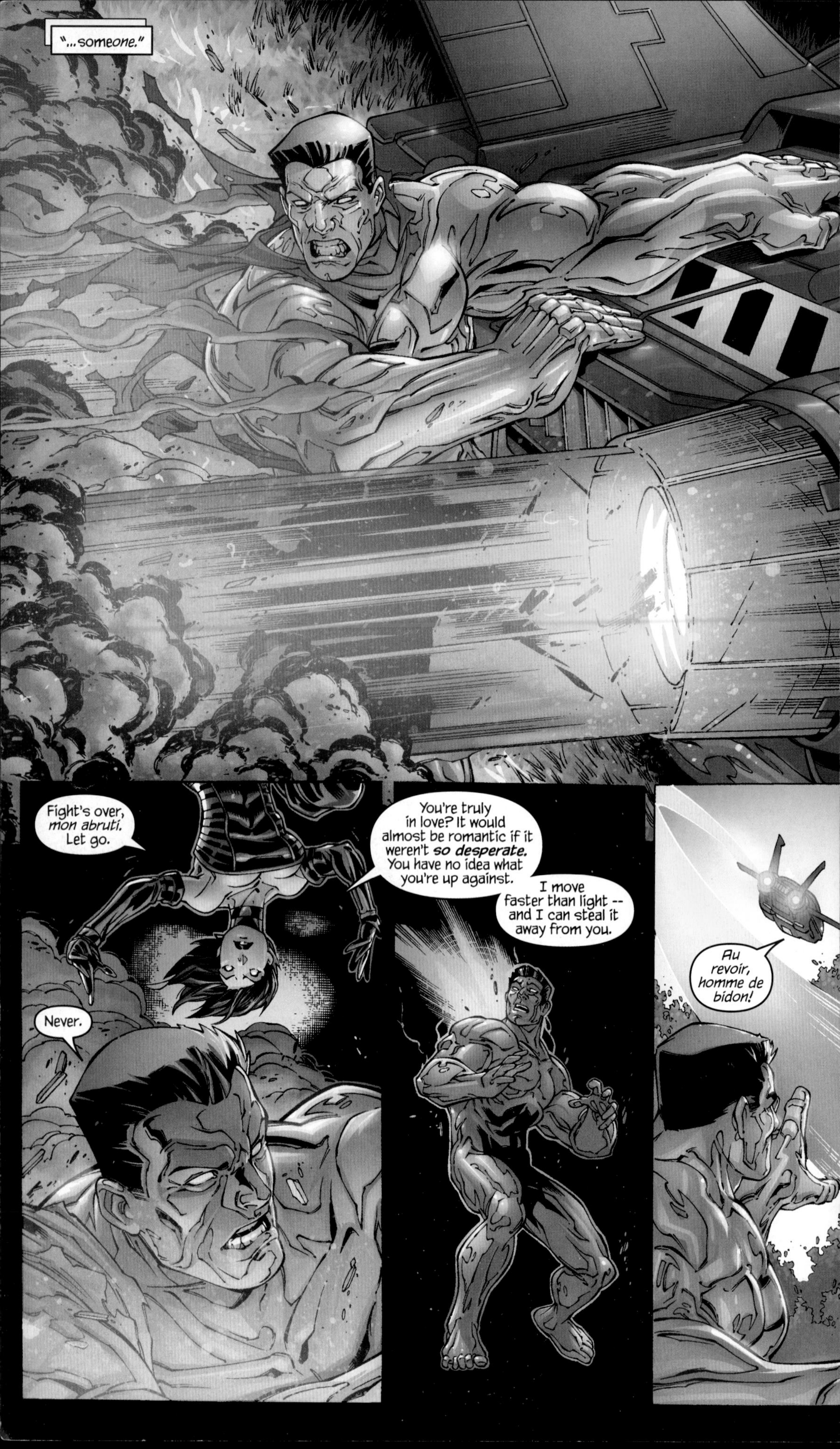

"...someone."
Fight's over, *mon abruti.* Let go.
Never.
You're truly in love? It would almost be romantic if it weren't ***so desperate.*** You have no idea what you're up against.
I move faster than light -- and I can steal it away from you.
Au revoir, homme de bidon!

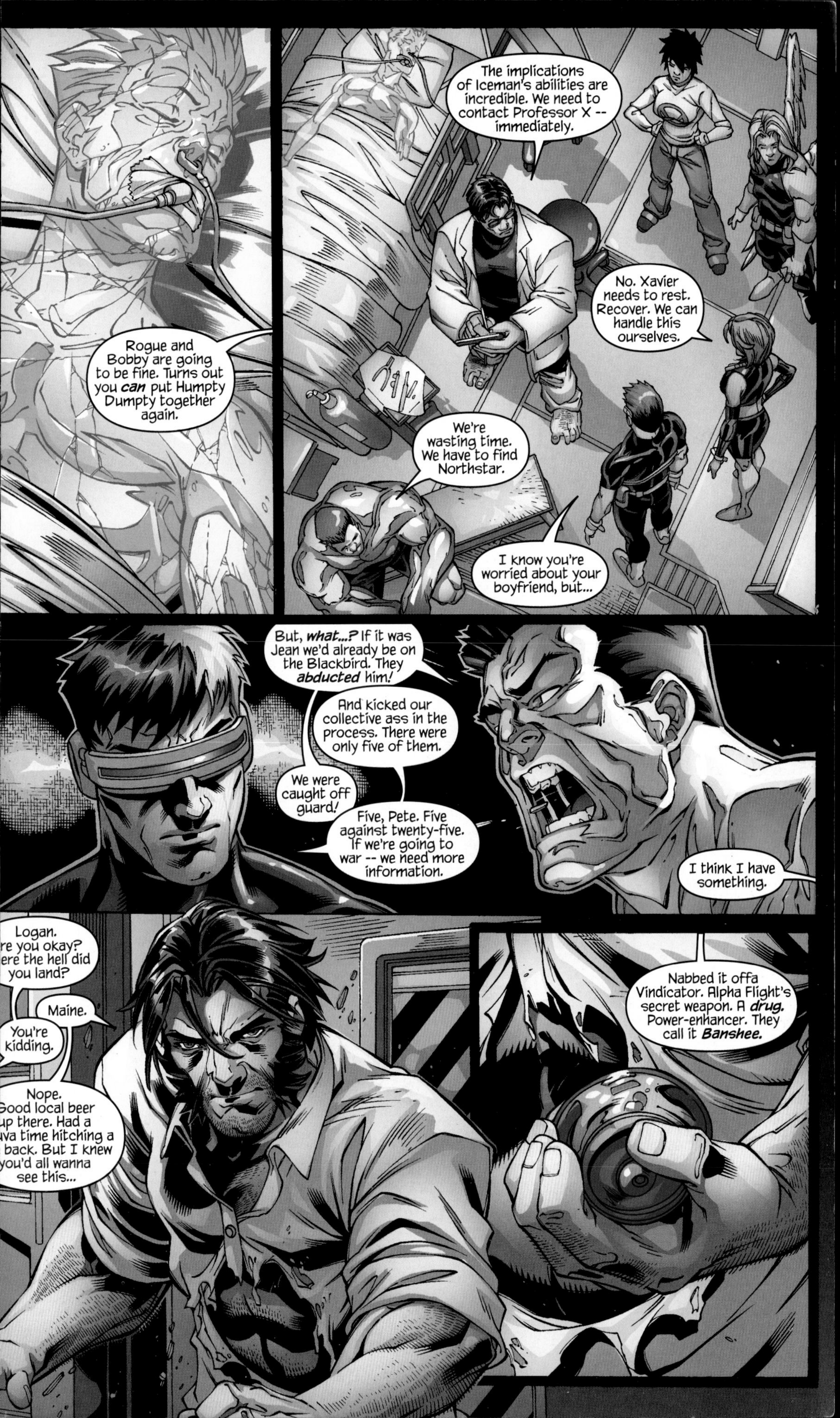
Rogue and Bobby are going to be fine. Turns out you *can* put Humpty Dumpty together again.
The implications of Iceman's abilities are incredible. We need to contact Professor X -- immediately.
No. Xavier needs to rest. Recover. We can handle this ourselves.
We're wasting time. We have to find Northstar.
I know you're worried about your boyfriend, but...
But, *what...?* If it was Jean we'd already be on the Blackbird. They *abducted* him!
And kicked our collective ass in the process. There were only five of them.
We were caught off guard!
Five, Pete. Five against twenty-five. If we're going to war -- we need more information.
I think I have something.
Logan. re you okay? ere the hell did you land?
Maine.
You're kidding.
Nope. Good local beer up there. Had a uva time hitching a back. But I knew you'd all wanna see this...
Nabbed it offa Vindicator. Alpha Flight's secret weapon. A *drug.* Power-enhancer. They call it *Banshee.*

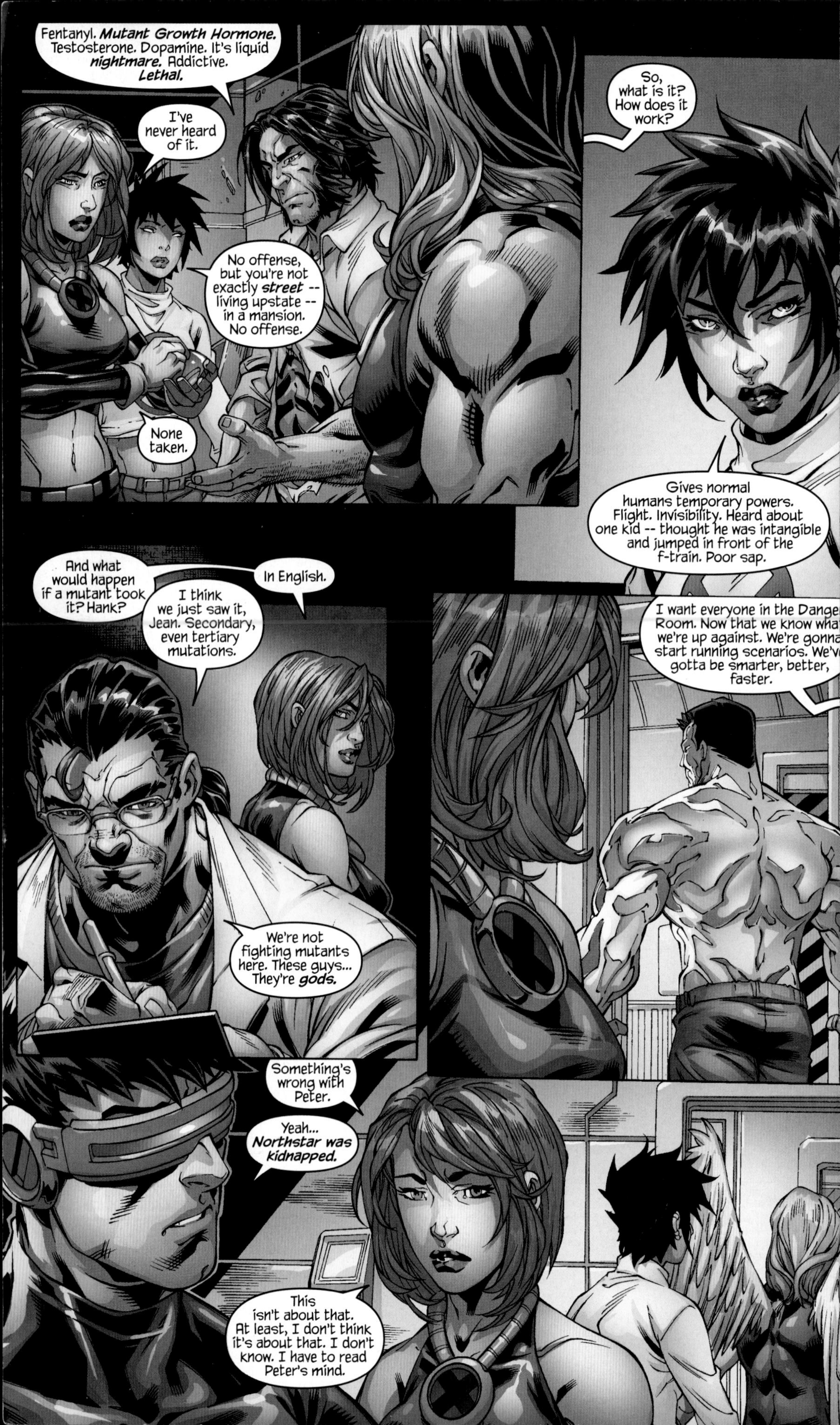

Fentanyl. Mutant Growth Hormone. Testosterone. Dopamine. It's liquid nightmare. Addictive. Lethal.
I've never heard of it.
No offense, but you're not exactly street -- living upstate -- in a mansion. No offense.
None taken.
So, what is it? How does it work?
Gives normal humans temporary powers. Flight. Invisibility. Heard about one kid -- thought he was intangible and jumped in front of the f-train. Poor sap.
And what would happen if a mutant took it? Hank?
In English.
I think we just saw it, Jean. Secondary, even tertiary mutations.
We're not fighting mutants here. These guys... They're gods.
I want everyone in the Dange Room. Now that we know wha we're up against. We're gonna start running scenarios. We'v gotta be smarter, better, faster.
Something's wrong with Peter.
Yeah... Northstar was kidnapped.
This isn't about that. At least, I don't think it's about that. I don't know. I have to read Peter's mind.

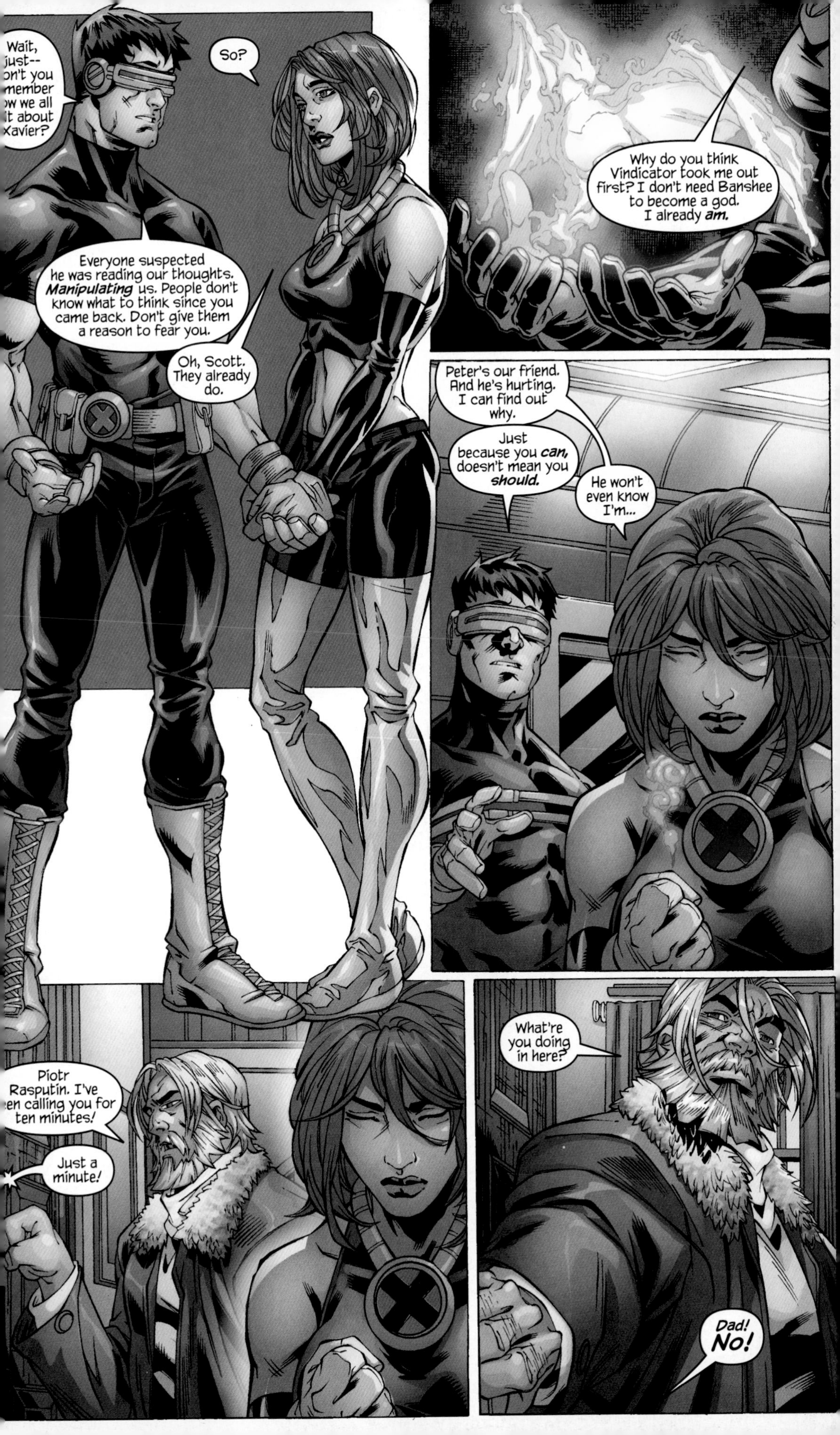

Wait, just-- on't you member ow we all it about Xavier?
So?
Everyone suspected he was reading our thoughts. *Manipulating* us. People don't know what to think since you came back. Don't give them a reason to fear you.
Oh, Scott. They already do.
Why do you think Vindicator took me out first? I don't need Banshee to become a god. I already *am.*
Peter's our friend. And he's hurting. I can find out why.
Just because you *can,* doesn't mean you *should.*
He won't even know I'm...
Piotr Rasputin. I've en calling you for ten minutes!
Just a minute!
What're you doing in here?
Dad! No!

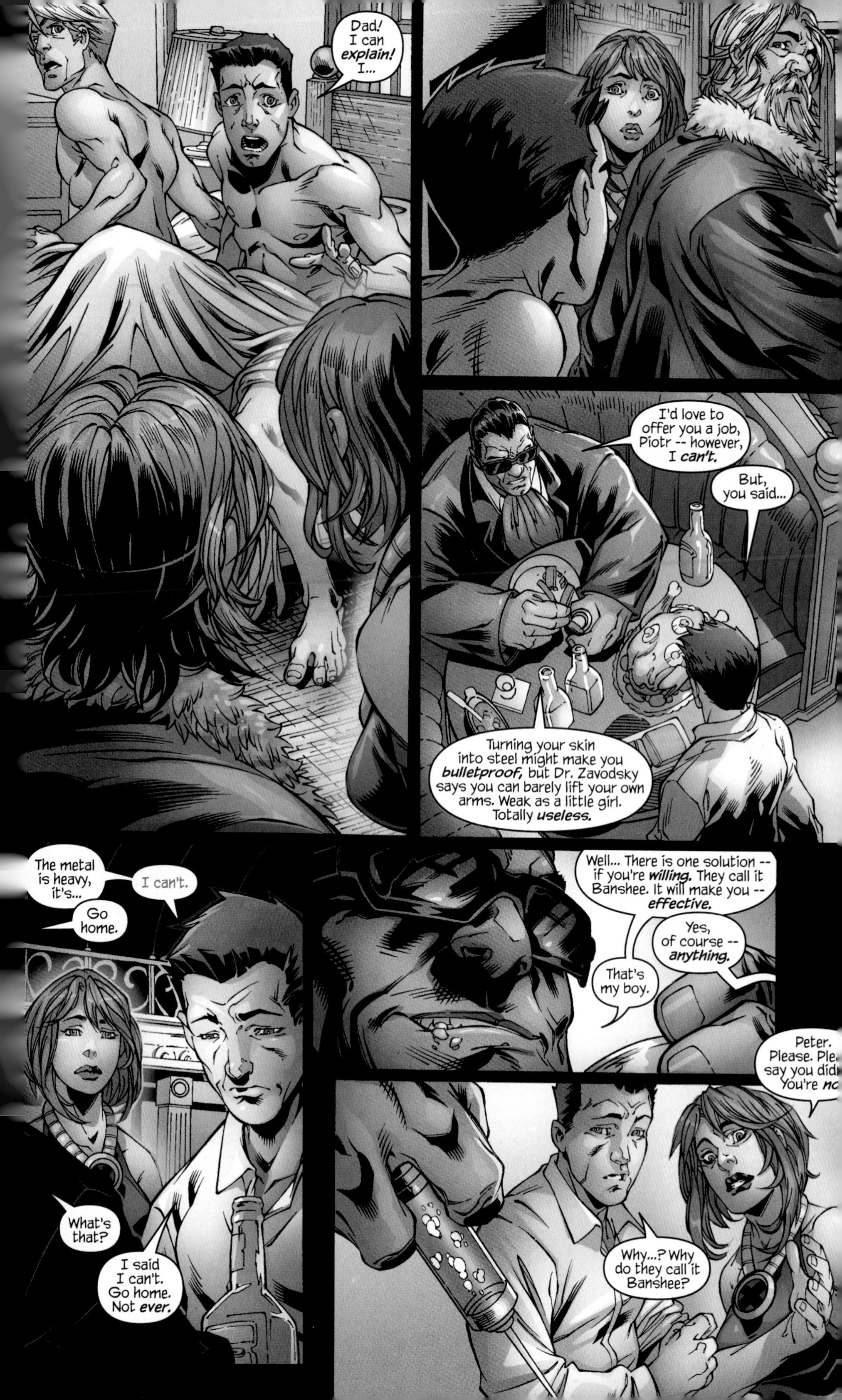
Dad! I can *explain!* I...
I'd love to offer you a job, Piotr -- however, I *can't.*
But, you said...
Turning your skin into steel might make you *bulletproof,* but Dr. Zavodsky says you can barely lift your own arms. Weak as a little girl. Totally *useless.*
The metal is heavy, it's...
I can't.
Go home.
What's that?
I said I can't. Go home. Not *ever.*
Well... There is one solution -- if you're *willing.* They call it Banshee. It will make you -- *effective.*
Yes, of course -- *anything.*
That's my boy.
Why...? Why do they call it Banshee?

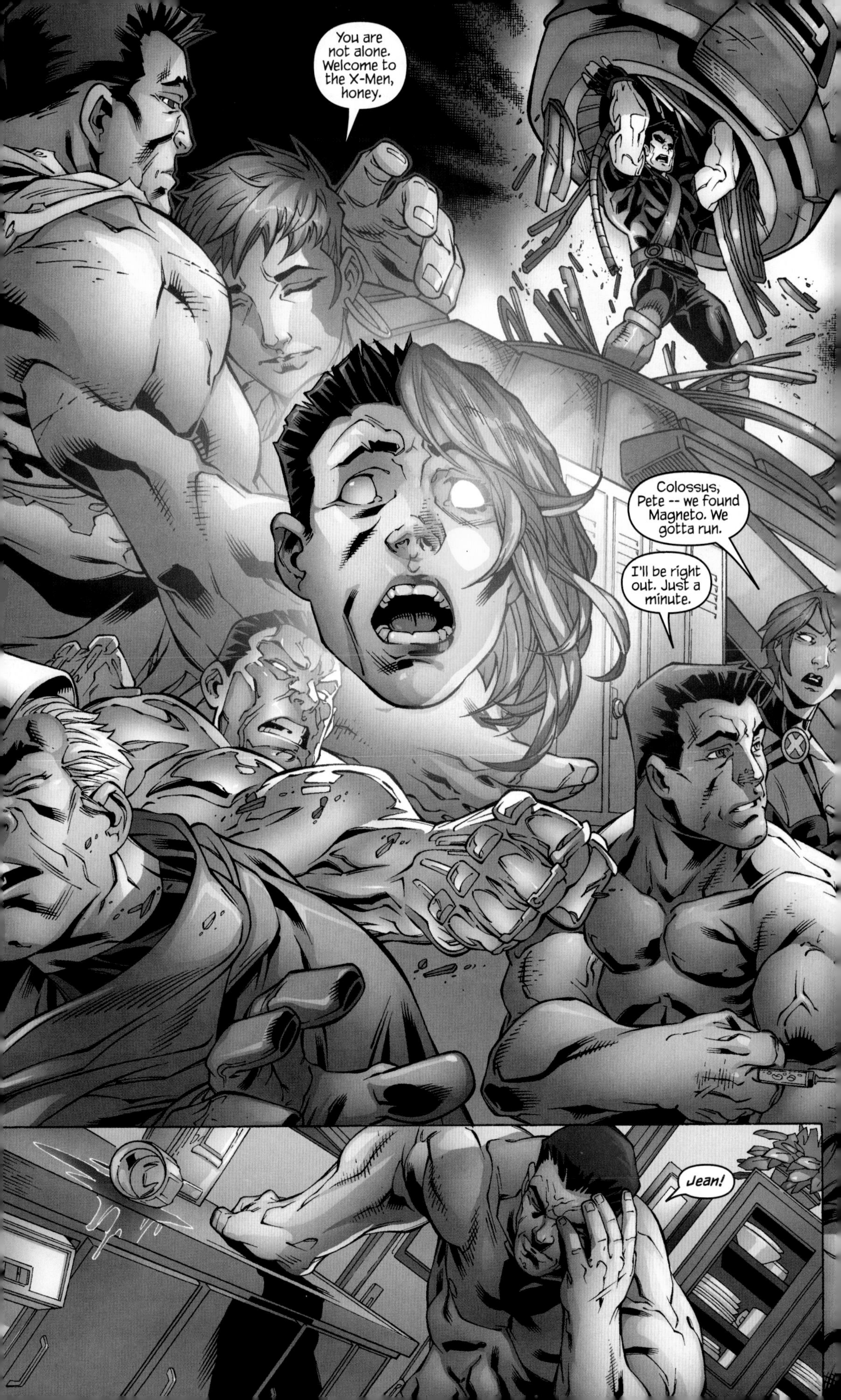
You are not alone. Welcome to the X-Men, honey.
Colossus, Pete -- we found Magneto. We gotta run.
I'll be right out. Just a minute.
Jean!

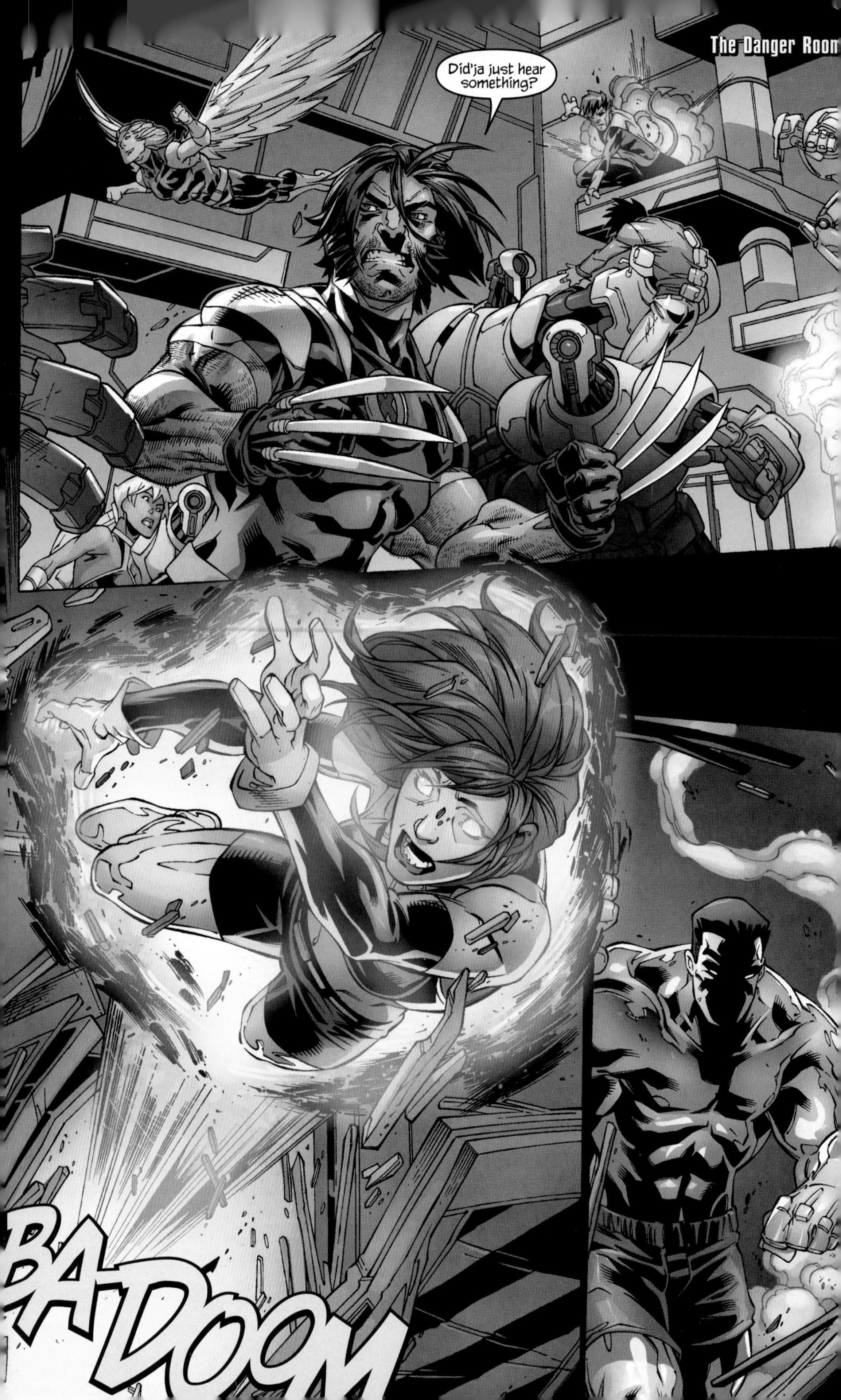
The Danger Room
Did'ja just hear something?
BADOOM

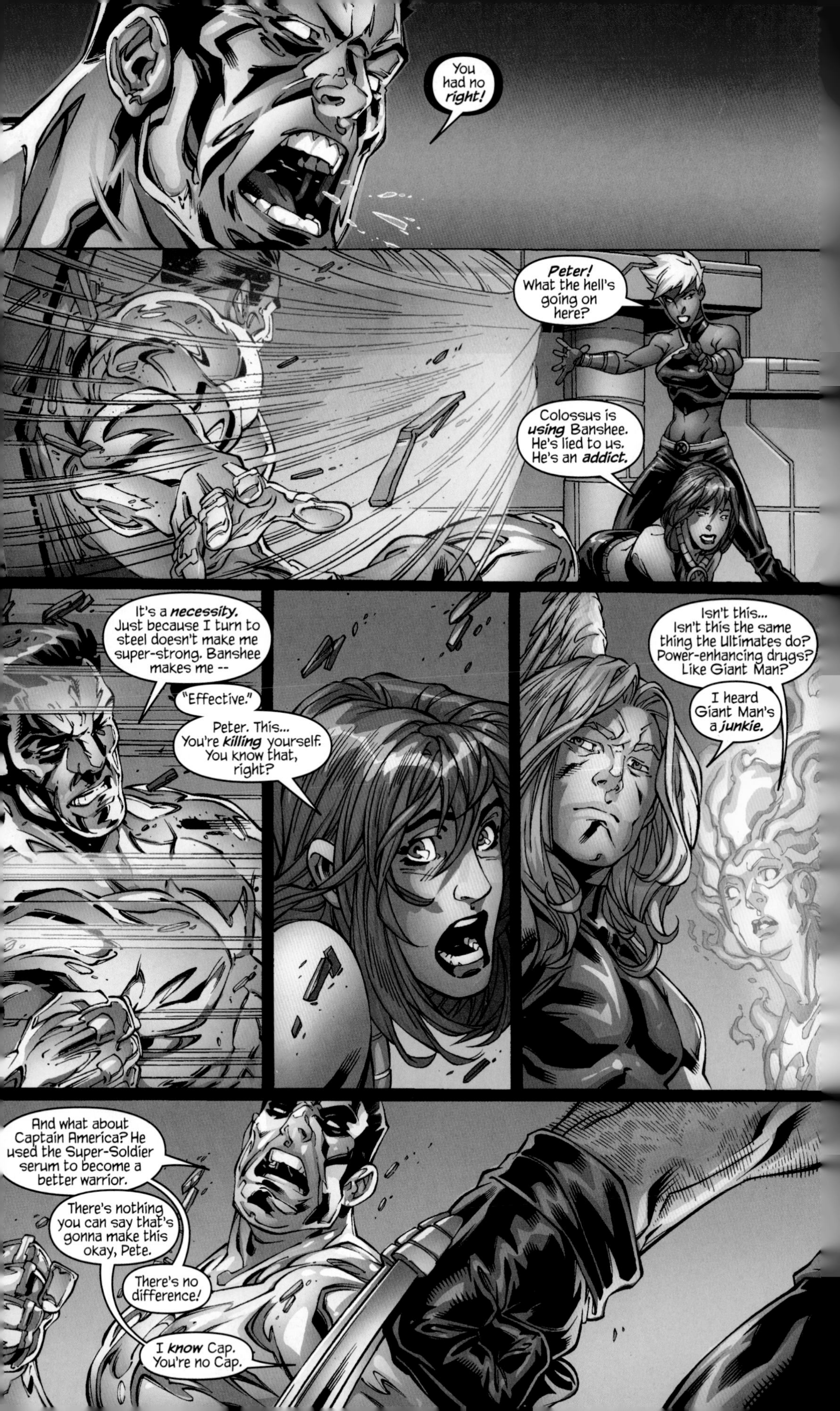

You had no right!
Peter! What the hell's going on here?
Colossus is using Banshee. He's lied to us. He's an addict.
It's a necessity. Just because I turn to steel doesn't make me super-strong. Banshee makes me --
"Effective."
Peter. This... You're killing yourself. You know that, right?
Isn't this... Isn't this the same thing the Ultimates do? Power-enhancing drugs? Like Giant Man?
I heard Giant Man's a junkie.
And what about Captain America? He used the Super-Soldier serum to become a better warrior.
There's nothing you can say that's gonna make this okay, Pete.
There's no difference!
I know Cap. You're no Cap.

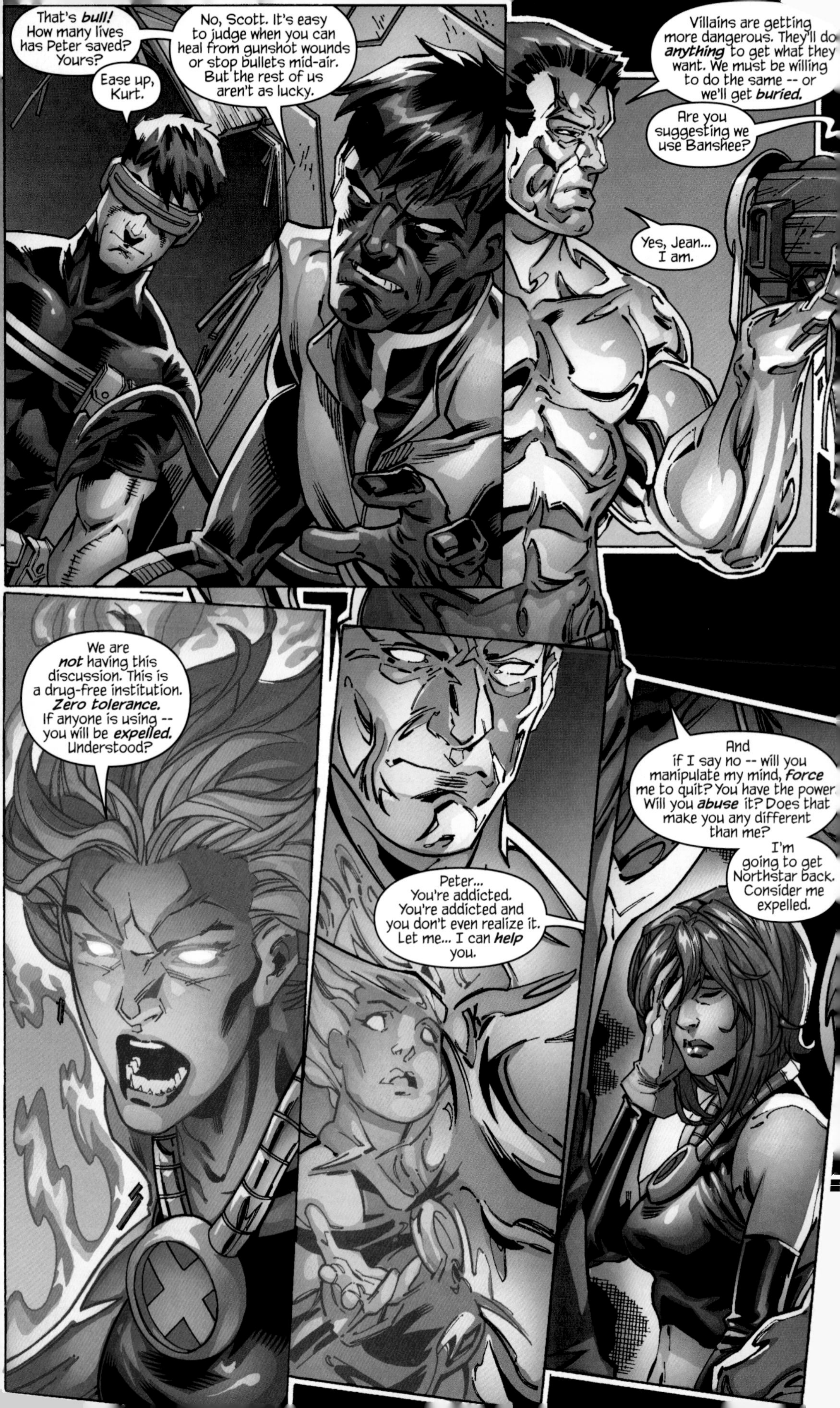

That's **bull!** How many lives has Peter saved? Yours?
Ease up, Kurt.
No, Scott. It's easy to judge when you can heal from gunshot wounds or stop bullets mid-air. But the rest of us aren't as lucky.
Villains are getting more dangerous. They'll do **anything** to get what they want. We must be willing to do the same -- or we'll get **buried.**
Are you suggesting we use Banshee?
Yes, Jean... I am.
We are **not** having this discussion. This is a drug-free institution. **Zero tolerance.** If anyone is using -- you will be **expelled.** Understood?
Peter... You're addicted. You're addicted and you don't even realize it. Let me... I can **help** you.
And if I say no -- will you manipulate my mind, **force** me to quit? You have the power Will you **abuse** it? Does that make you any different than me?
I'm going to get Northstar back. Consider me expelled.

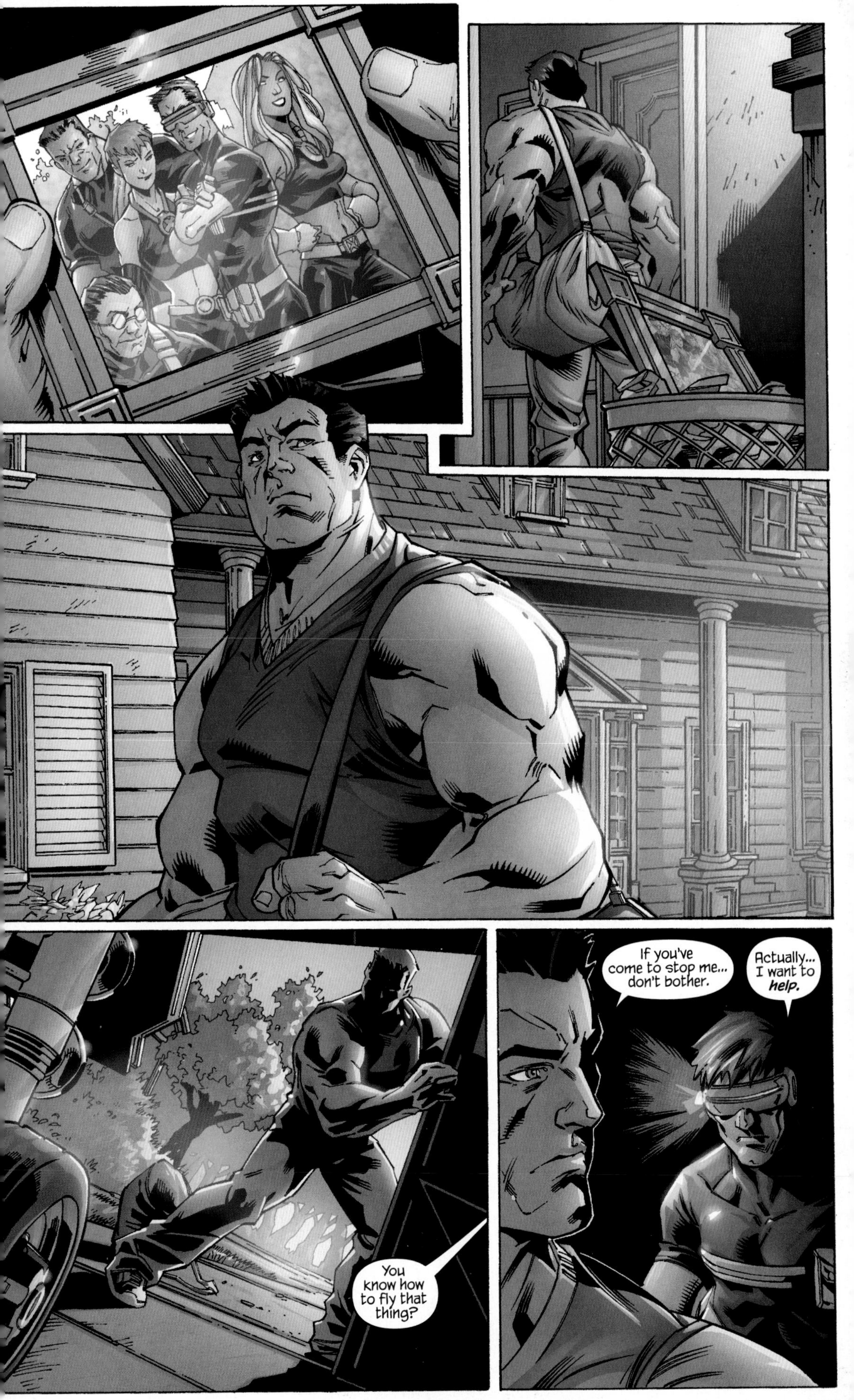
You know how to fly that thing?
If you've come to stop me... don't bother.
Actually... I want to **help.**

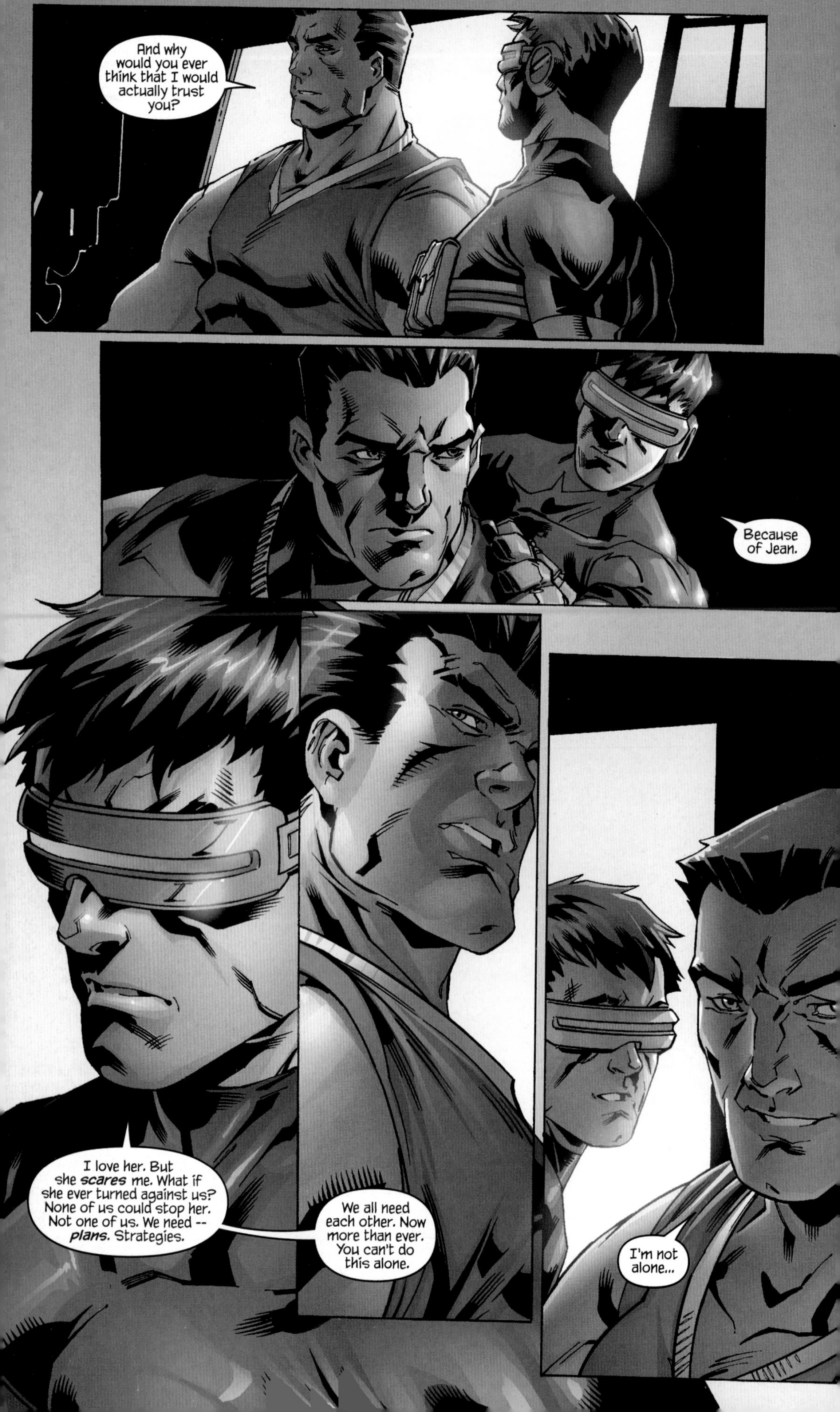
And why would you ever think that I would actually trust you?
Because of Jean.
I love her. But she *scares* me. What if she ever turned against us? None of us could stop her. Not one of us. We need -- *plans*. Strategies.
We all need each other. Now more than ever. You can't do this alone.
I'm not alone...

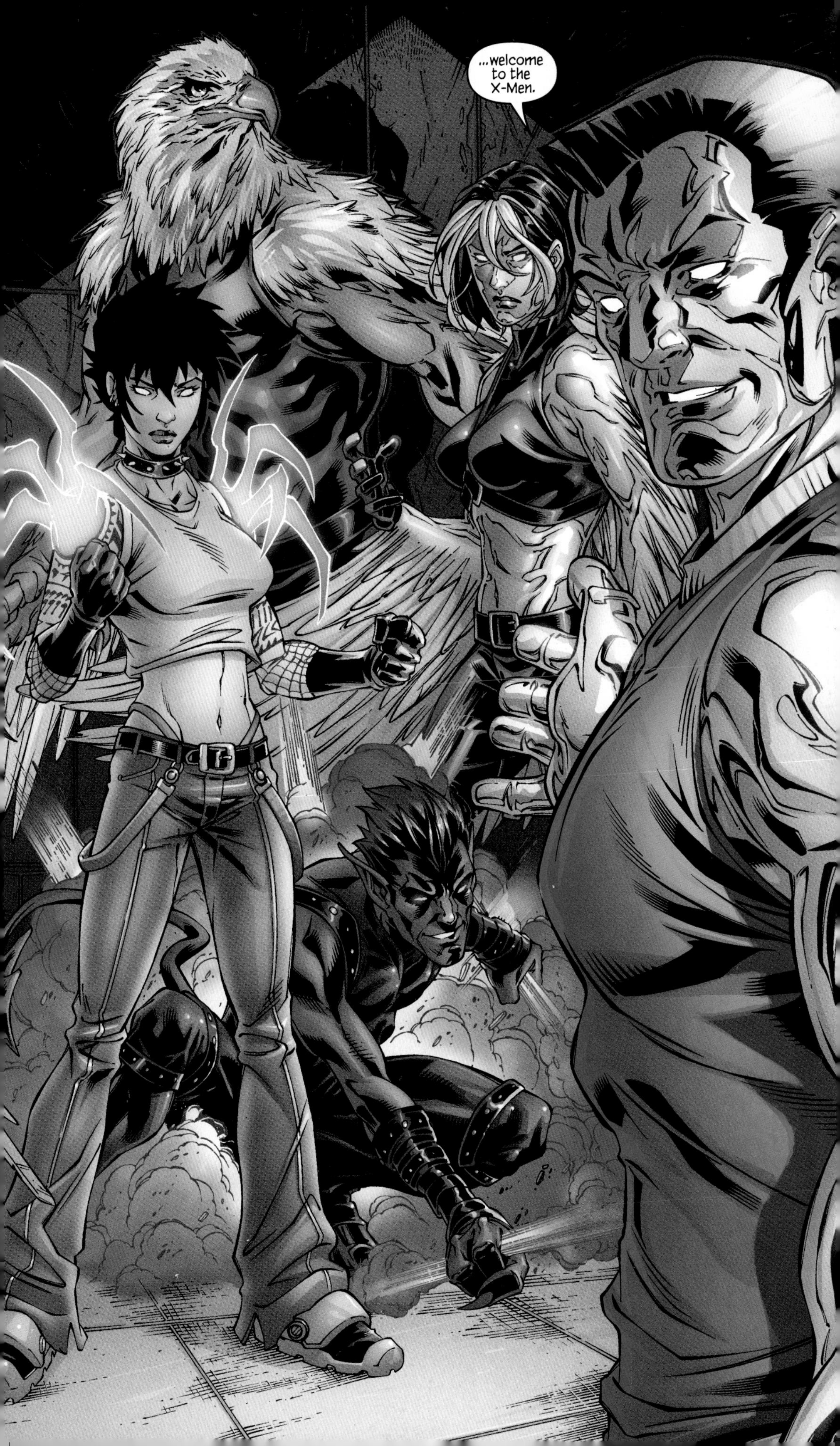
...welcome to the X-Men.

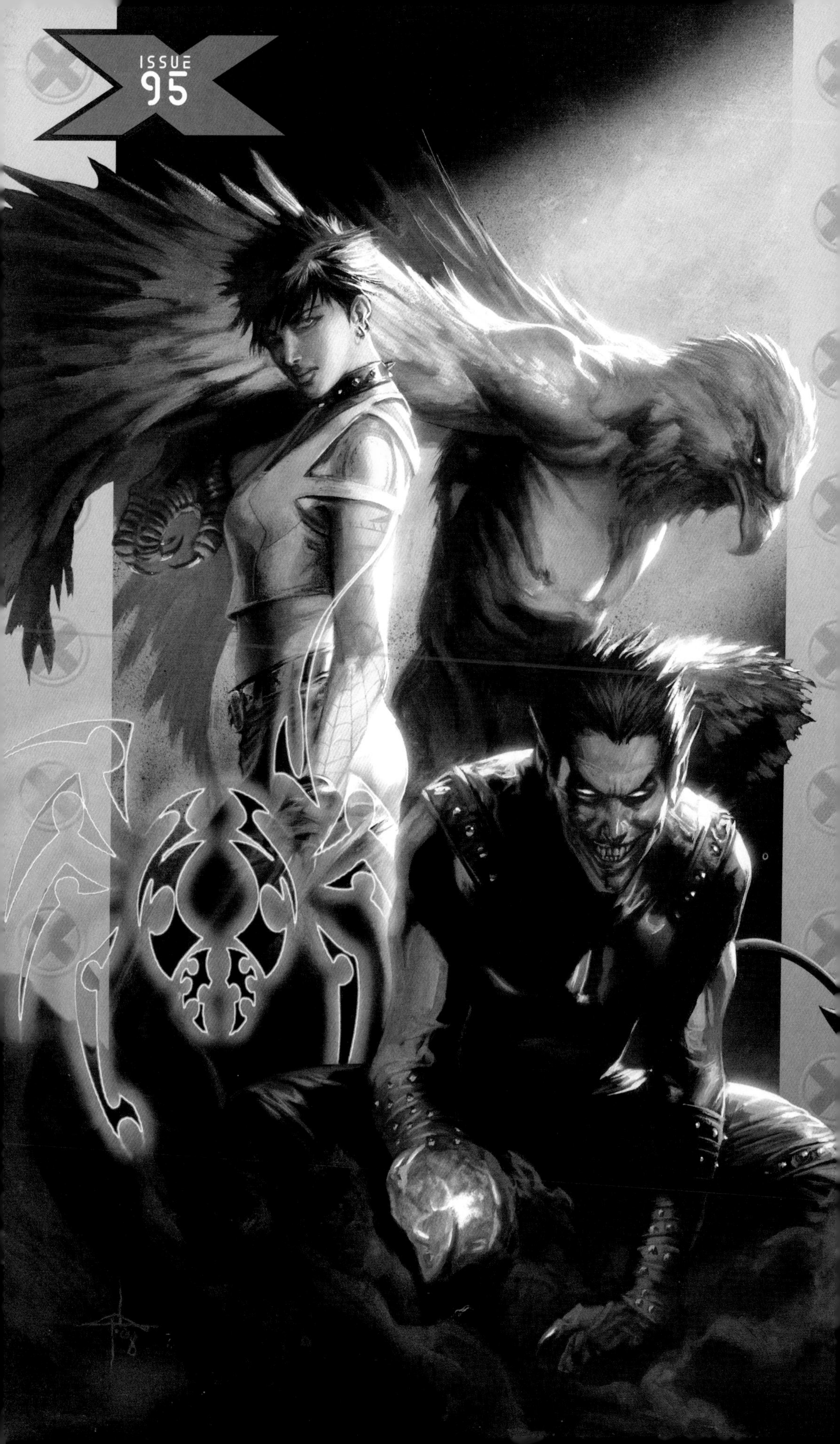
ISSUE
95

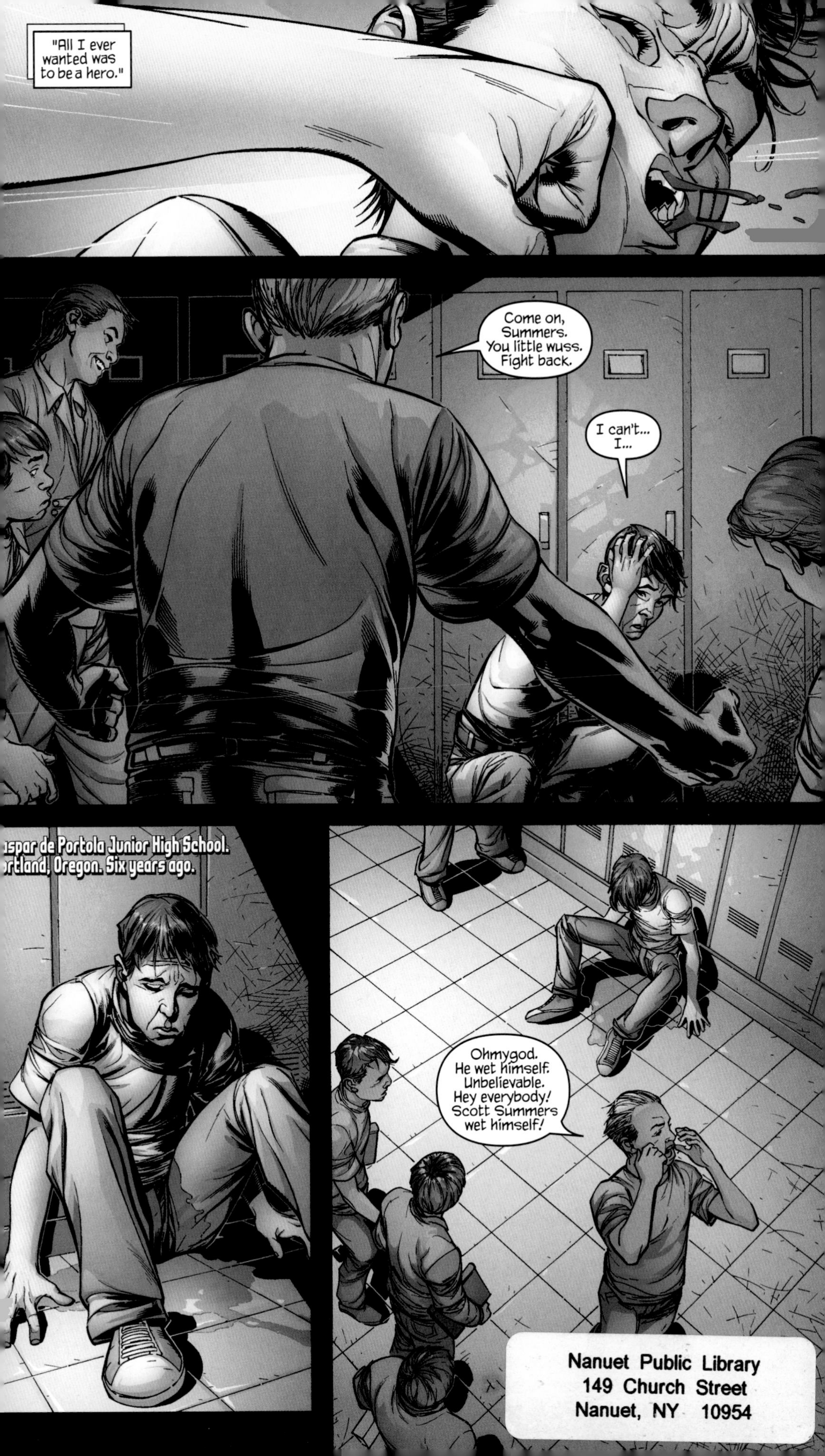
"All I ever wanted was to be a hero."
Come on, Summers. You little wuss. Fight back.
I can't... I...
aspar de Portola Junior High School. ortland, Oregon. Six years ago.
Ohmygod. He wet himself. Unbelievable. Hey everybody! Scott Summers wet himself!

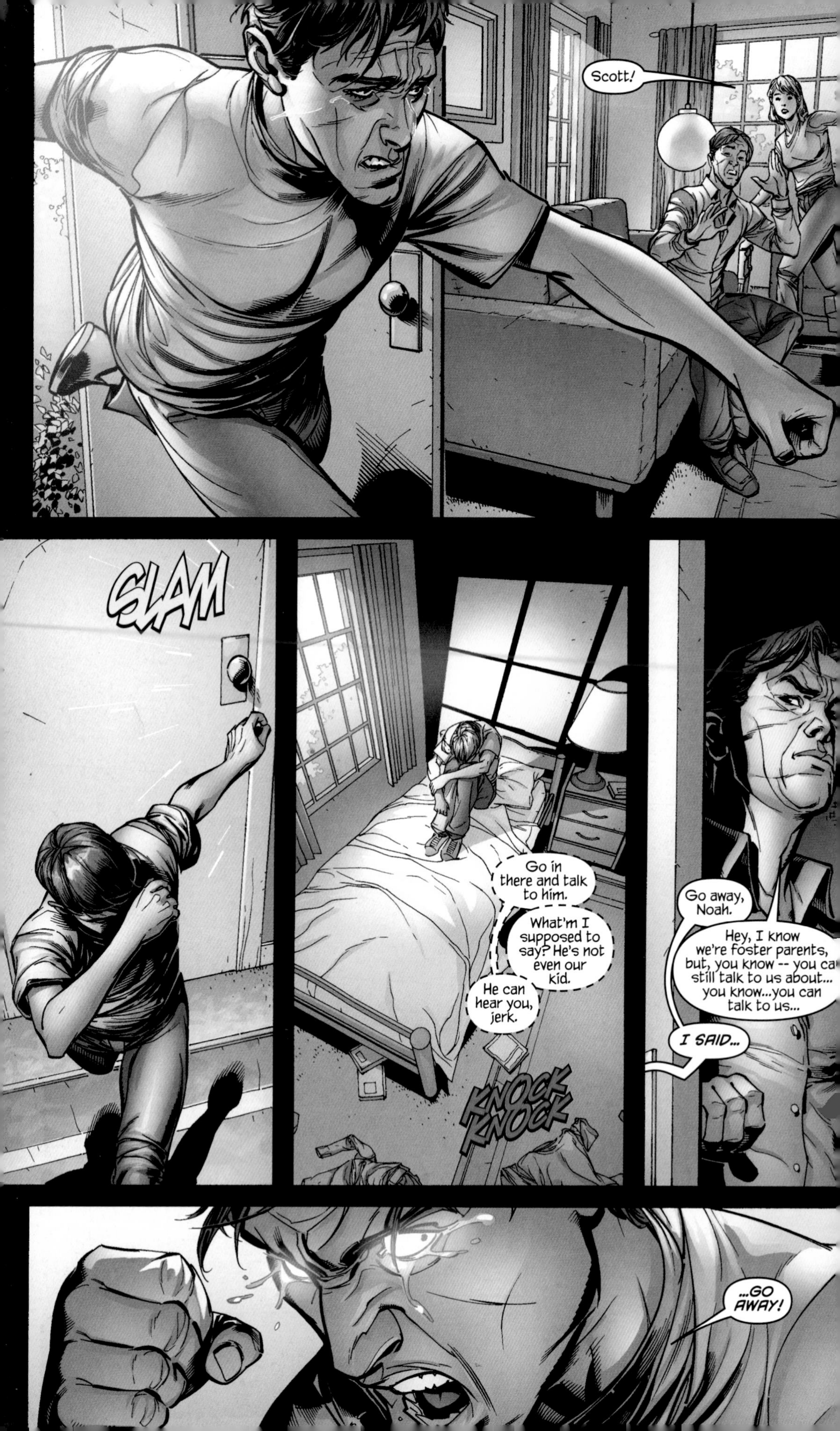
Scott!
SLAM
Go in there and talk to him.
What'm I supposed to say? He's not even our kid.
He can hear you, jerk.
KNOCK KNOCK
Go away, Noah.
Hey, I know we're foster parents, but, you know -- you ca still talk to us about... you know...you can talk to us...
I SAID...
...GO AWAY!

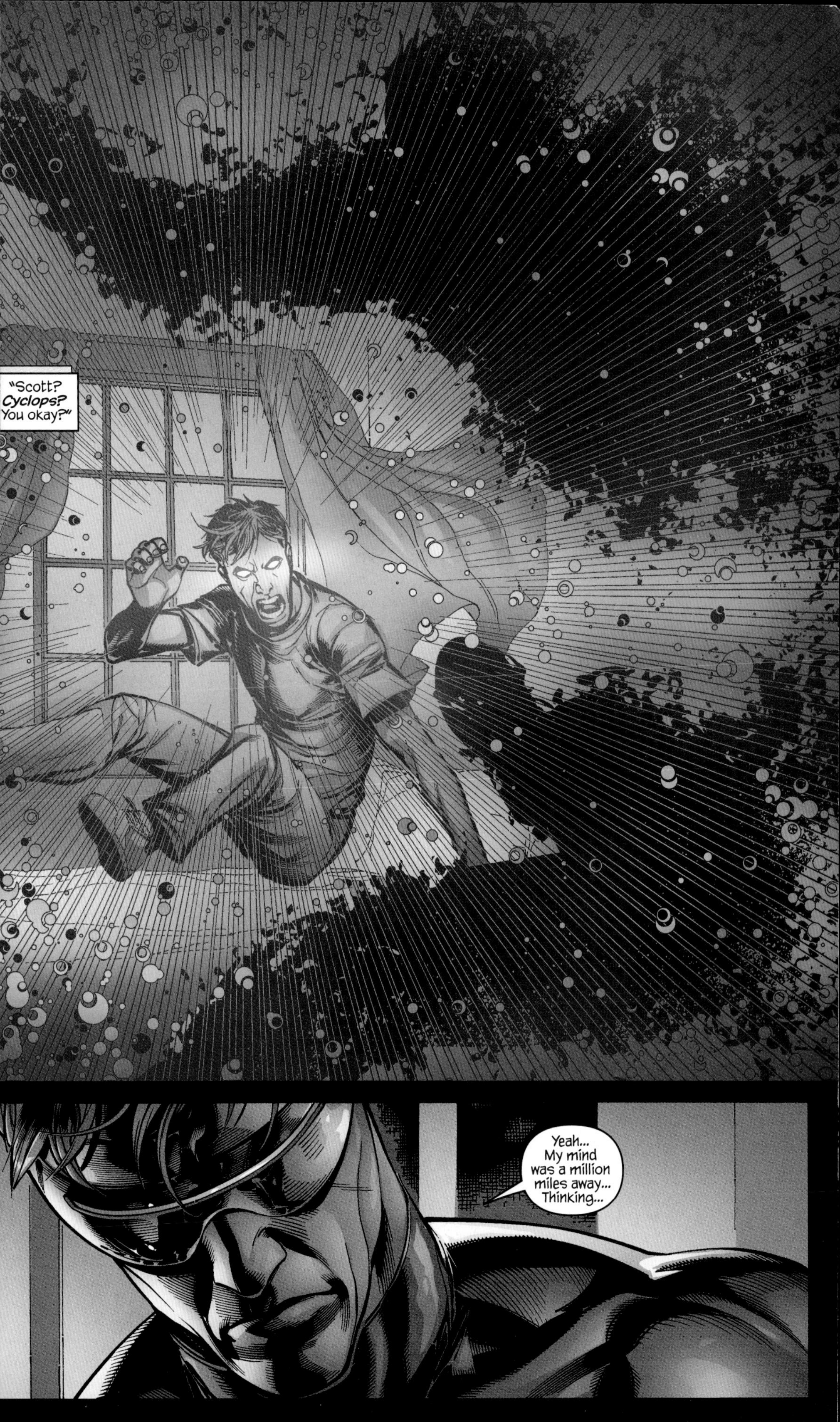
"Scott? *Cyclops?* You okay?"
Yeah... My mind was a million miles away... Thinking...

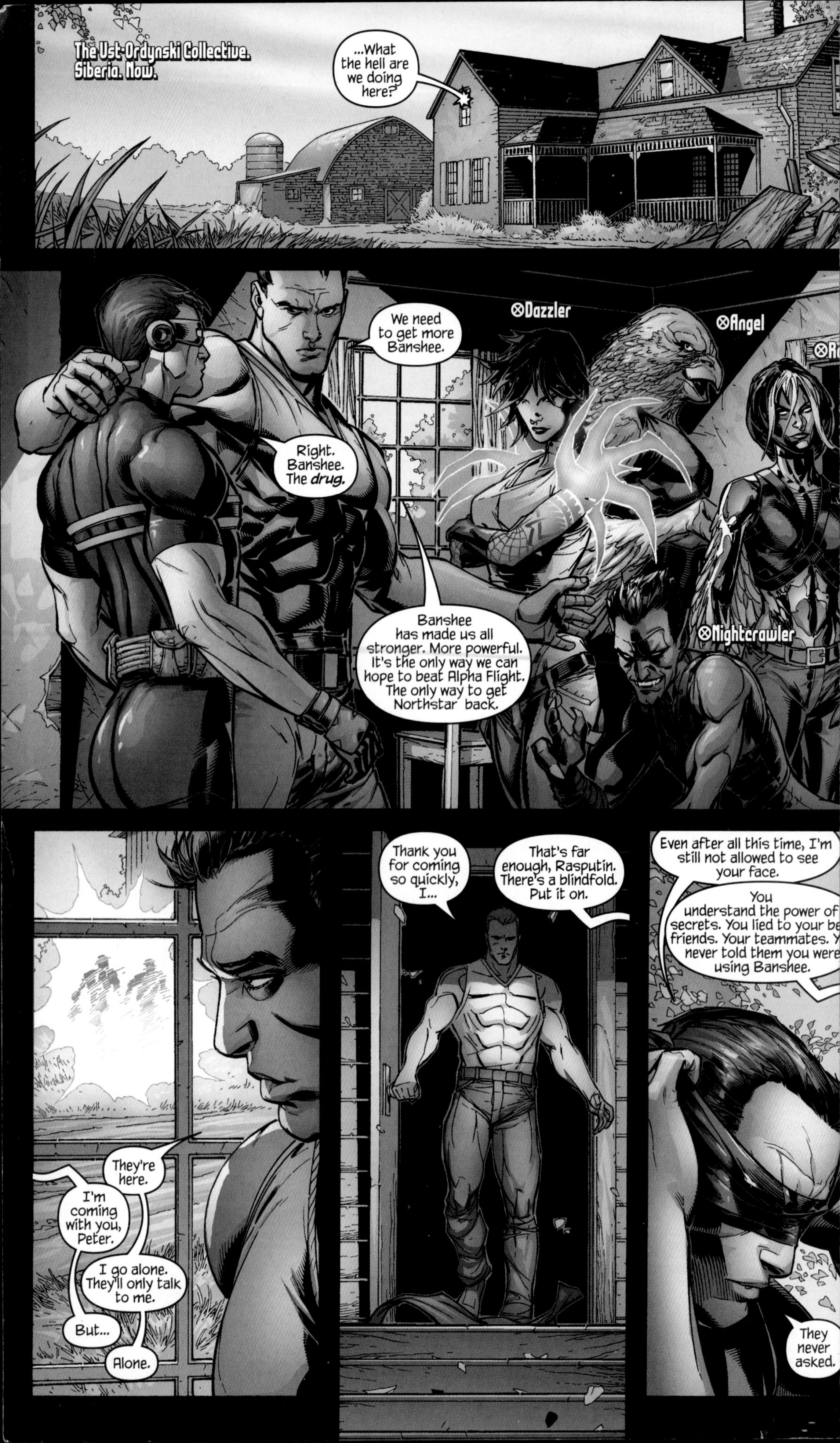
The Ust-Ordynski Collective. Siberia. Now.
...What the hell are we doing here?
We need to get more Banshee.
Right. Banshee. The *drug.*
Banshee has made us all stronger. More powerful. It's the only way we can hope to beat Alpha Flight. The only way to get Northstar back.
⊗Dazzler
⊗Angel
⊗Nightcrawler
They're here.
I'm coming with you, Peter.
I go alone. They'll only talk to me.
But...
Alone.
Thank you for coming so quickly, I...
That's far enough, Rasputin. There's a blindfold. Put it on.
Even after all this time, I'm still not allowed to see your face.
You understand the power of secrets. You lied to your be friends. Your teammates. Y never told them you were using Banshee.
They never asked.

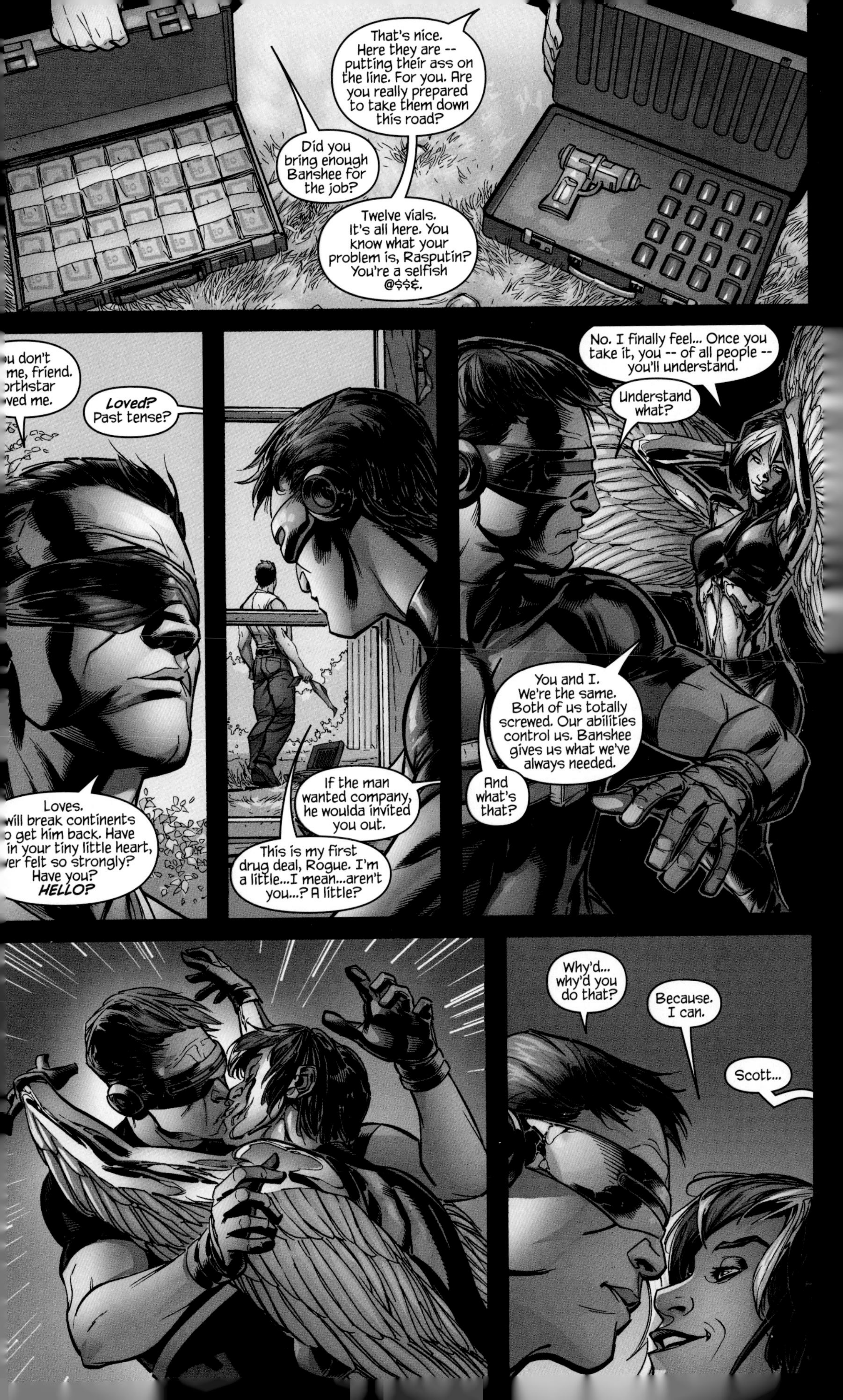

That's nice. Here they are -- putting their ass on the line. For you. Are you really prepared to take them down this road?
Did you bring enough Banshee for the job?
Twelve vials. It's all here. You know what your problem is, Rasputin? You're a selfish @$$£.
u don't me, friend. orthstar ved me.
Loved? Past tense?
Loves. will break continents o get him back. Have in your tiny little heart, er felt so strongly? Have you? ***HELLO?***
If the man wanted company, he woulda invited you out.
This is my first drug deal, Rogue. I'm a little...I mean...aren't you...? A little?
No. I finally feel... Once you take it, you -- of all people -- you'll understand.
Understand what?
You and I. We're the same. Both of us totally screwed. Our abilities control us. Banshee gives us what we've always needed.
And what's that?
Why'd... why'd you do that?
Because. I can.
Scott...

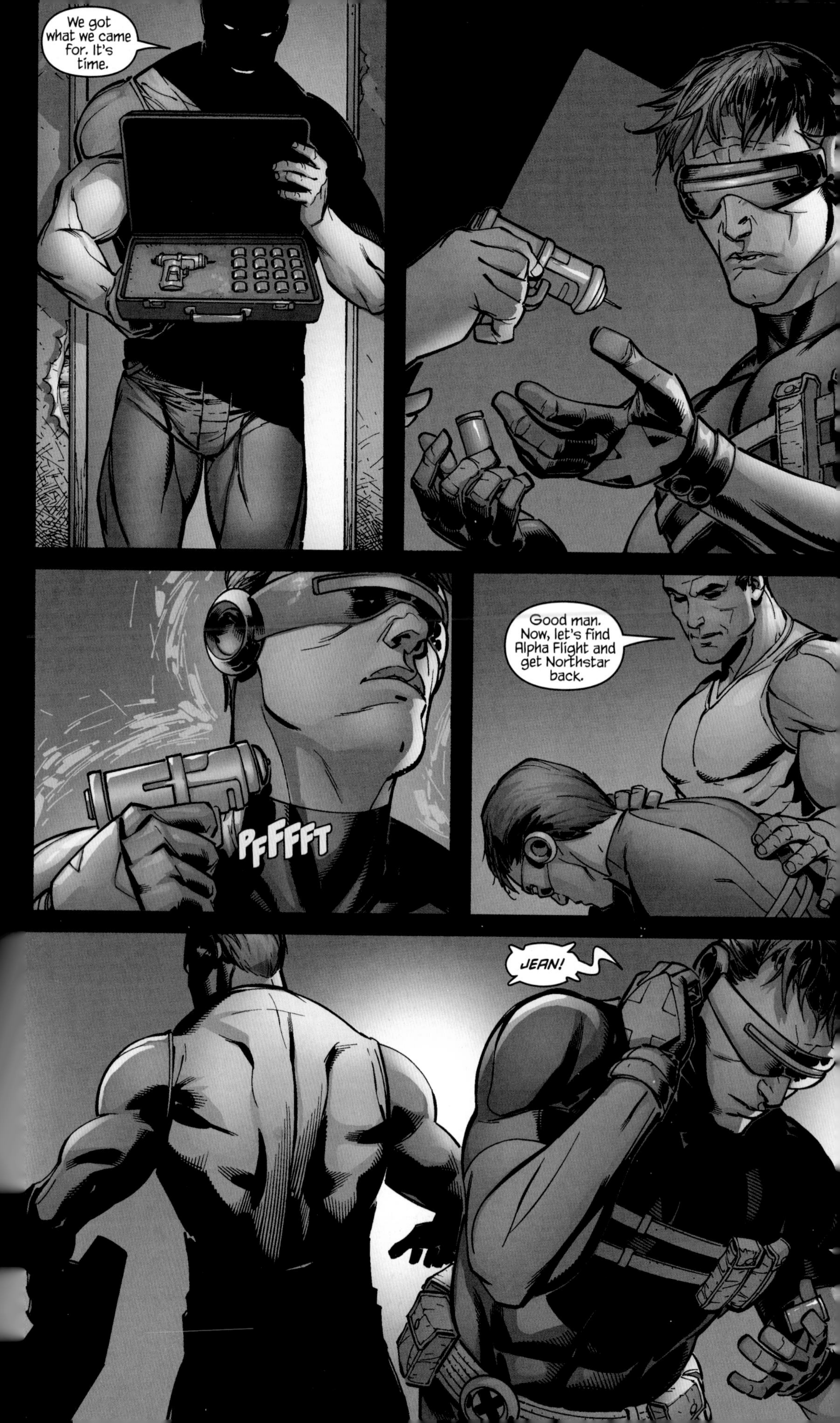
We got what we came for. It's time.
PFFFFT
Good man. Now, let's find Alpha Flight and get Northstar back.
JEAN!

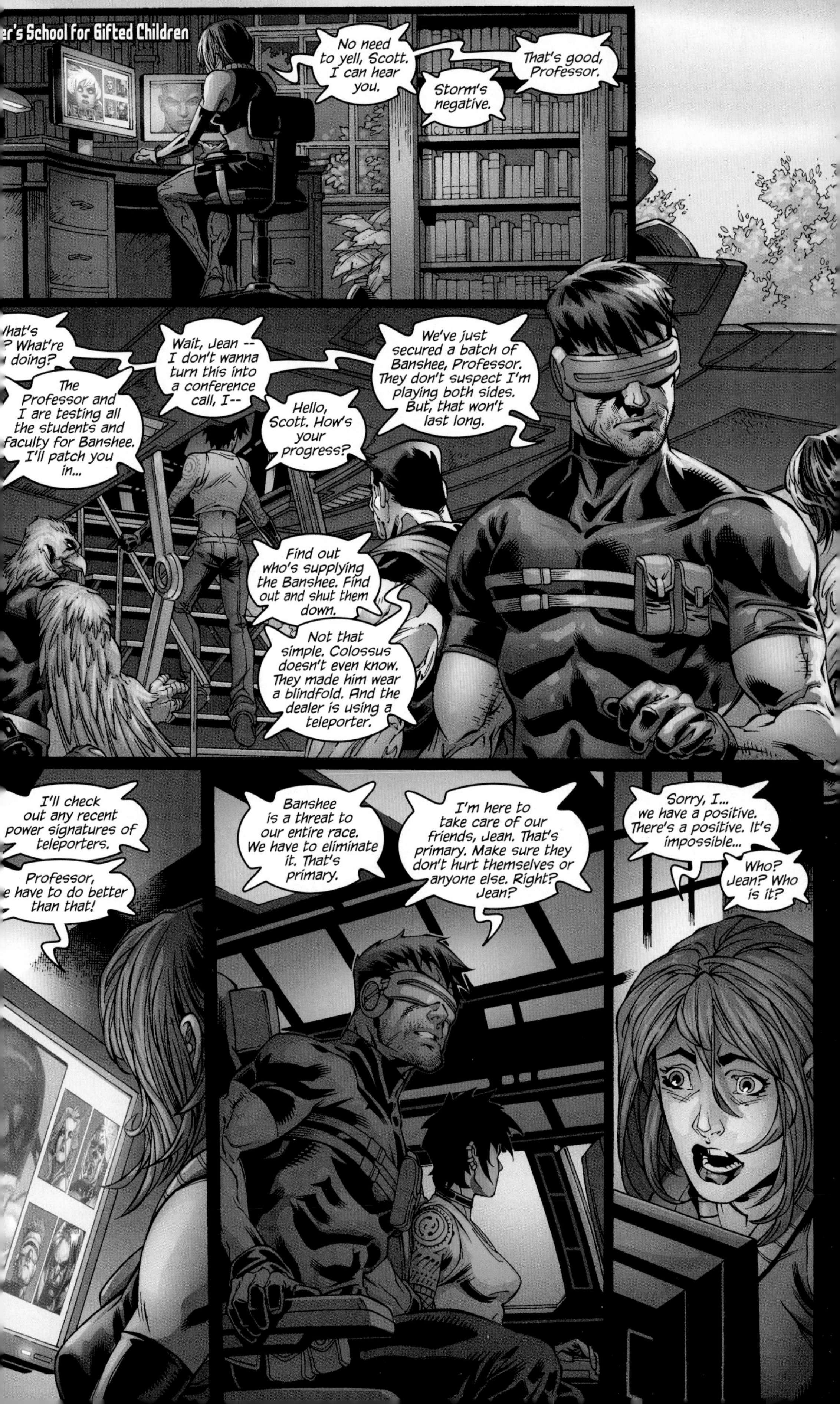

er's School for Gifted Children
No need to yell, Scott. I can hear you.
Storm's negative.
That's good, Professor.
hat's ? What're doing?
The Professor and I are testing all the students and faculty for Banshee. I'll patch you in...
Wait, Jean -- I don't wanna turn this into a conference call, I--
Hello, Scott. How's your progress?
We've just secured a batch of Banshee, Professor. They don't suspect I'm playing both sides. But, that won't last long.
Find out who's supplying the Banshee. Find out and shut them down.
Not that simple. Colossus doesn't even know. They made him wear a blindfold. And the dealer is using a teleporter.
I'll check out any recent power signatures of teleporters.
Professor, e have to do better than that!
Banshee is a threat to our entire race. We have to eliminate it. That's primary.
I'm here to take care of our friends, Jean. That's primary. Make sure they don't hurt themselves or anyone else. Right? Jean?
Sorry, I... we have a positive. There's a positive. It's impossible...
Who? Jean? Who is it?

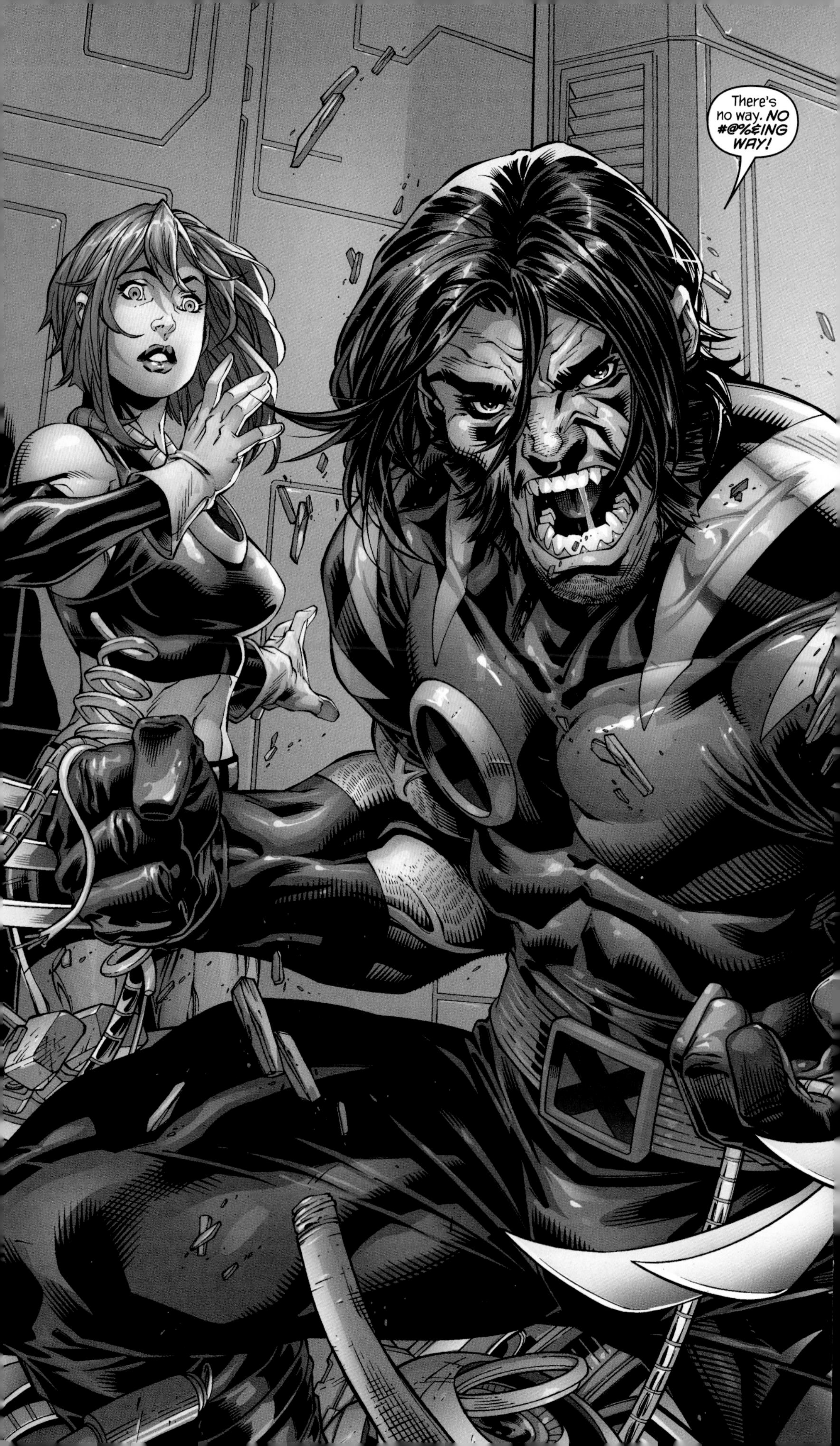
There's no way. NO #@%&ING WAY!

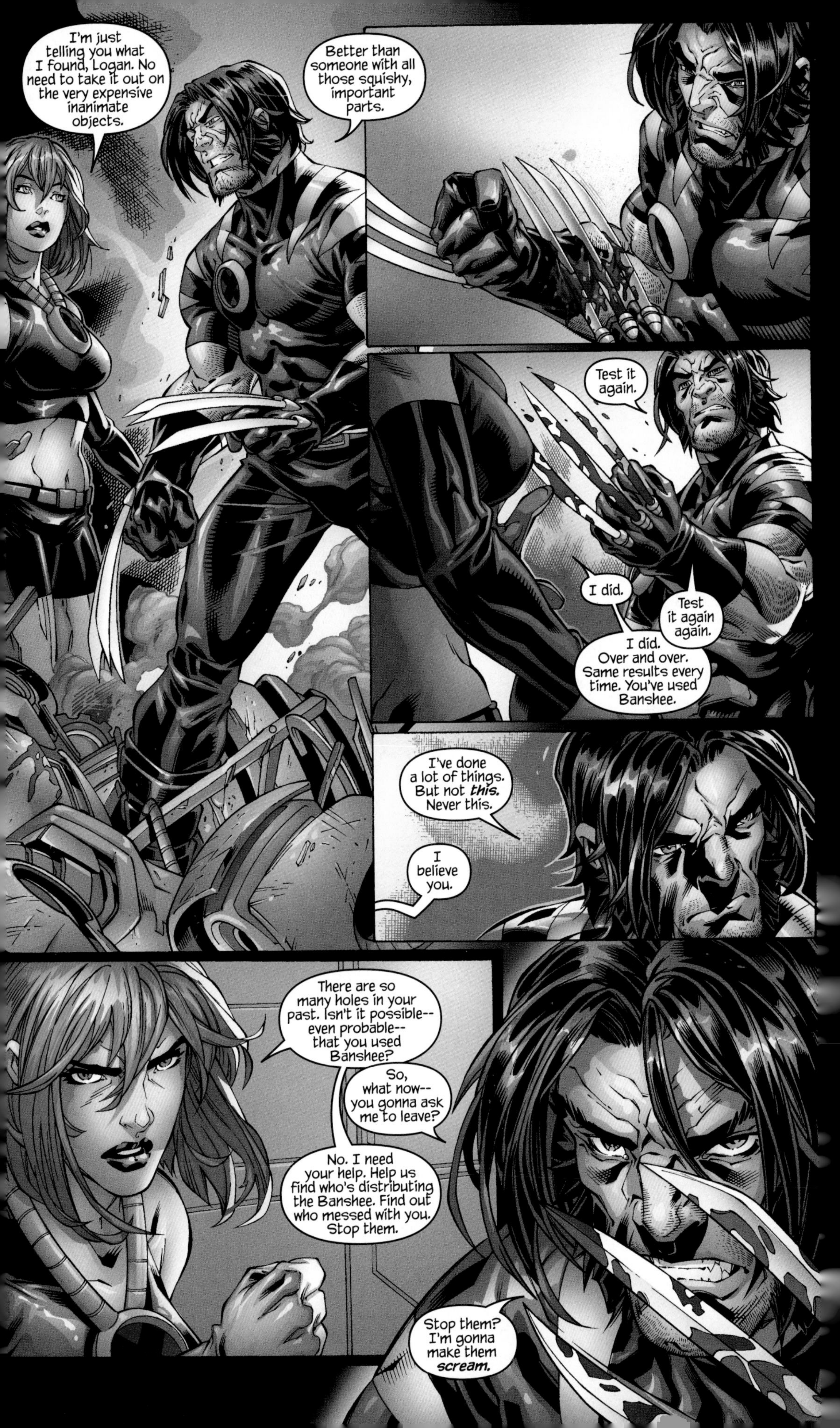

I'm just telling you what I found, Logan. No need to take it out on the very expensive inanimate objects.
Better than someone with all those squishy, important parts.
Test it again.
I did.
Test it again again.
I did. Over and over. Same results every time. You've used Banshee.
I've done a lot of things. But not *this.* Never this.
I believe you.
There are so many holes in your past. Isn't it possible-- even probable-- that you used Banshee?
So, what now-- you gonna ask me to leave?
No. I need your help. Help us find who's distributing the Banshee. Find out who messed with you. Stop them.
Stop them? I'm gonna make them ***scream.***

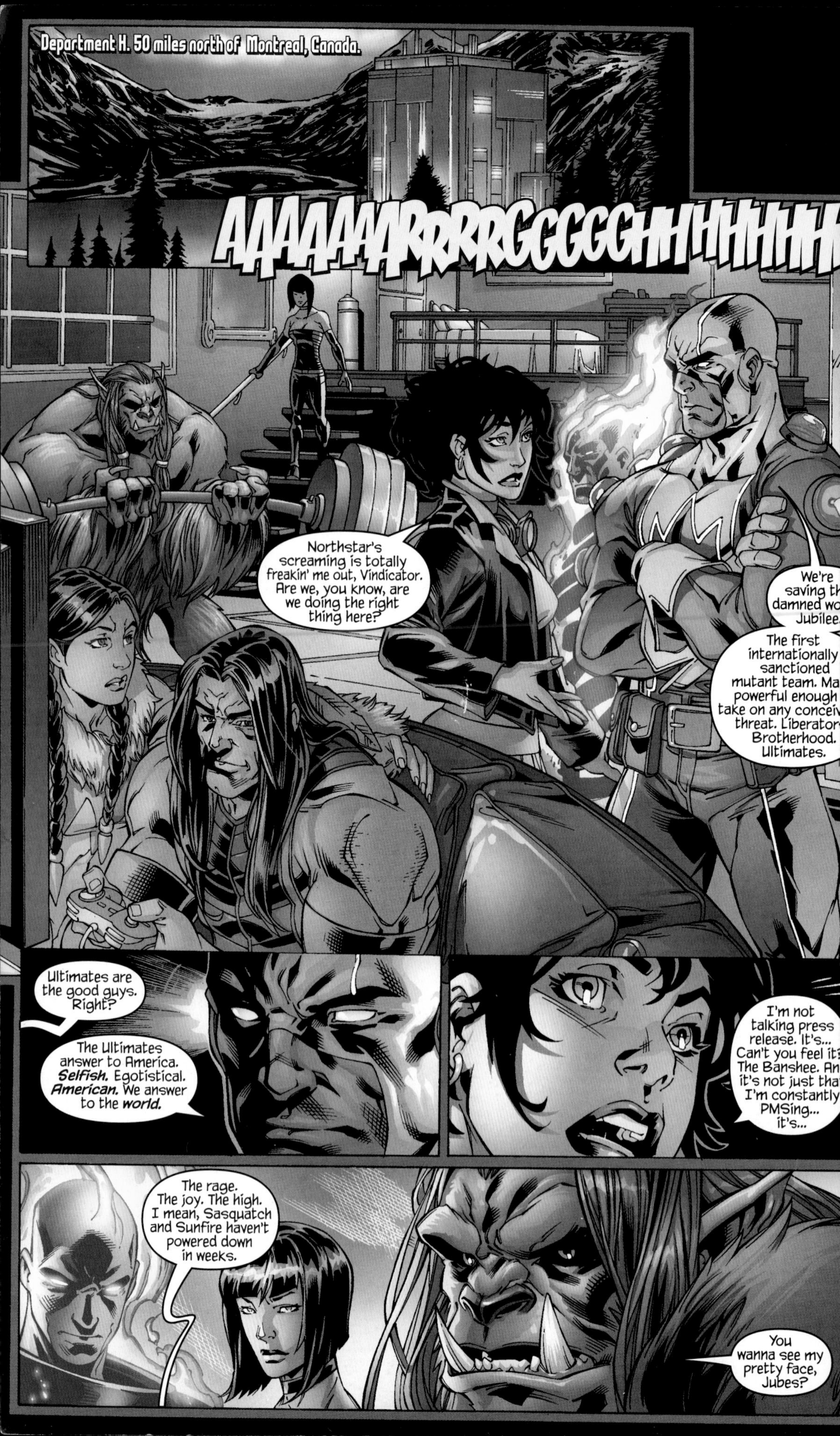

Department H. 50 miles north of Montreal, Canada.
AAAAAAARRRRGGGGGHHHHHHH
Northstar's screaming is totally freakin' me out, Vindicator. Are we, you know, are we doing the right thing here?
We're saving th damned wo Jubilee.
The first internationally sanctioned mutant team. Ma powerful enough take on any conceiv threat. Liberator Brotherhood. Ultimates.
Ultimates are the good guys. Right?
The Ultimates answer to America. *Selfish.* Egotistical. *American.* We answer to the *world.*
I'm not talking press release. It's... Can't you feel it The Banshee. An it's not just tha I'm constantly PMSing... it's...
The rage. The joy. The high. I mean, Sasquatch and Sunfire haven't powered down in weeks.
You wanna see my pretty face, Jubes?

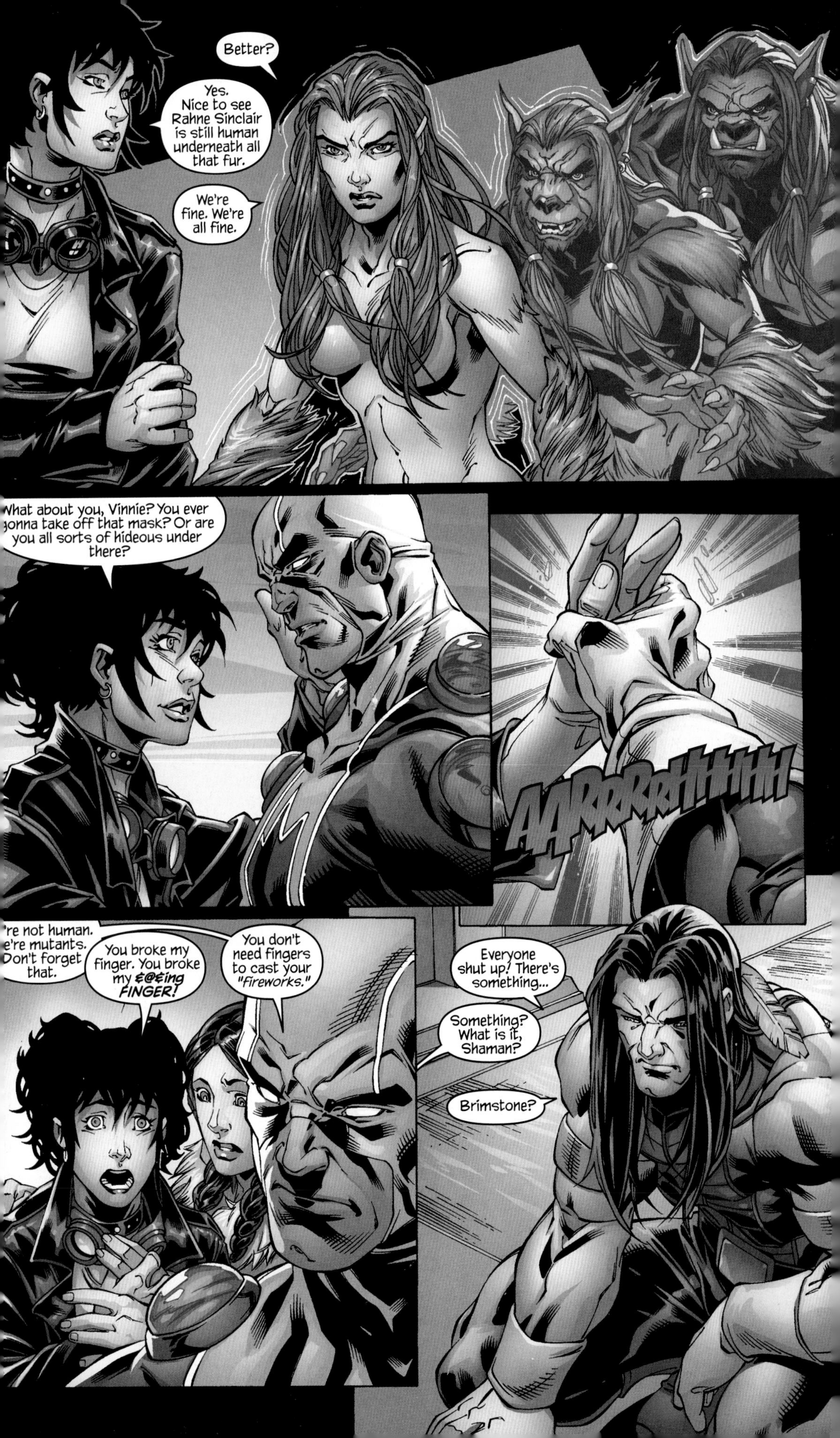
Better?
Yes. Nice to see Rahne Sinclair is still human underneath all that fur.
We're fine. We're all fine.
What about you, Vinnie? You ever gonna take off that mask? Or are you all sorts of hideous under there?
AARRRRHHHHH
're not human. e're mutants. Don't forget that.
You broke my finger. You broke my €@€ing FINGER!
You don't need fingers to cast your "Fireworks."
Everyone shut up! There's something...
Something? What is it, Shaman?
Brimstone?

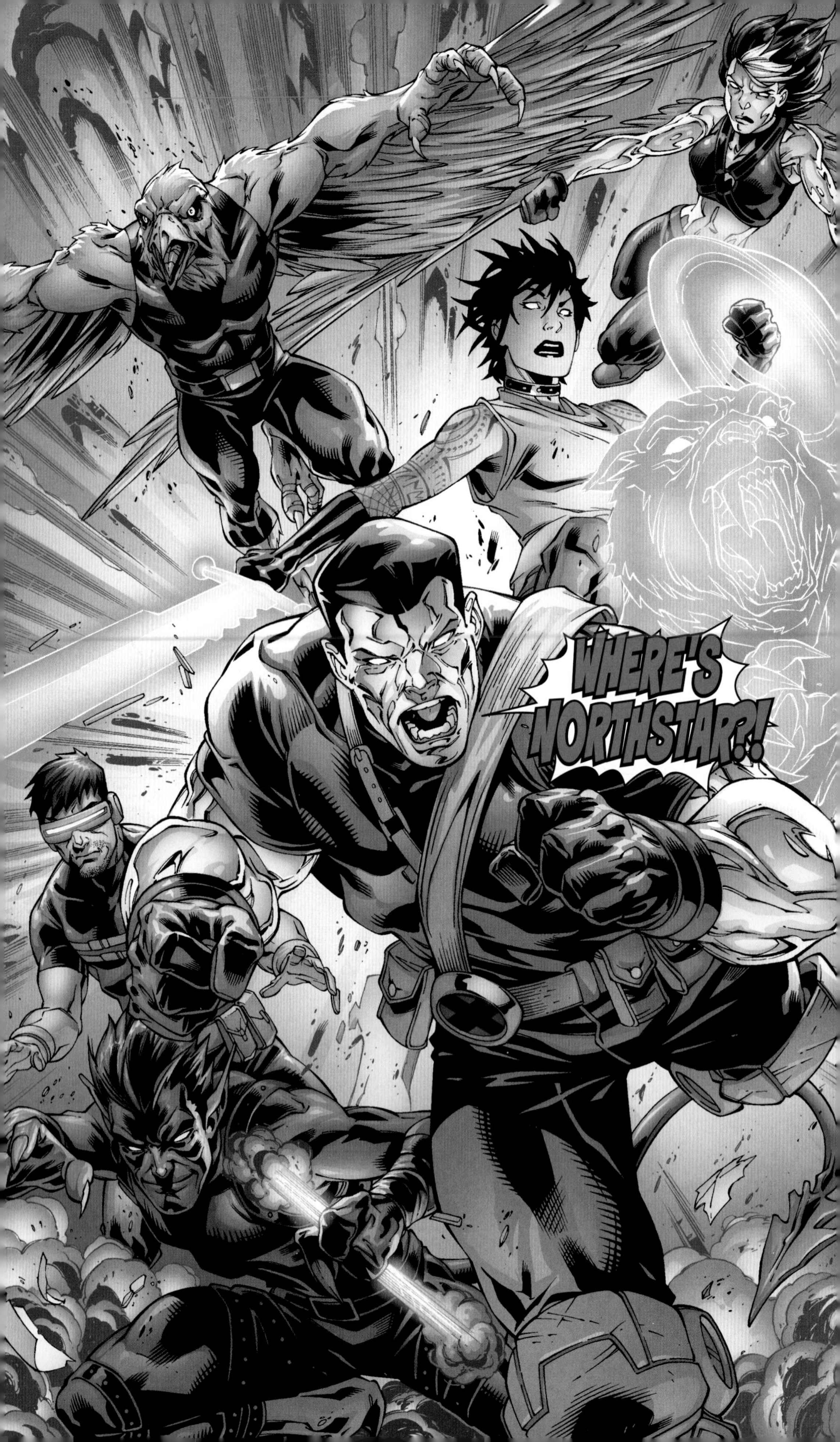
WHERE'S NORTHSTAR?!

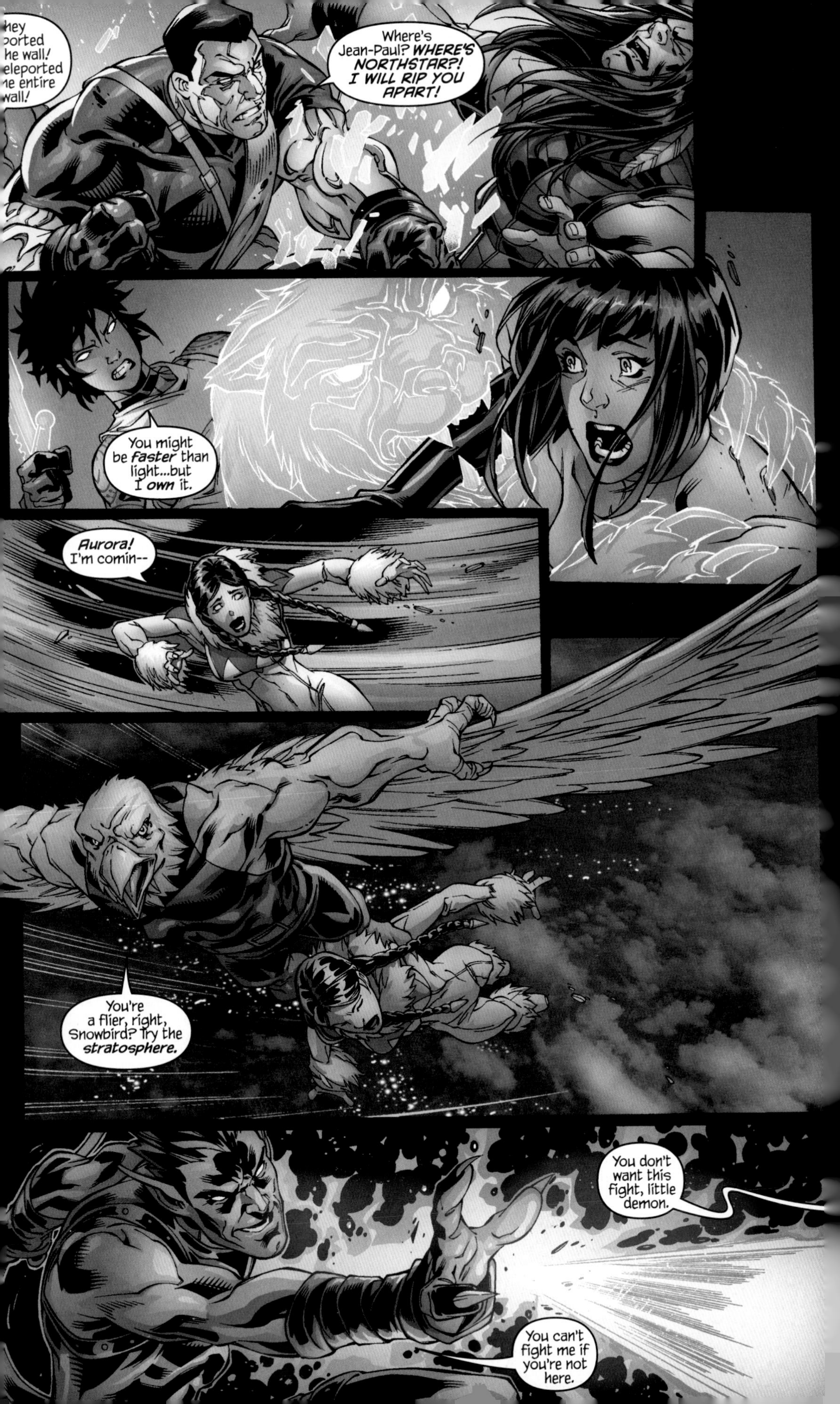

hey
ported
he wall!
eleported
e entire
wall!
Where's Jean-Paul? WHERE'S NORTHSTAR?! I WILL RIP YOU APART!
You might be faster than light...but I own it.
Aurora! I'm comin--
You're a flier, right, Snowbird? Try the stratosphere.
You don't want this fight, little demon.
You can't fight me if you're not here.

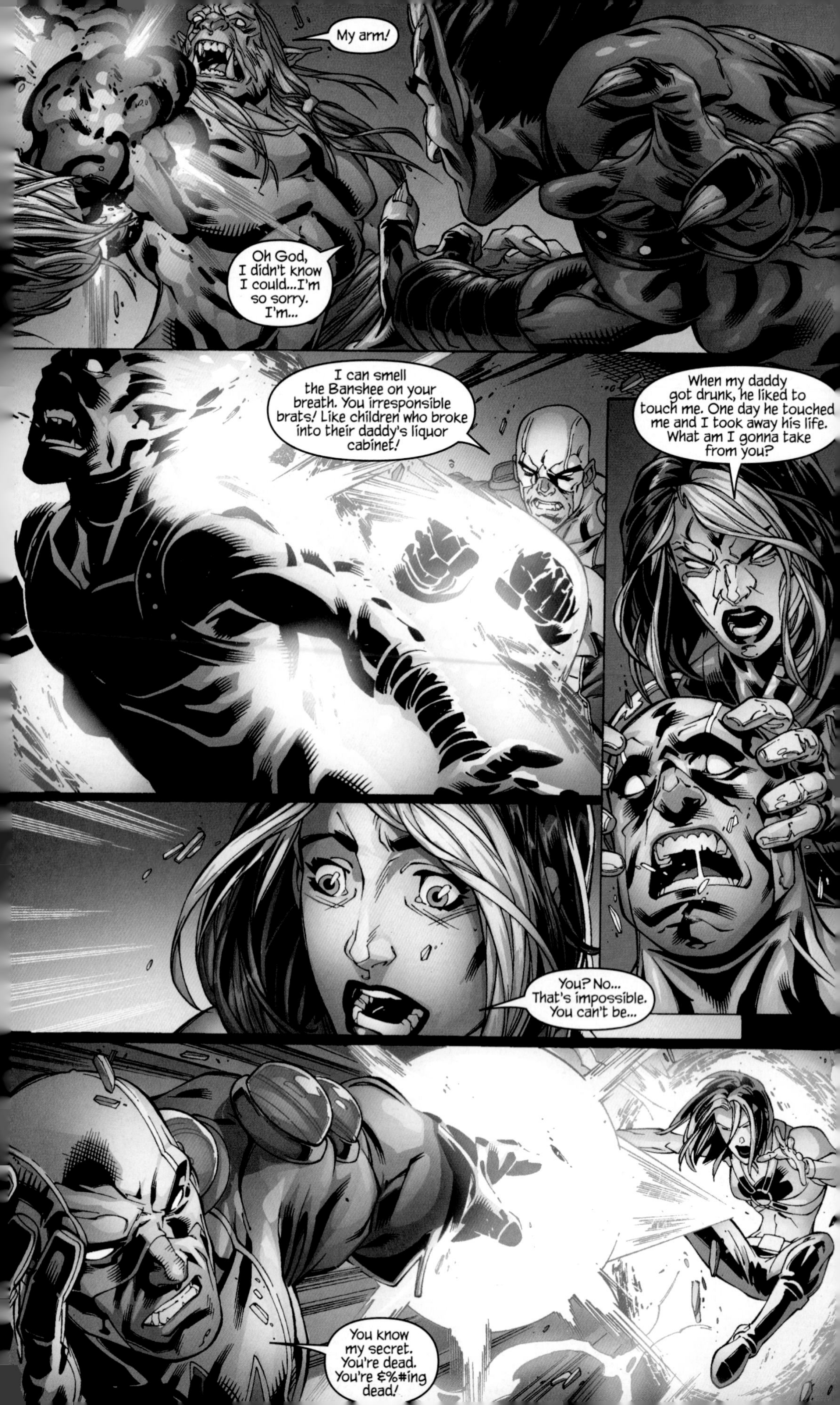
My arm!
Oh God, I didn't know I could...I'm so sorry. I'm...
I can smell the Banshee on your breath. You irresponsible brats! Like children who broke into their daddy's liquor cabinet!
When my daddy got drunk, he liked to touch me. One day he touched me and I took away his life. What am I gonna take from you?
You? No... That's impossible. You can't be...
You know my secret. You're dead. You're £%#ing dead!

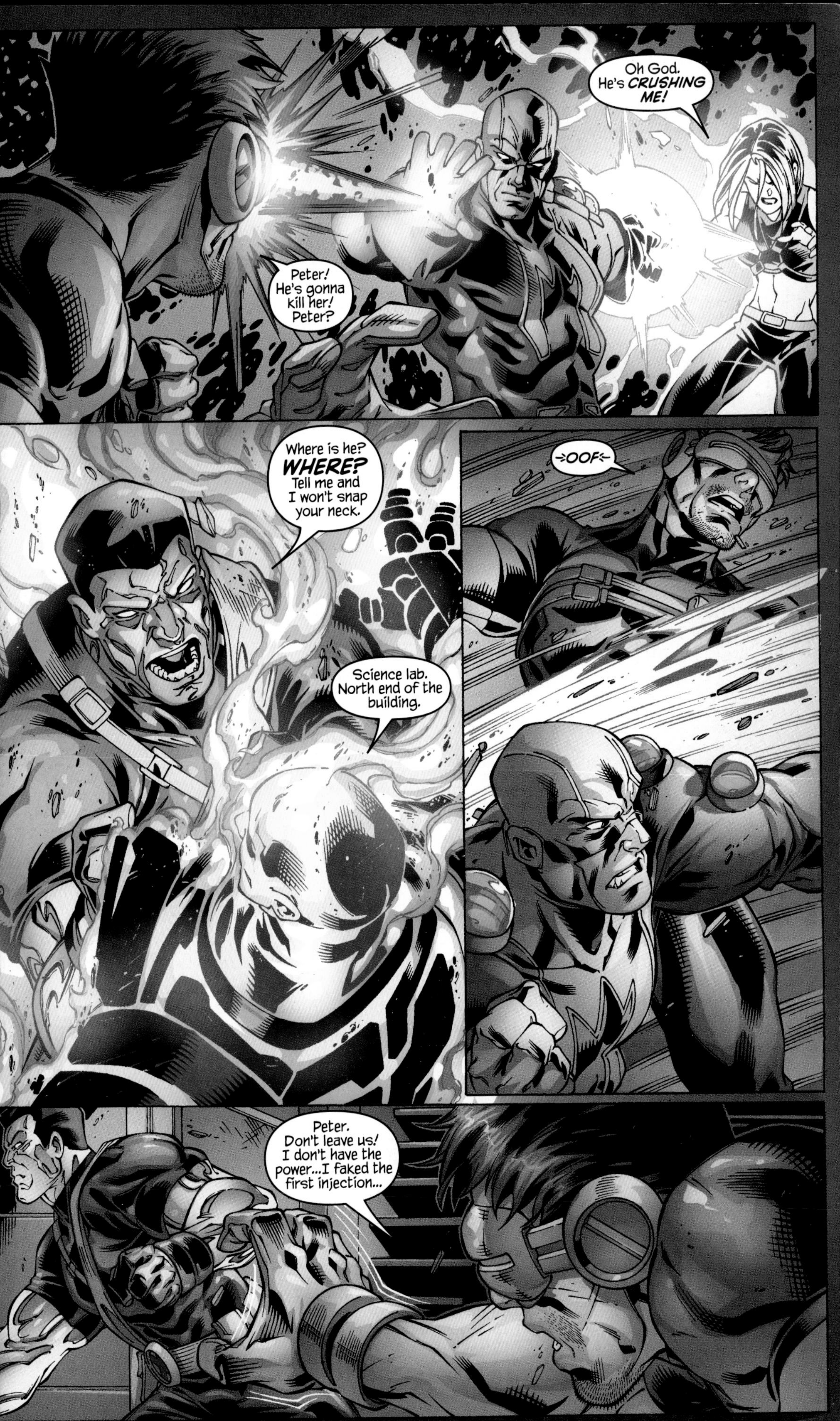
Oh God. He's CRUSHING ME!
Peter! He's gonna kill her! Peter?
Where is he? WHERE? Tell me and I won't snap your neck.
Science lab. North end of the building.
OOF
Peter. Don't leave us! I don't have the power...I faked the first injection...

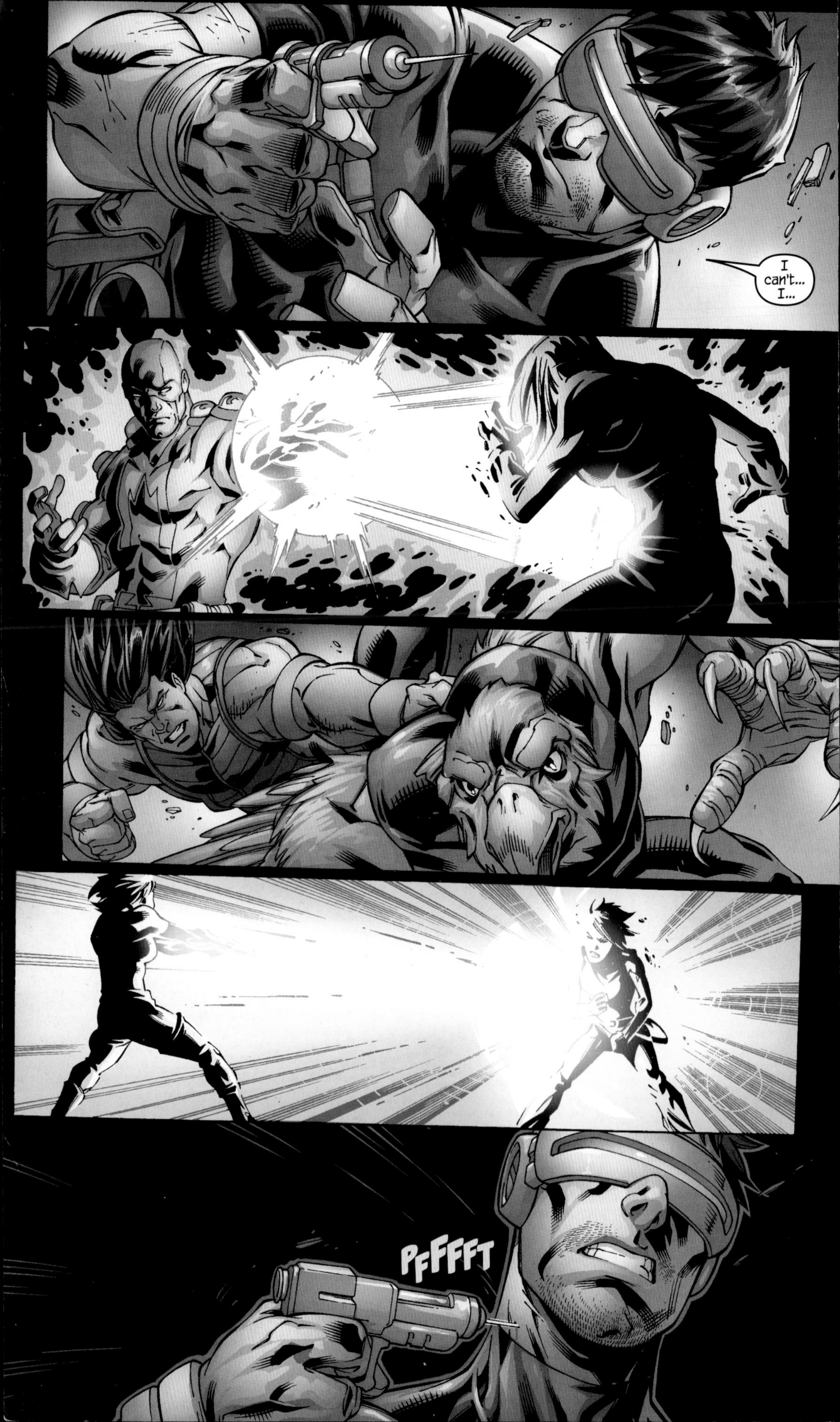
I can't... I...
PFFFFT

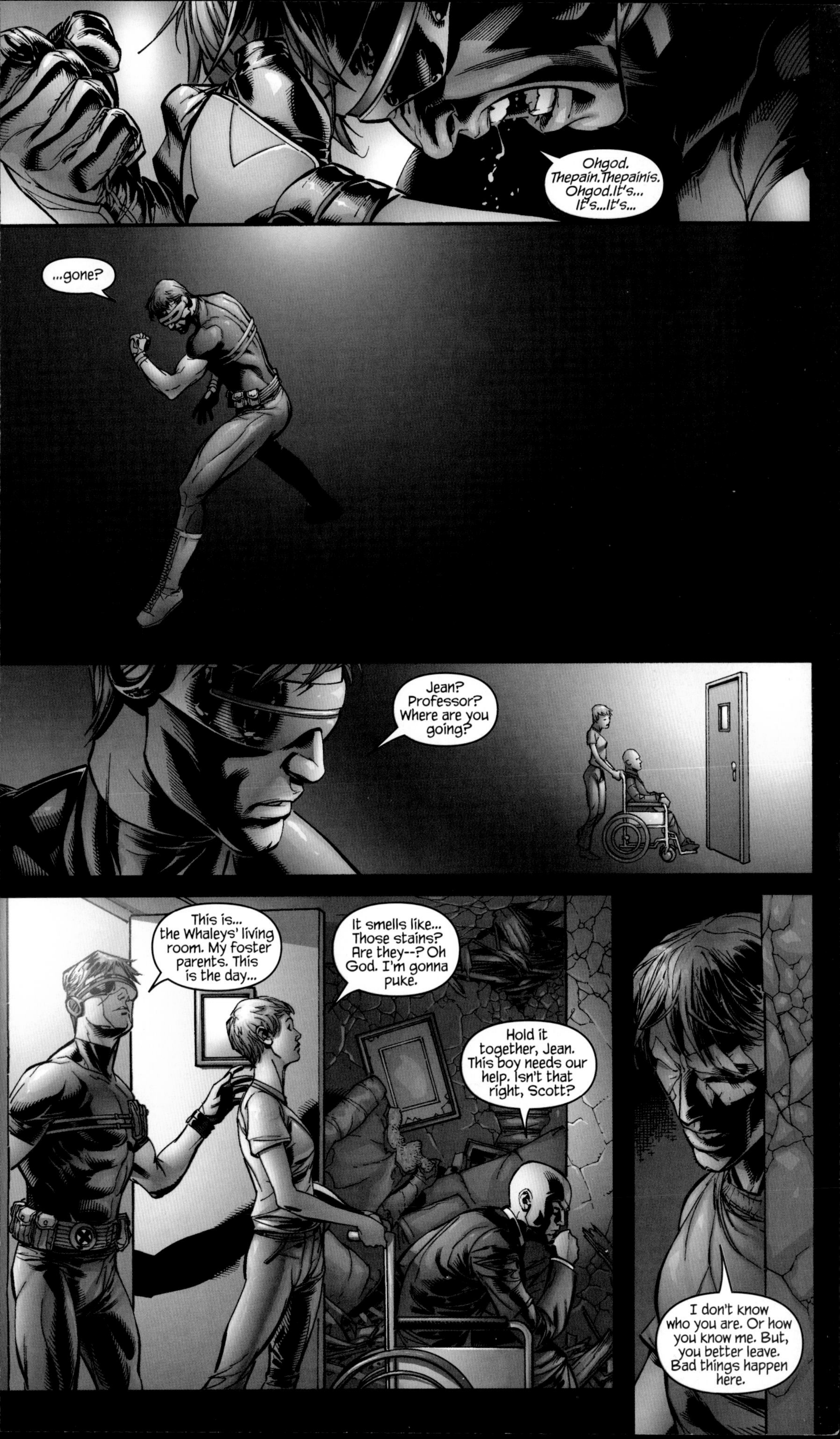
Ohgod.
Thepain.Thepainis.
Ohgod.It's...
It's...It's...
...gone?
Jean?
Professor?
Where are you
going?
This is...
the Whaleys' living
room. My foster
parents. This
is the day...
It smells like...
Those stains?
Are they--? Oh
God. I'm gonna
puke.
Hold it
together, Jean.
This boy needs our
help. Isn't that
right, Scott?
I don't know
who you are. Or how
you know me. But,
you better leave.
Bad things happen
here.

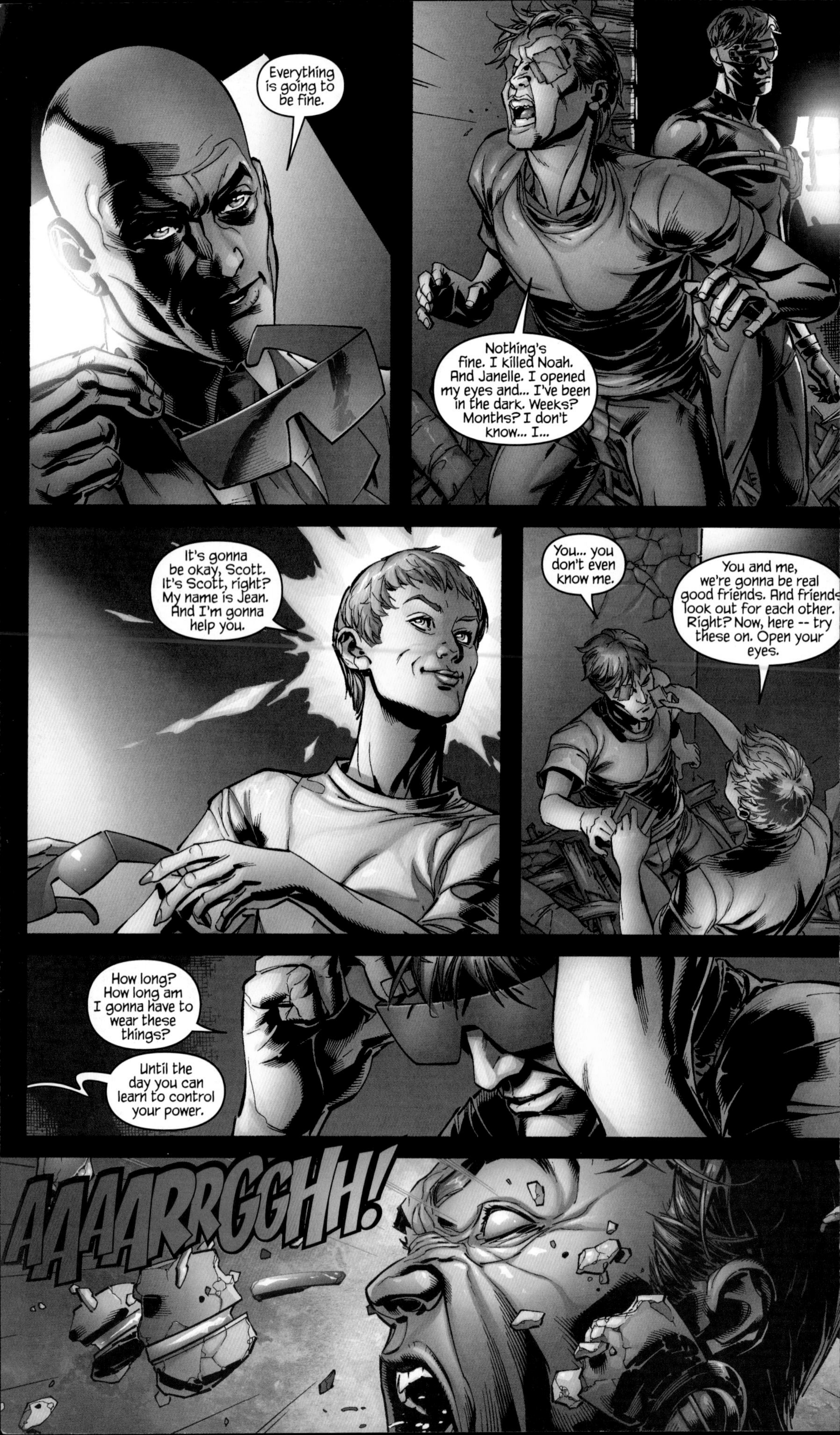
Everything is going to be fine.
Nothing's fine. I killed Noah. And Janelle. I opened my eyes and... I've been in the dark. Weeks? Months? I don't know... I...
It's gonna be okay, Scott. It's Scott, right? My name is Jean. And I'm gonna help you.
You... you don't even know me.
You and me, we're gonna be real good friends. And friends look out for each other. Right? Now, here -- try these on. Open your eyes.
How long? How long am I gonna have to wear these things?
Until the day you can learn to control your power.
AAAARRGGHH!

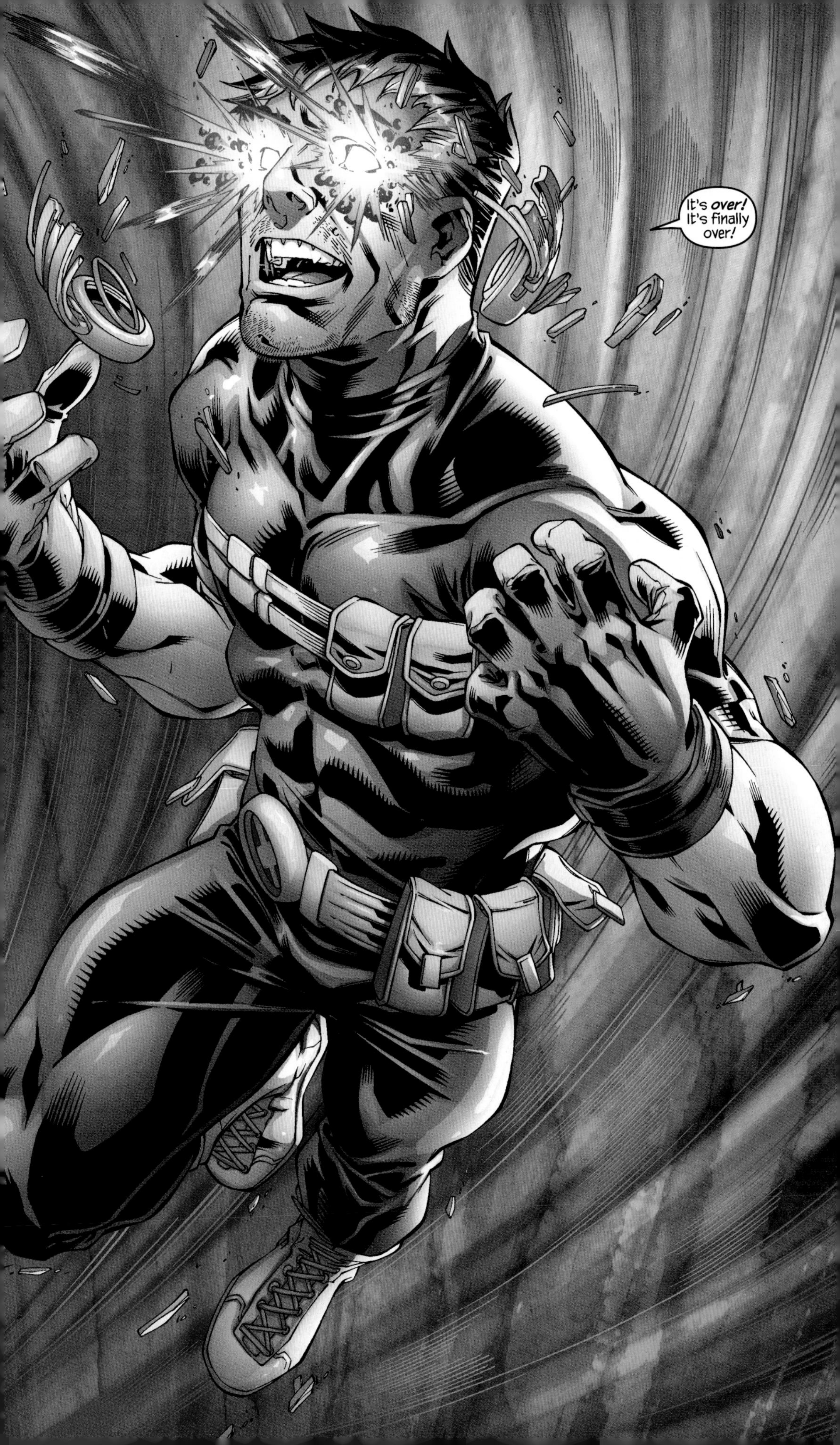
It's *over!* It's finally over!

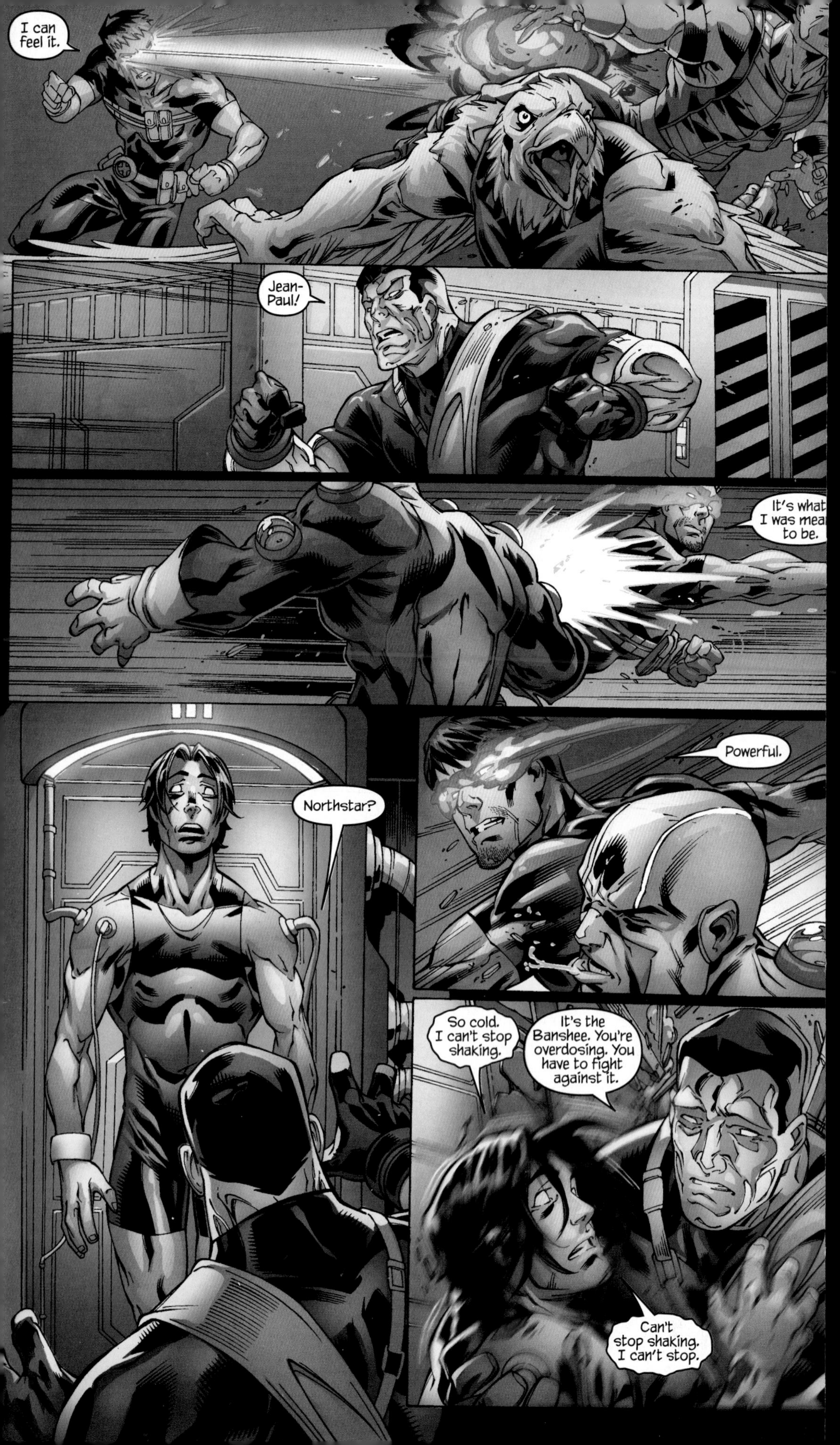
I can feel it.
Jean-Paul!
It's what I was mea
to be.
Northstar?
Powerful.
So cold. I can't stop shaking.
It's the Banshee. You're overdosing. You have to fight against it.
Can't stop shaking. I can't stop.

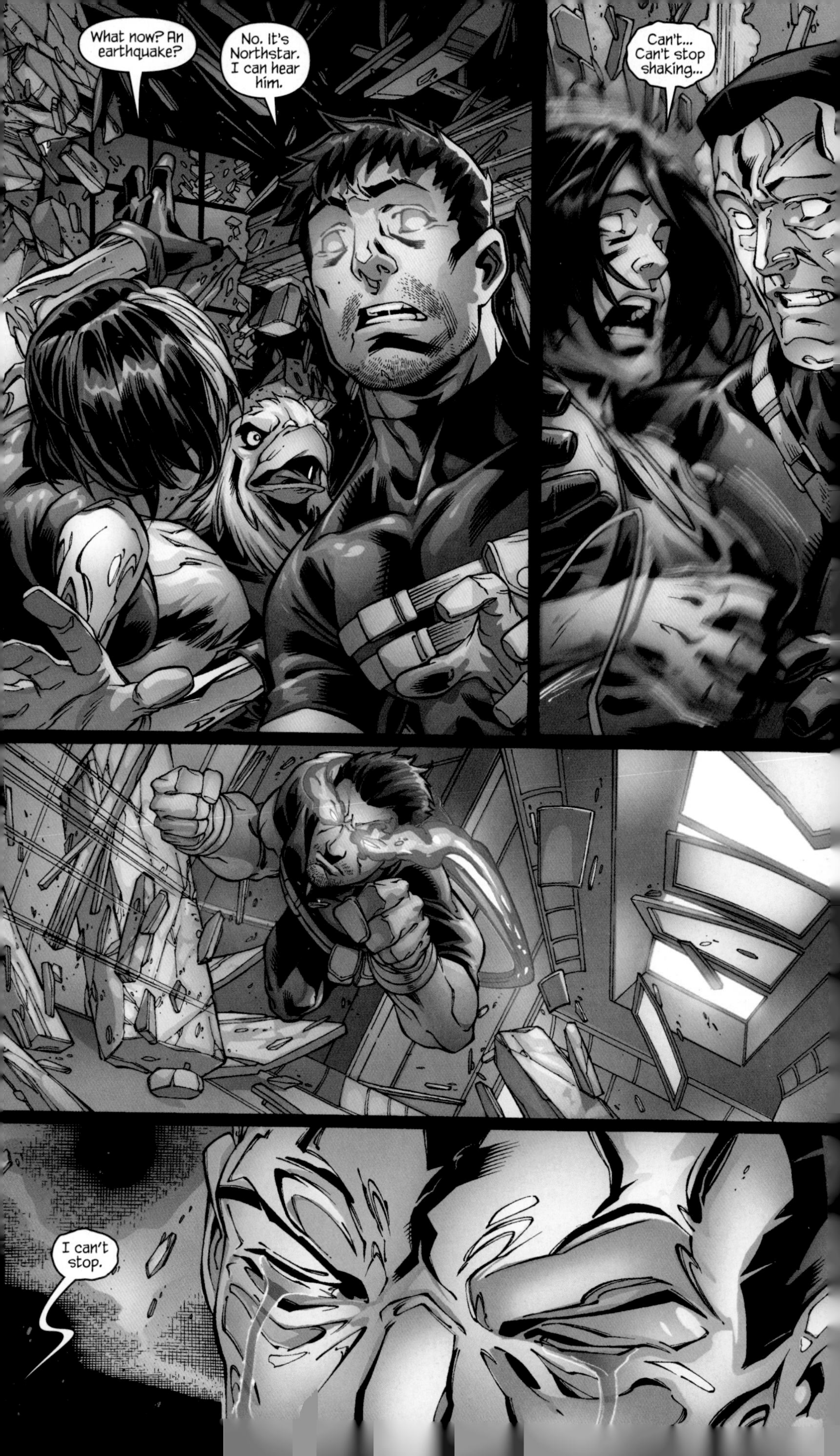
What now? An earthquake?
No. It's Northstar. I can hear him.
Can't... Can't stop shaking...
I can't stop.

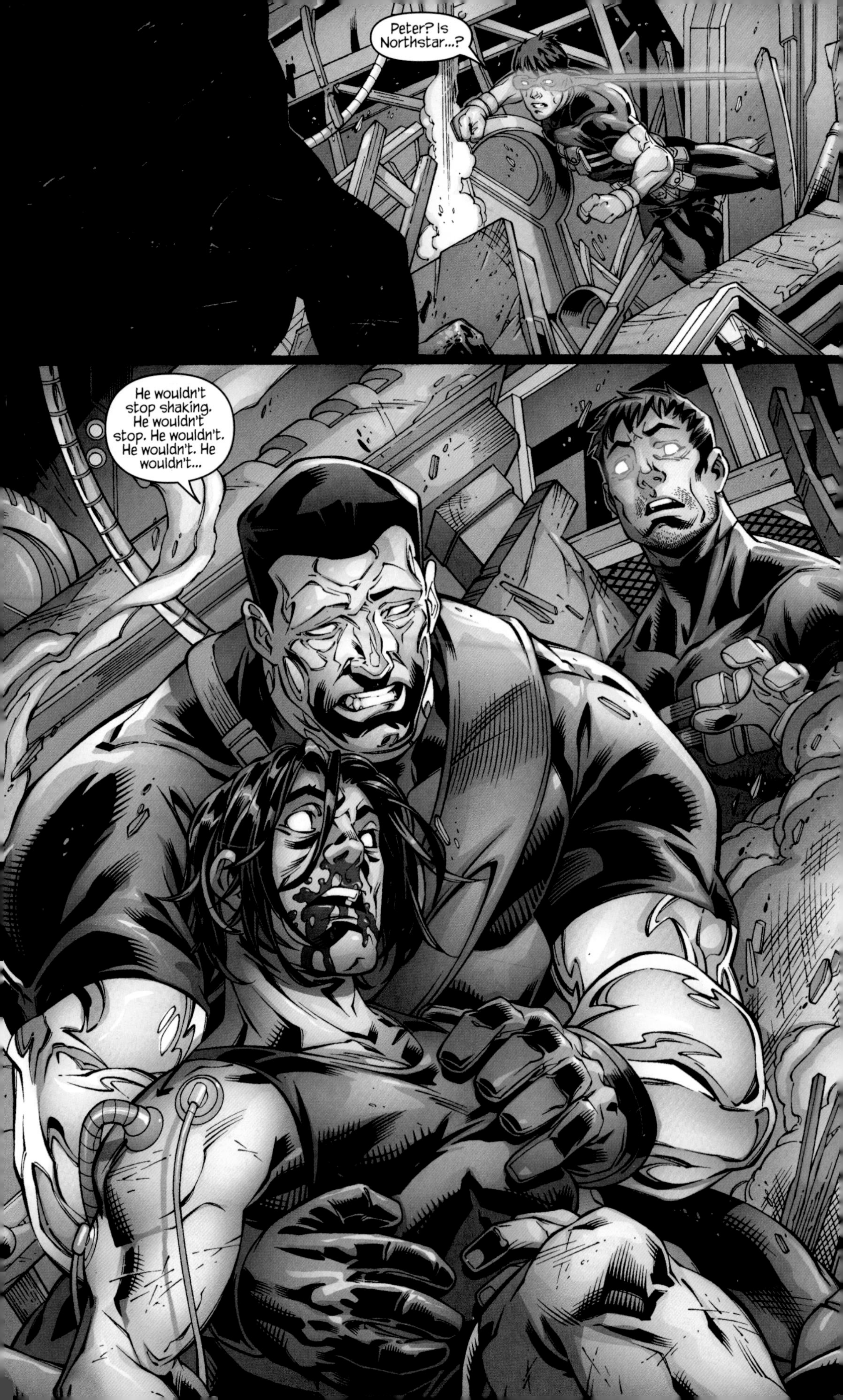
Peter? Is Northstar...?
He wouldn't stop shaking. He wouldn't stop. He wouldn't. He wouldn't. He wouldn't...

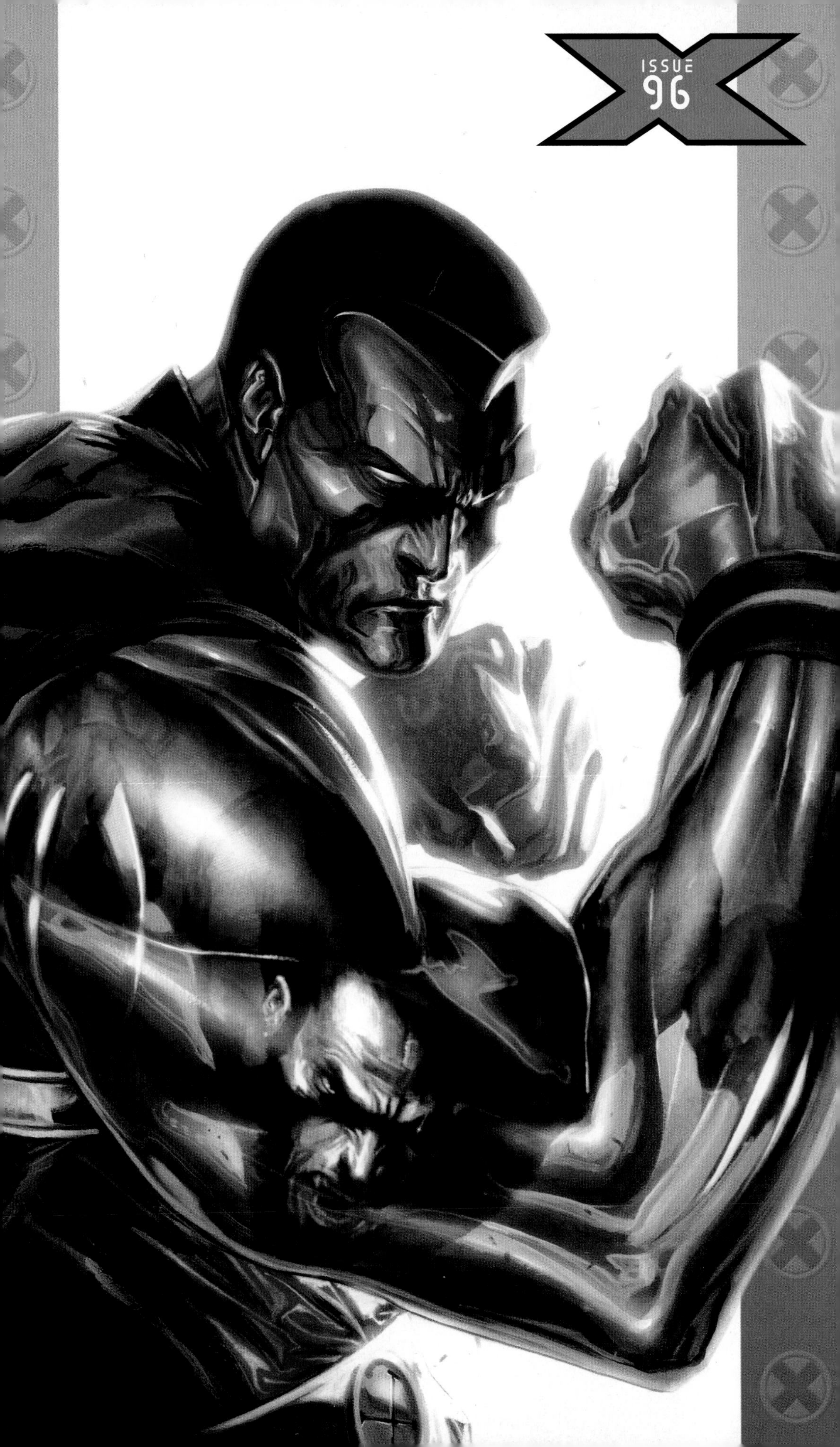
ISSUE
96

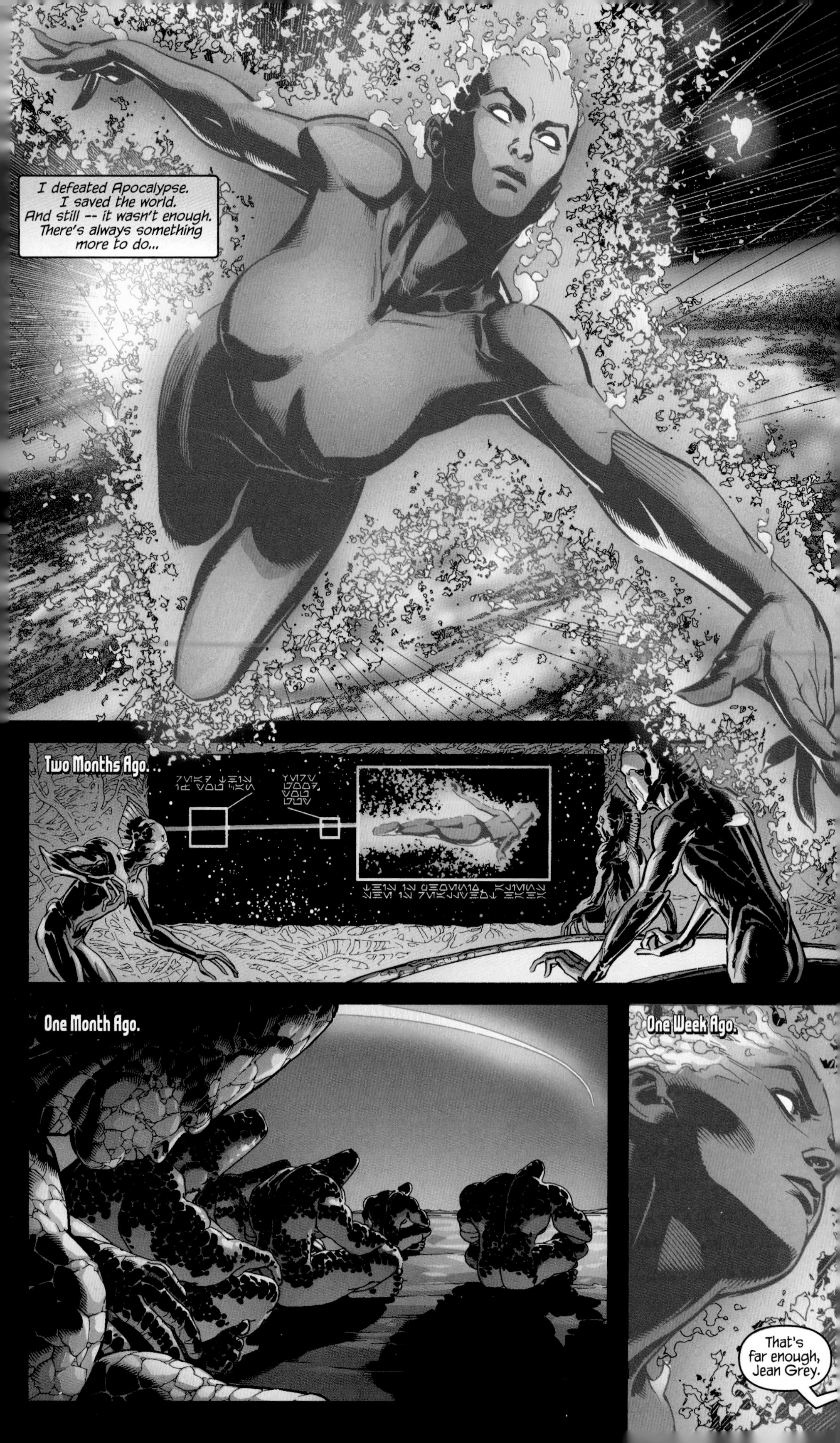
I defeated Apocalypse. I saved the world. And still -- it wasn't enough. There's always something more to do...
Two Months Ago...
One Month Ago.
One Week Ago.
That's far enough, Jean Grey.

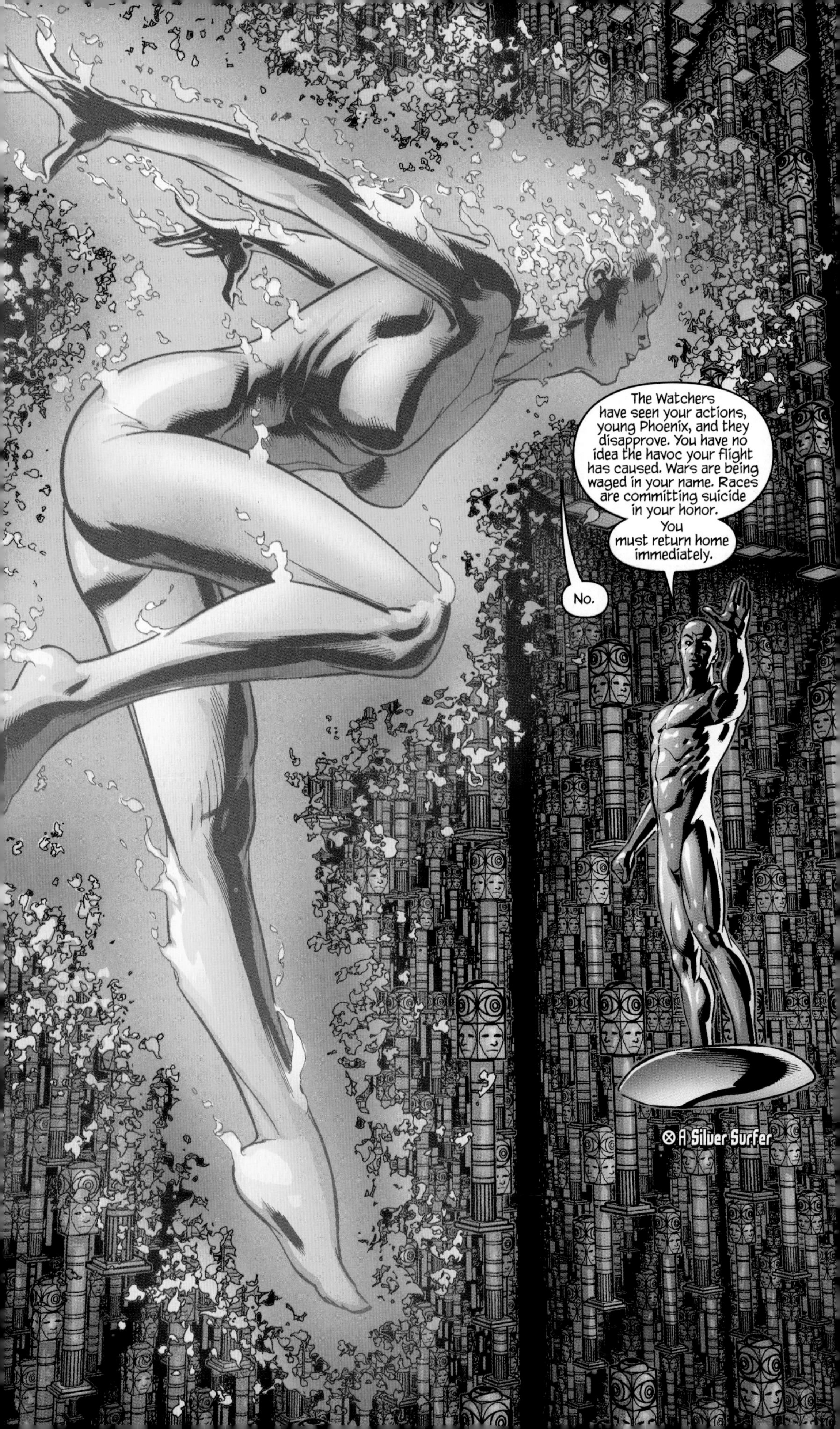
The Watchers have seen your actions, young Phoenix, and they disapprove. You have no idea the havoc your flight has caused. Wars are being waged in your name. Races are committing suicide in your honor.
You must return home immediately.
No.
⊗ A Silver Surfer

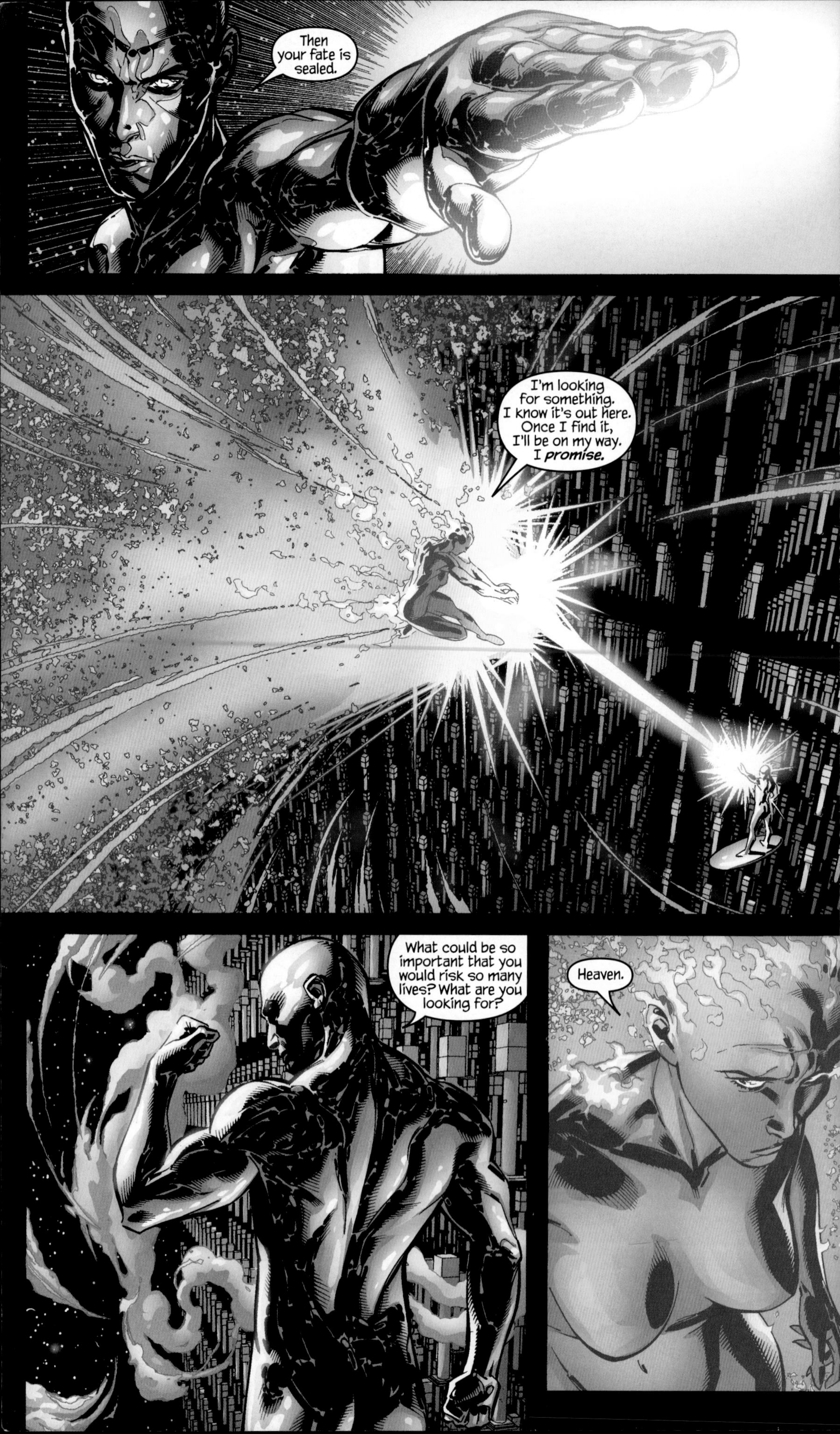
Then your fate is sealed.
I'm looking for something. I know it's out here. Once I find it, I'll be on my way. I *promise.*
What could be so important that you would risk so many lives? What are you looking for?
Heaven.

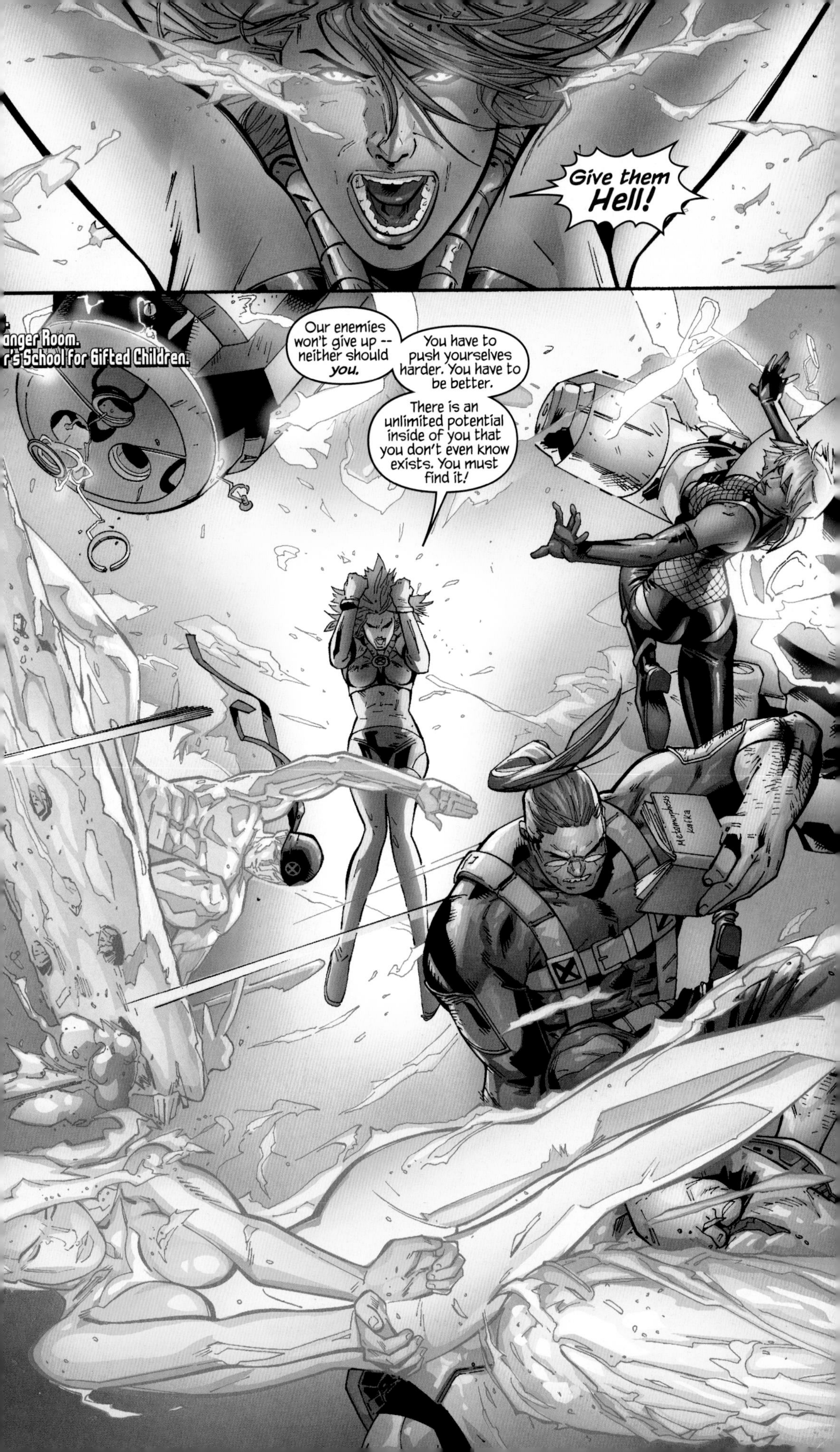
Give them Hell!
...anger Room.
...r's School for Gifted Children.
Our enemies won't give up -- neither should you.
You have to push yourselves harder. You have to be better.
There is an unlimited potential inside of you that you don't even know exists. You must find it!

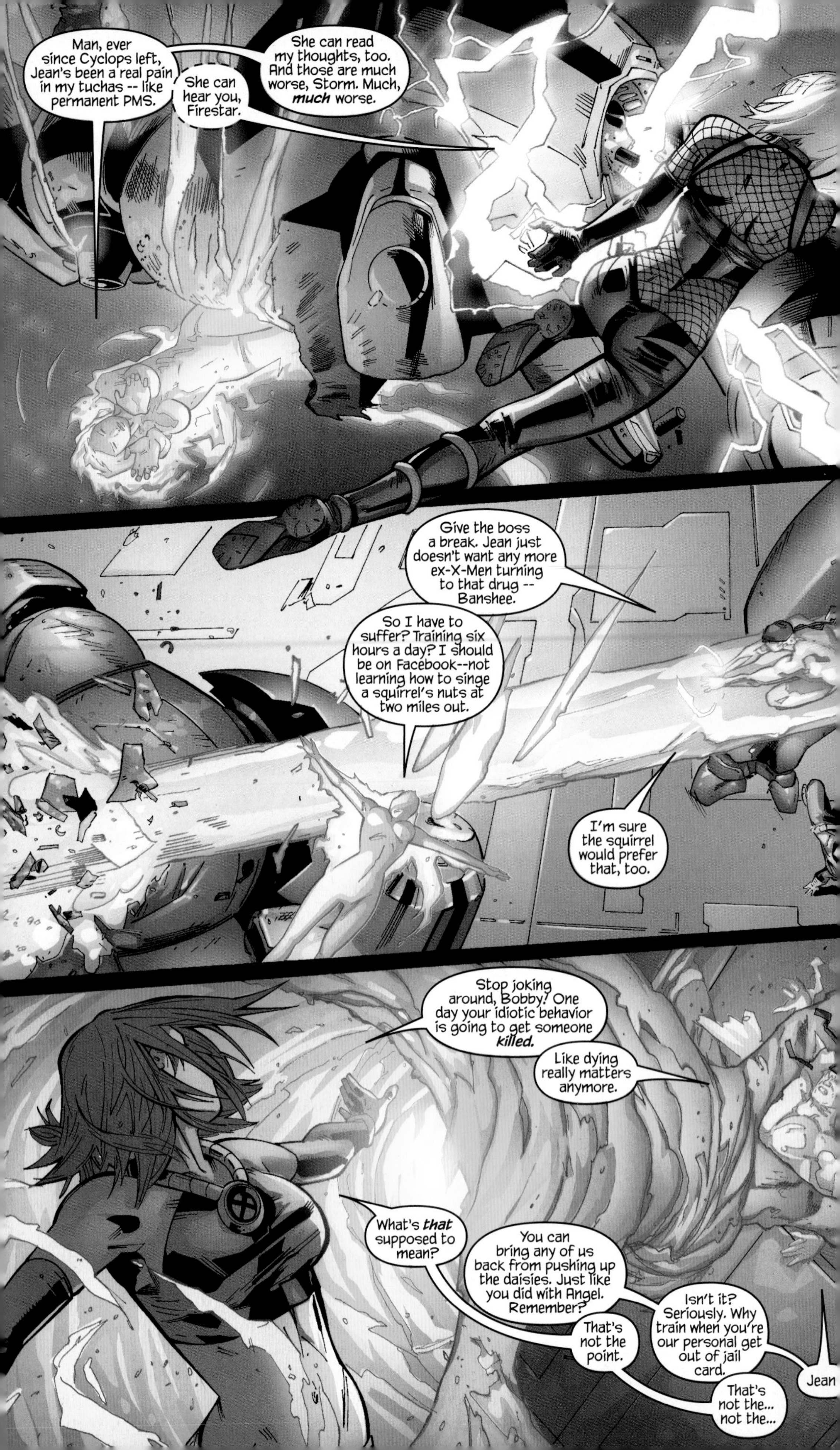

Man, ever since Cyclops left, Jean's been a real pain in my tuchas -- like permanent PMS.
She can hear you, Firestar.
She can read my thoughts, too. And those are much worse, Storm. Much, *much* worse.
Give the boss a break. Jean just doesn't want any more ex-X-Men turning to that drug -- Banshee.
So I have to suffer? Training six hours a day? I should be on Facebook--not learning how to singe a squirrel's nuts at two miles out.
I'm sure the squirrel would prefer that, too.
Stop joking around, Bobby! One day your idiotic behavior is going to get someone ***killed.***
Like dying really matters anymore.
What's ***that*** supposed to mean?
You can bring any of us back from pushing up the daisies. Just like you did with Angel. Remember?
That's not the point.
Isn't it? Seriously. Why train when you're our personal get out of jail card.
That's not the... not the...
Jean

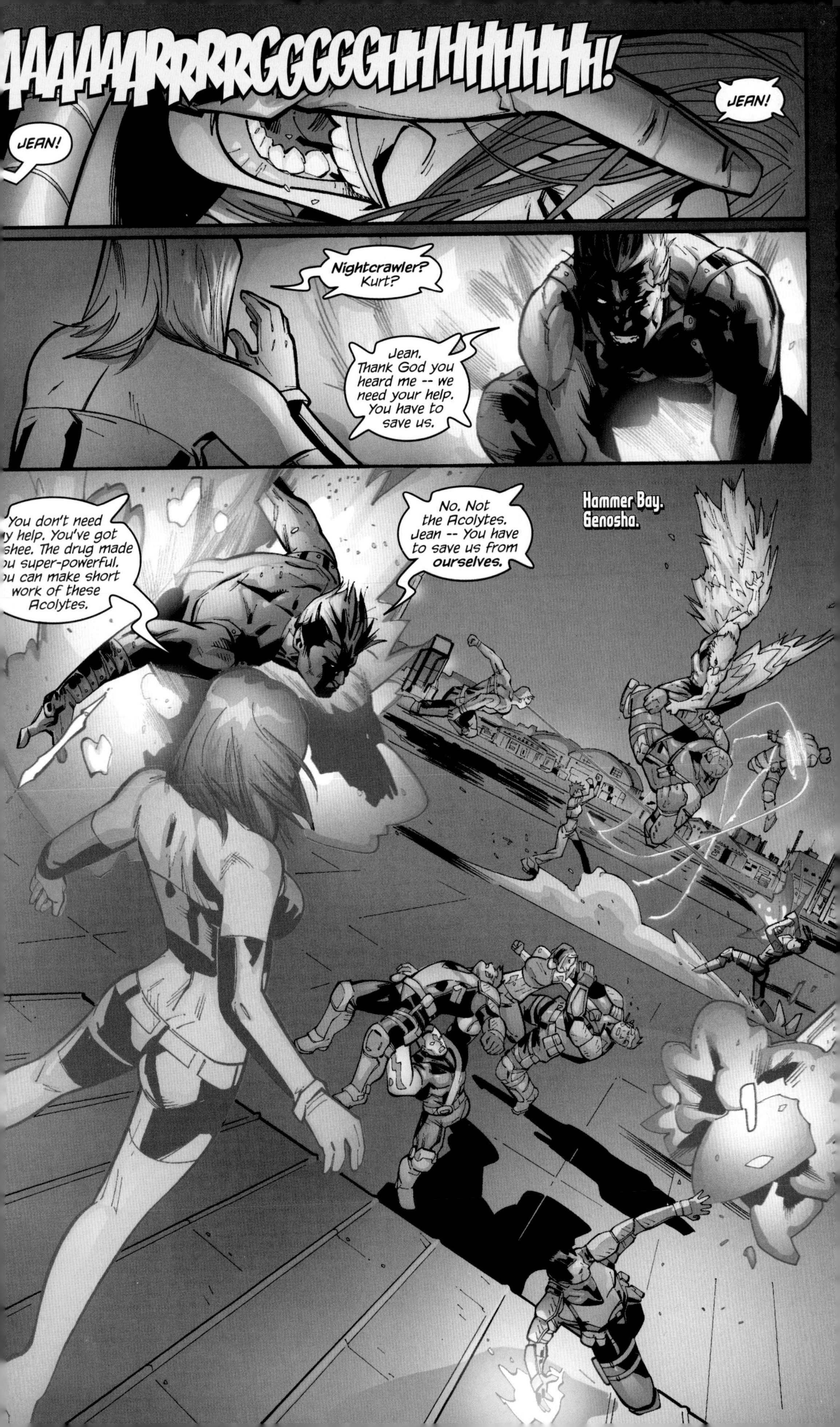
AAAAARRRRGGGGGHHHHHHHH!
JEAN!
JEAN!
Nightcrawler? Kurt?
Jean. Thank God you heard me -- we need your help. You have to save us.
You don't need y help. You've got shee. The drug made ou super-powerful. ou can make short work of these Acolytes.
No. Not the Acolytes. Jean -- You have to save us from **ourselves.**
Hammer Bay. Genosha.

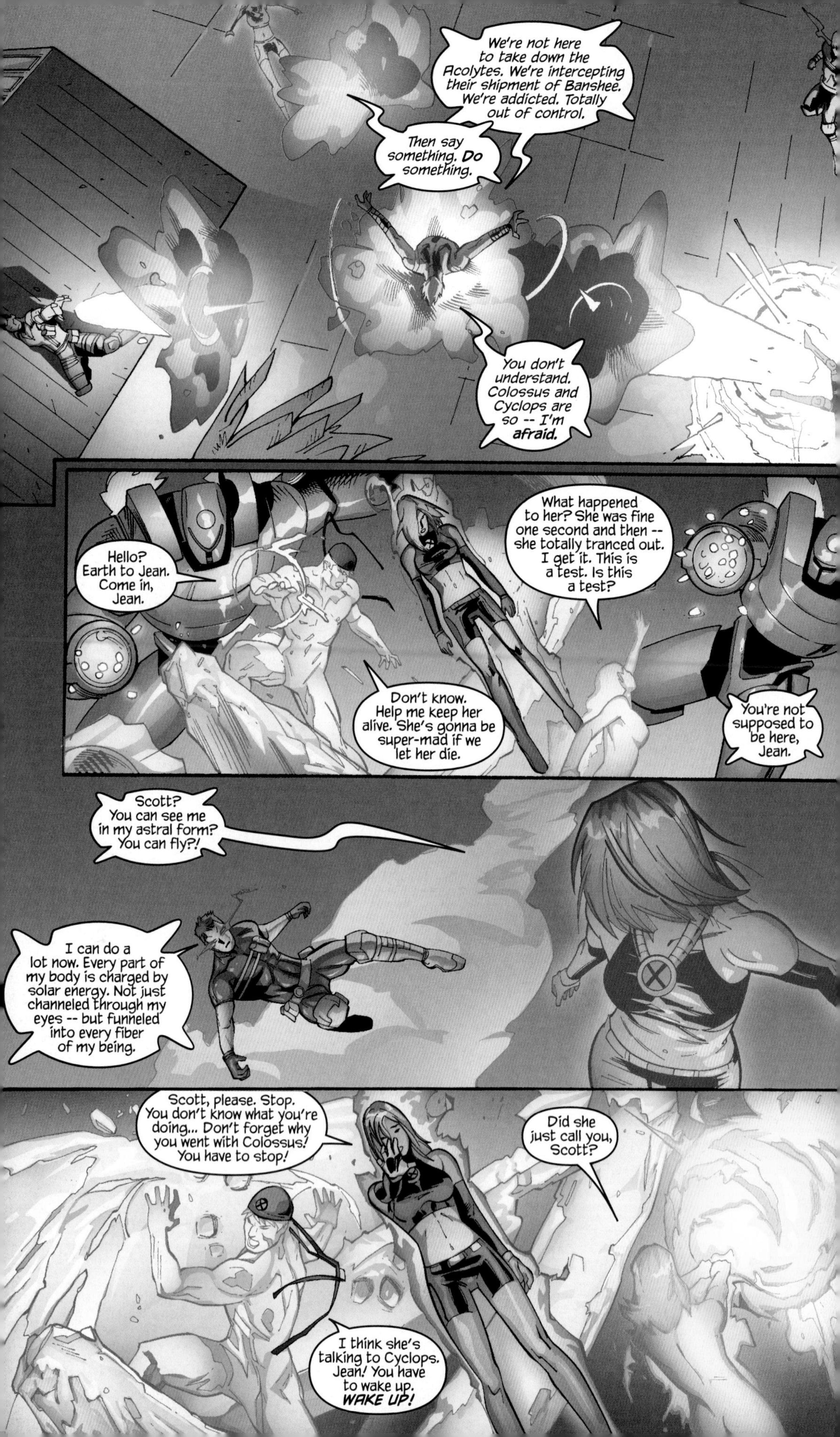
We're not here to take down the Acolytes. We're intercepting their shipment of Banshee. We're addicted. Totally out of control.
Then say something. Do something.
You don't understand. Colossus and Cyclops are so -- I'm afraid.
Hello? Earth to Jean. Come in, Jean.
What happened to her? She was fine one second and then -- she totally tranced out. I get it. This is a test. Is this a test?
Don't know. Help me keep her alive. She's gonna be super-mad if we let her die.
You're not supposed to be here, Jean.
Scott? You can see me in my astral form? You can fly?!
I can do a lot now. Every part of my body is charged by solar energy. Not just channeled through my eyes -- but funneled into every fiber of my being.
Scott, please. Stop. You don't know what you're doing... Don't forget why you went with Colossus! You have to stop!
Did she just call you, Scott?
I think she's talking to Cyclops. Jean! You have to wake up. WAKE UP!

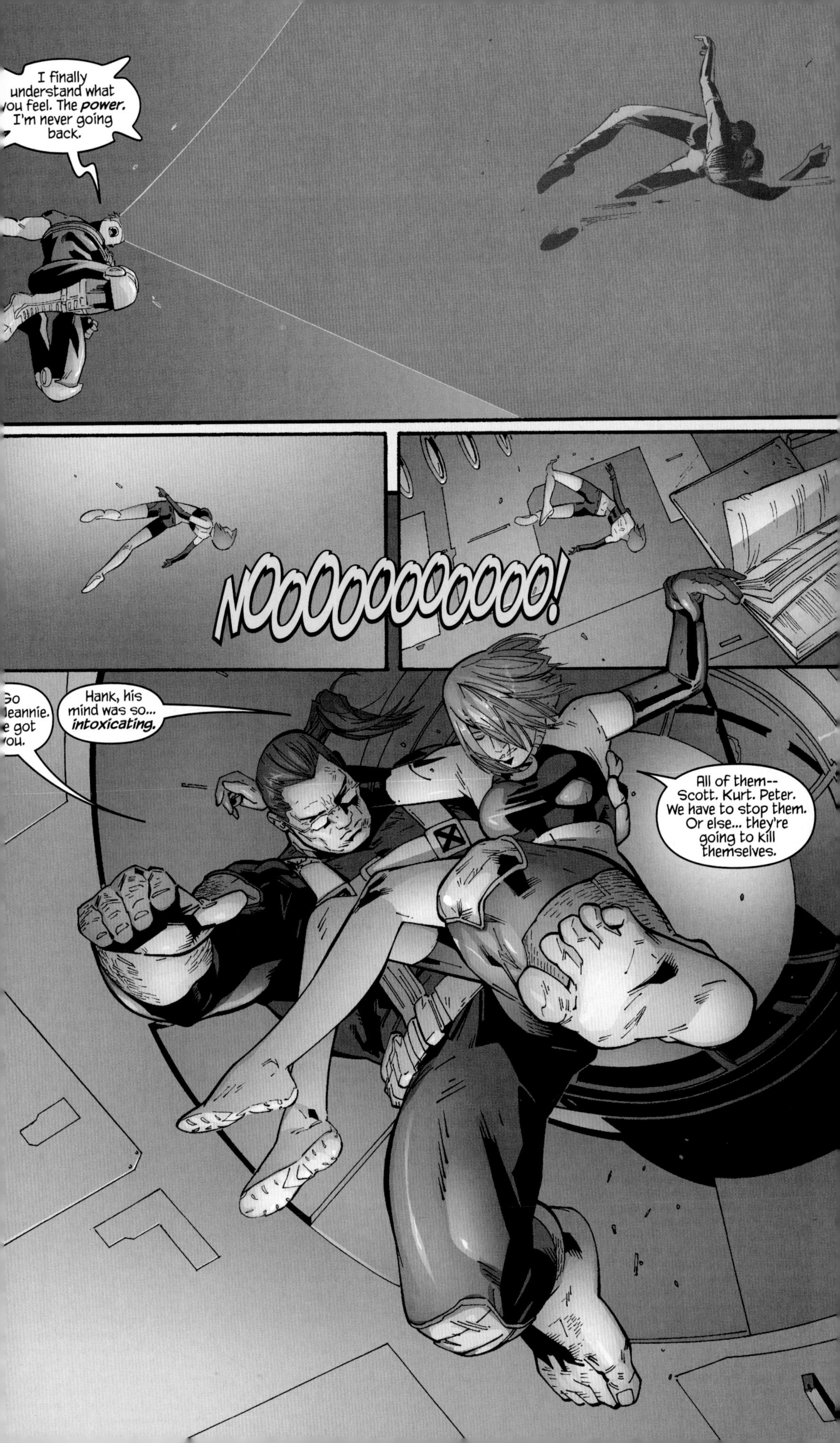

I finally understand what ou feel. The *power.* I'm never going back.
NOOOOOOOOOOO!
So eannie. e got ou.
Hank, his mind was so... *intoxicating.*
All of them-- Scott. Kurt. Peter. We have to stop them. Or else... they're going to kill themselves.

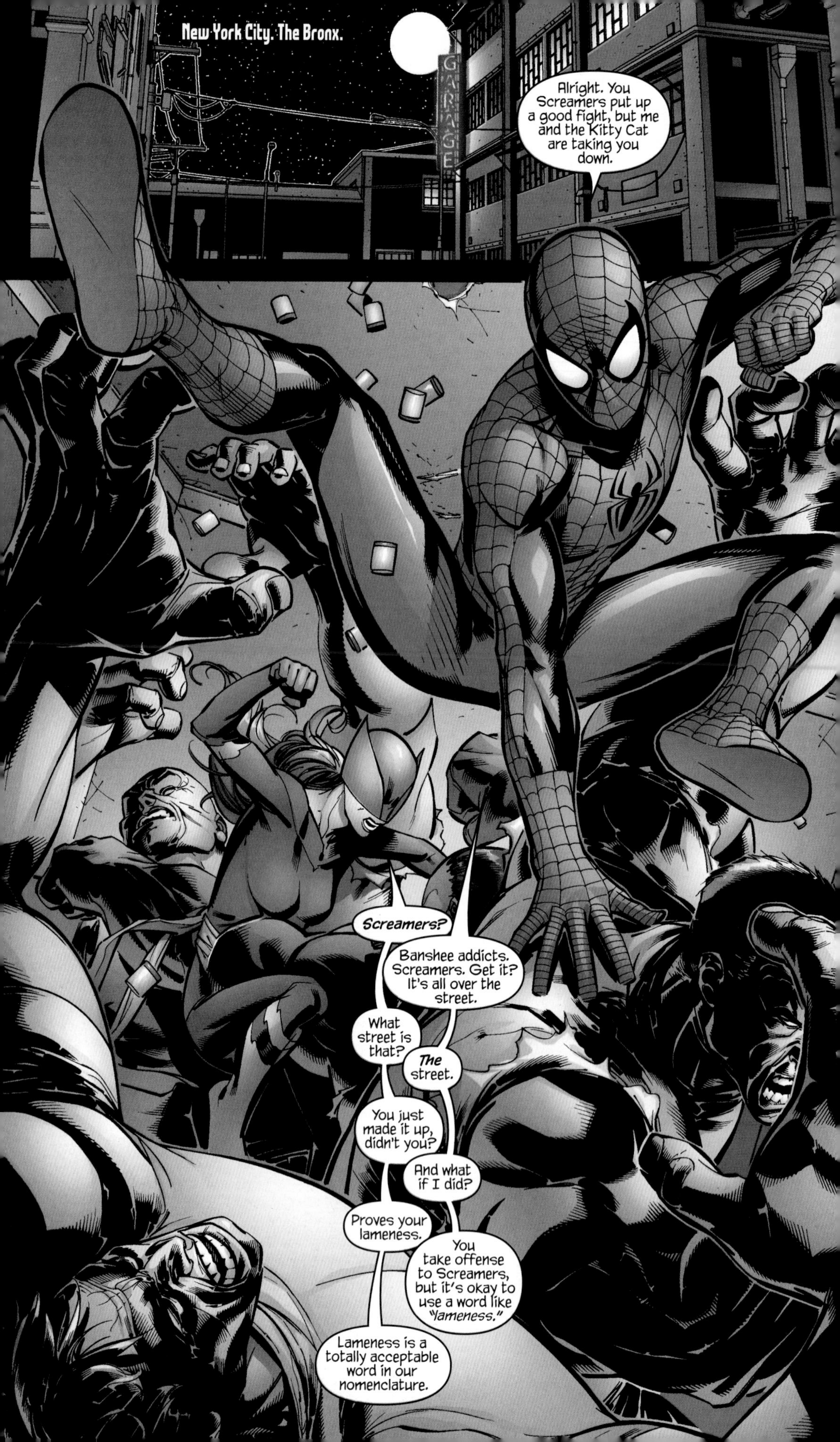
New York City. The Bronx.
Alright. You Screamers put up a good fight, but me and the Kitty Cat are taking you down.
Screamers?
Banshee addicts. Screamers. Get it? It's all over the street.
What street is that?
The street.
You just made it up, didn't you?
And what if I did?
Proves your lameness.
You take offense to Screamers, but it's okay to use a word like "lameness."
Lameness is a totally acceptable word in our nomenclature.

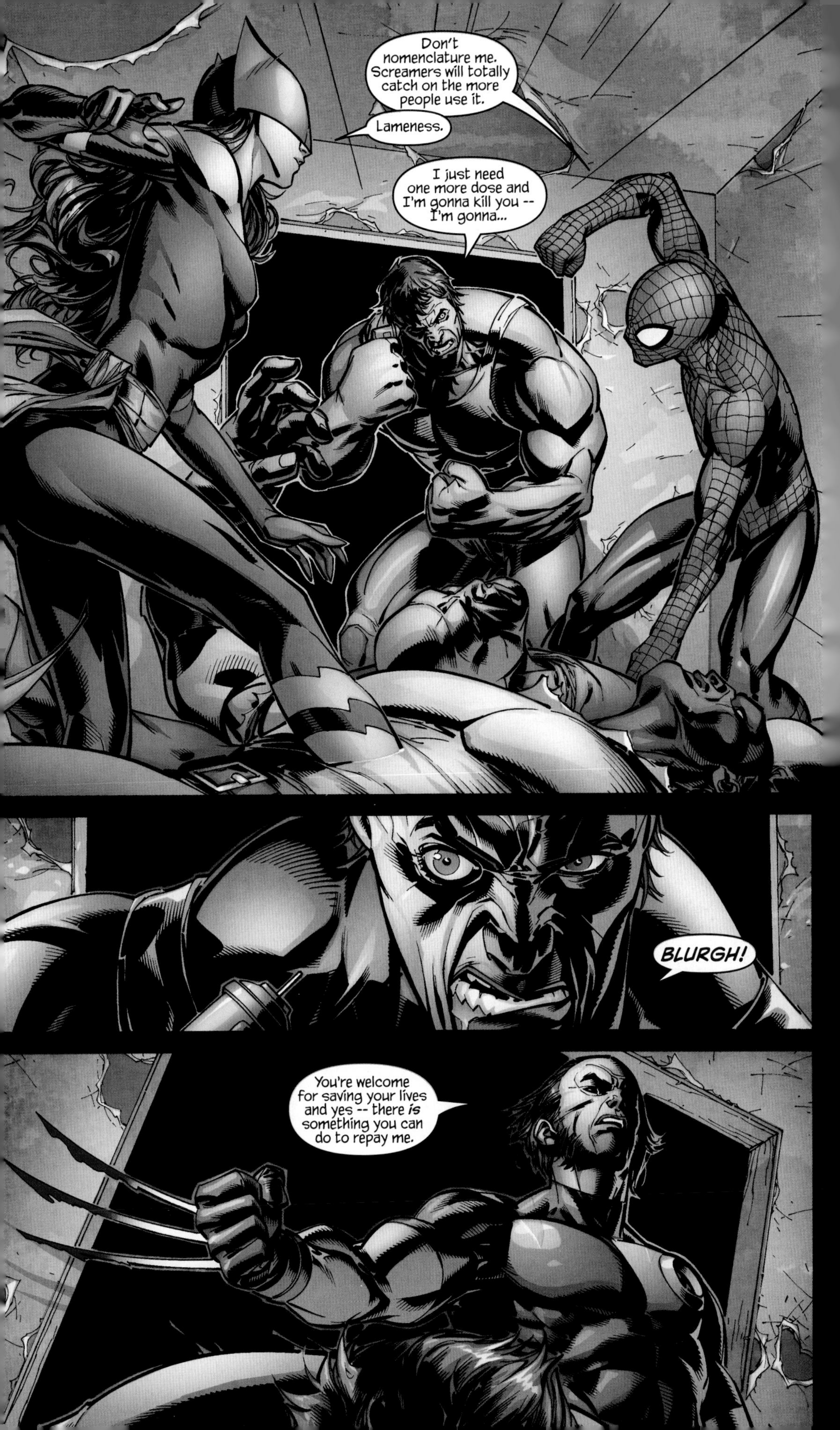
Don't nomenclature me. Screamers will totally catch on the more people use it.
Lameness.
I just need one more dose and I'm gonna kill you -- I'm gonna...
BLURGH!
You're welcome for saving your lives and yes -- there *is* something you can do to repay me.

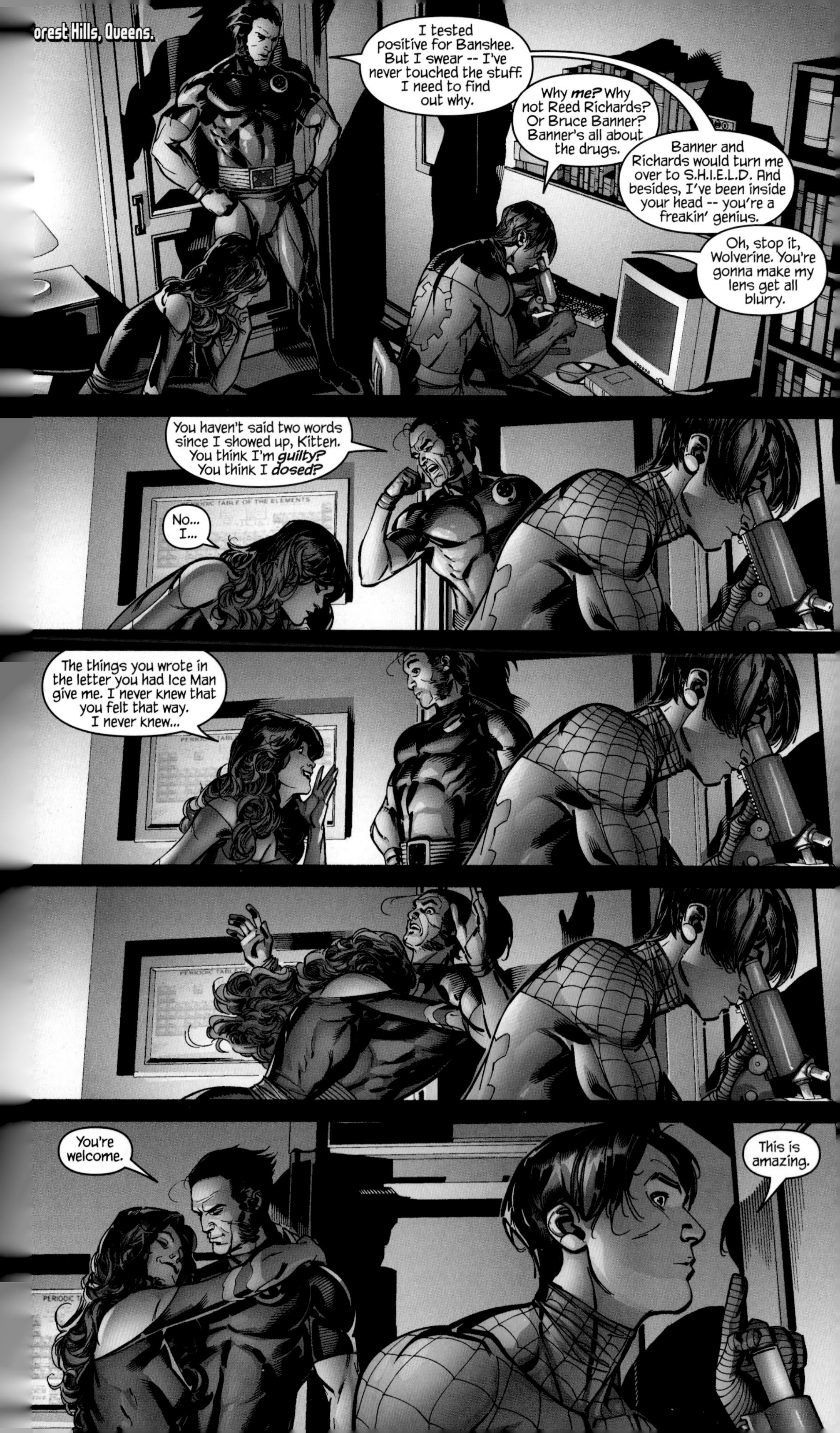

orest Hills, Queens.
I tested positive for Banshee. But I swear -- I've never touched the stuff. I need to find out why.
Why *me?* Why not Reed Richards? Or Bruce Banner? Banner's all about the drugs.
Banner and Richards would turn me over to S.H.I.E.L.D. And besides, I've been inside your head -- you're a freakin' genius.
Oh, stop it, Wolverine. You're gonna make my lens get all blurry.
You haven't said two words since I showed up, Kitten. You think I'm *guilty?* You think I *dosed?*
No... I...
PERIODIC TABLE OF THE ELEMENTS
The things you wrote in the letter you had Ice Man give me. I never knew that you felt that way. I never knew...
You're welcome.
This is amazing.

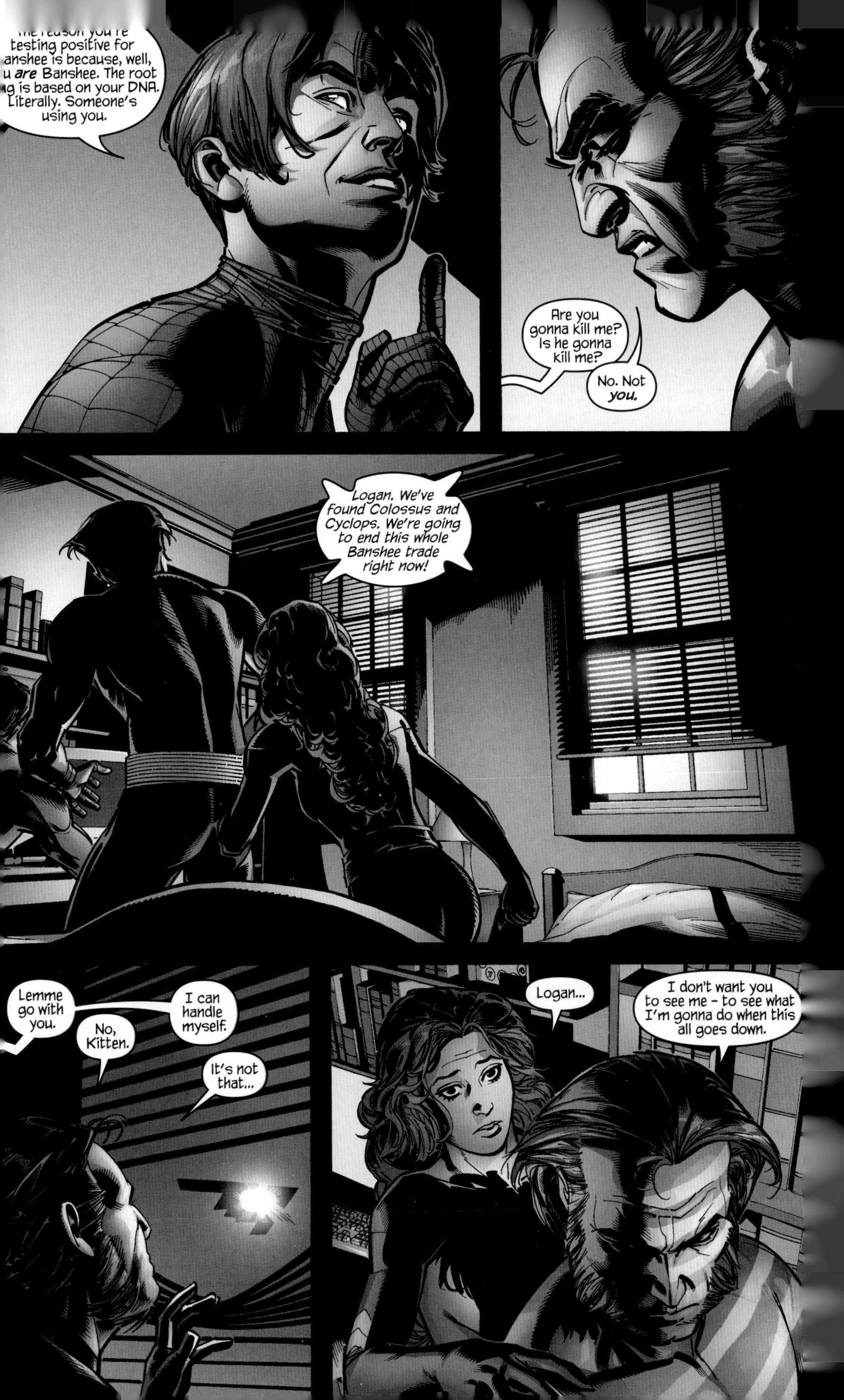

testing positive for anshee is because, well, u are Banshee. The root g is based on your DNA. Literally. Someone's using you.
Are you gonna kill me? Is he gonna kill me?
No. Not you.
Logan. We've found Colossus and Cyclops. We're going to end this whole Banshee trade right now!
Lemme go with you.
No, Kitten.
I can handle myself.
It's not that...
Logan...
I don't want you to see me - to see what I'm gonna do when this all goes down.

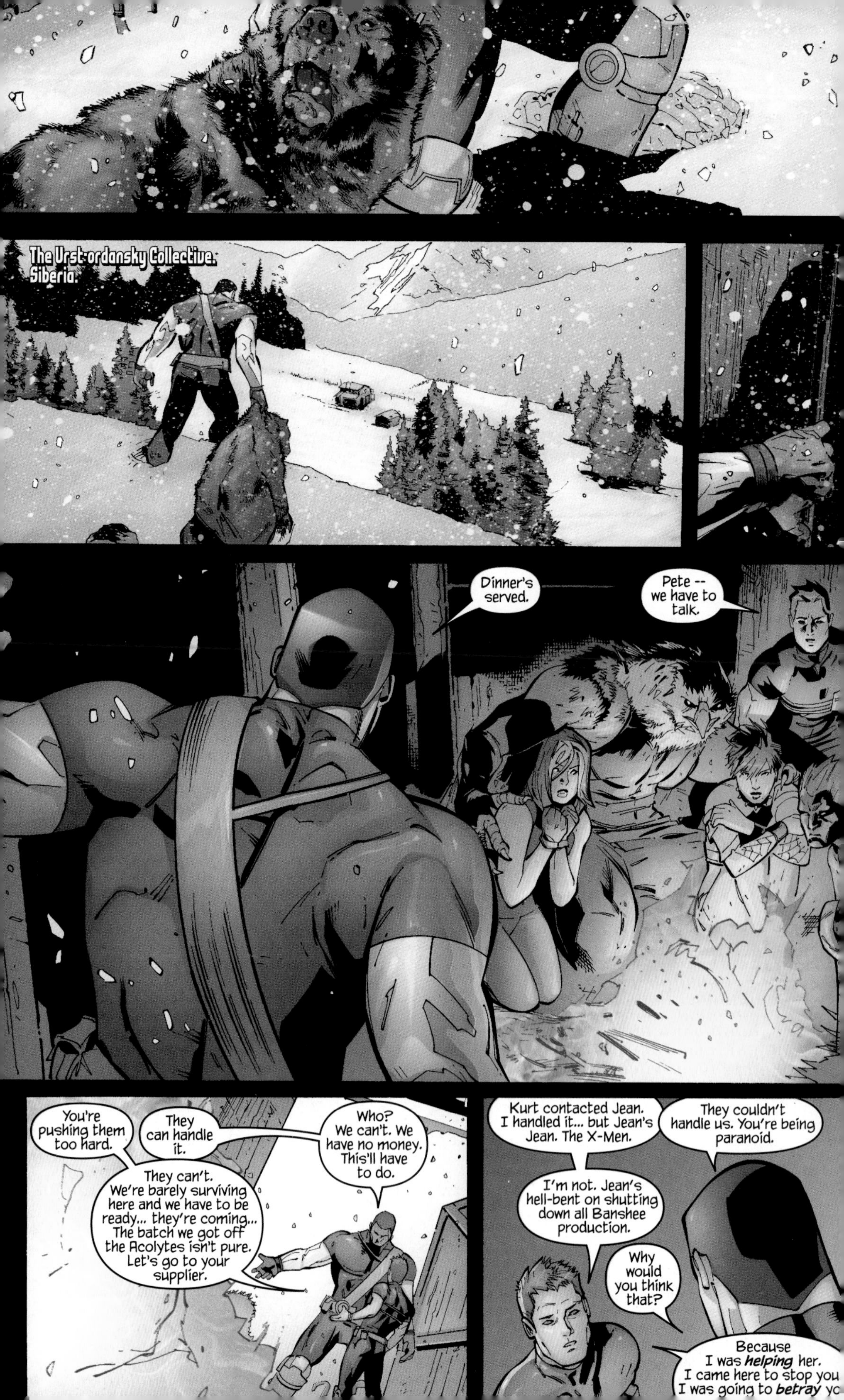

The Urst-ordansky Collective.
Siberia.
Dinner's served.
Pete -- we have to talk.
You're pushing them too hard.
They can handle it.
They can't. We're barely surviving here and we have to be ready... they're coming... The batch we got off the Acolytes isn't pure. Let's go to your supplier.
Who? We can't. We have no money. This'll have to do.
Kurt contacted Jean. I handled it... but Jean's Jean. The X-Men.
They couldn't handle us. You're being paranoid.
I'm not. Jean's hell-bent on shutting down all Banshee production.
Why would you think that?
Because I was *helping* her. I came here to stop you
I was going to *betray* yo

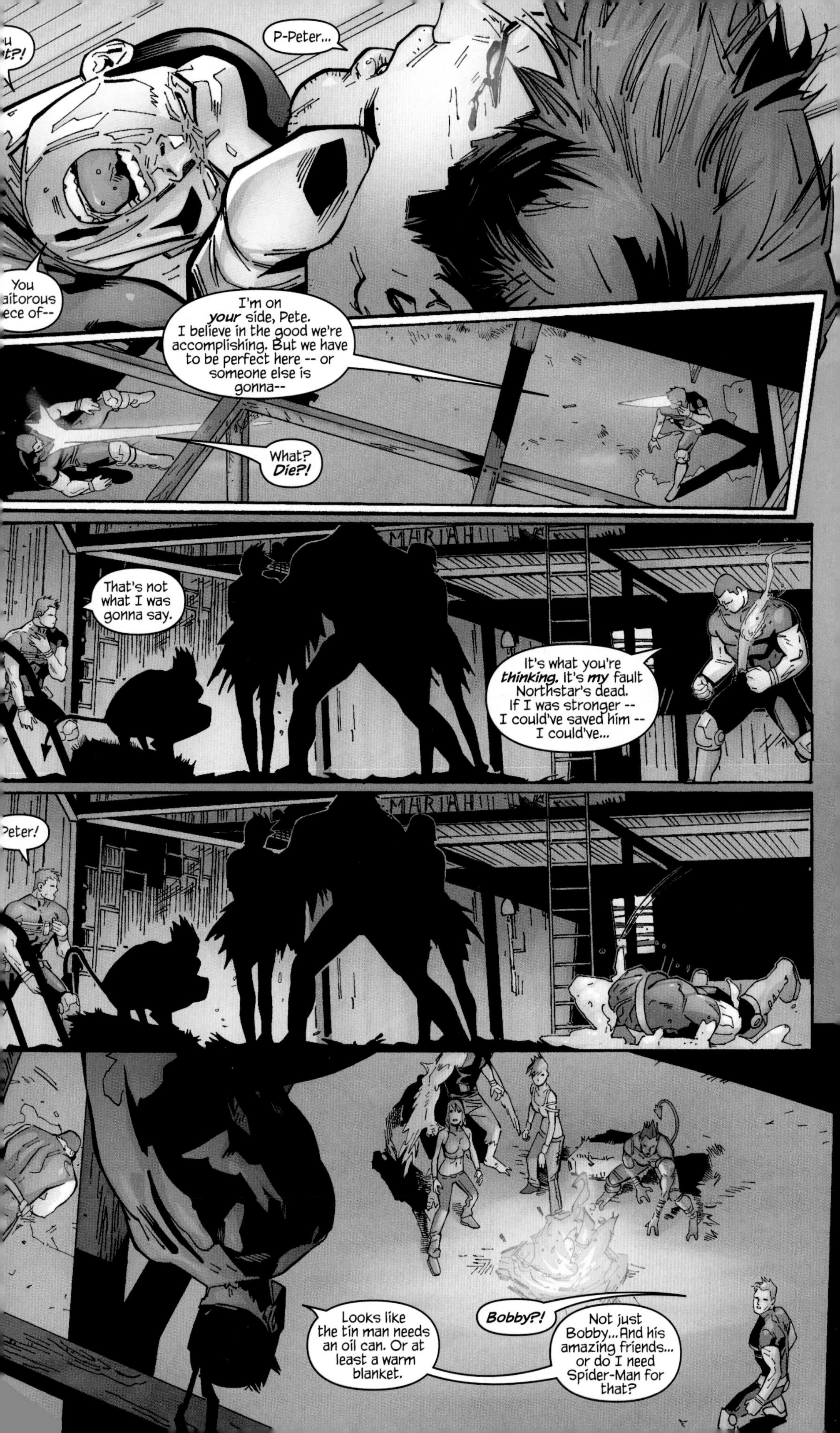

...u ...t?!
P-Peter...
You ...aitorous ...ece of--
I'm on *your* side, Pete. I believe in the good we're accomplishing. But we have to be perfect here -- or someone else is gonna--
What? *Die?!*
That's not what I was gonna say.
It's what you're *thinking.* It's *my* fault Northstar's dead. If I was stronger -- I could've saved him -- I could've...
MARIAH
...eter!
MARIAH
Looks like the tin man needs an oil can. Or at least a warm blanket.
Bobby?!
Not just Bobby... And his amazing friends... or do I need Spider-Man for that?

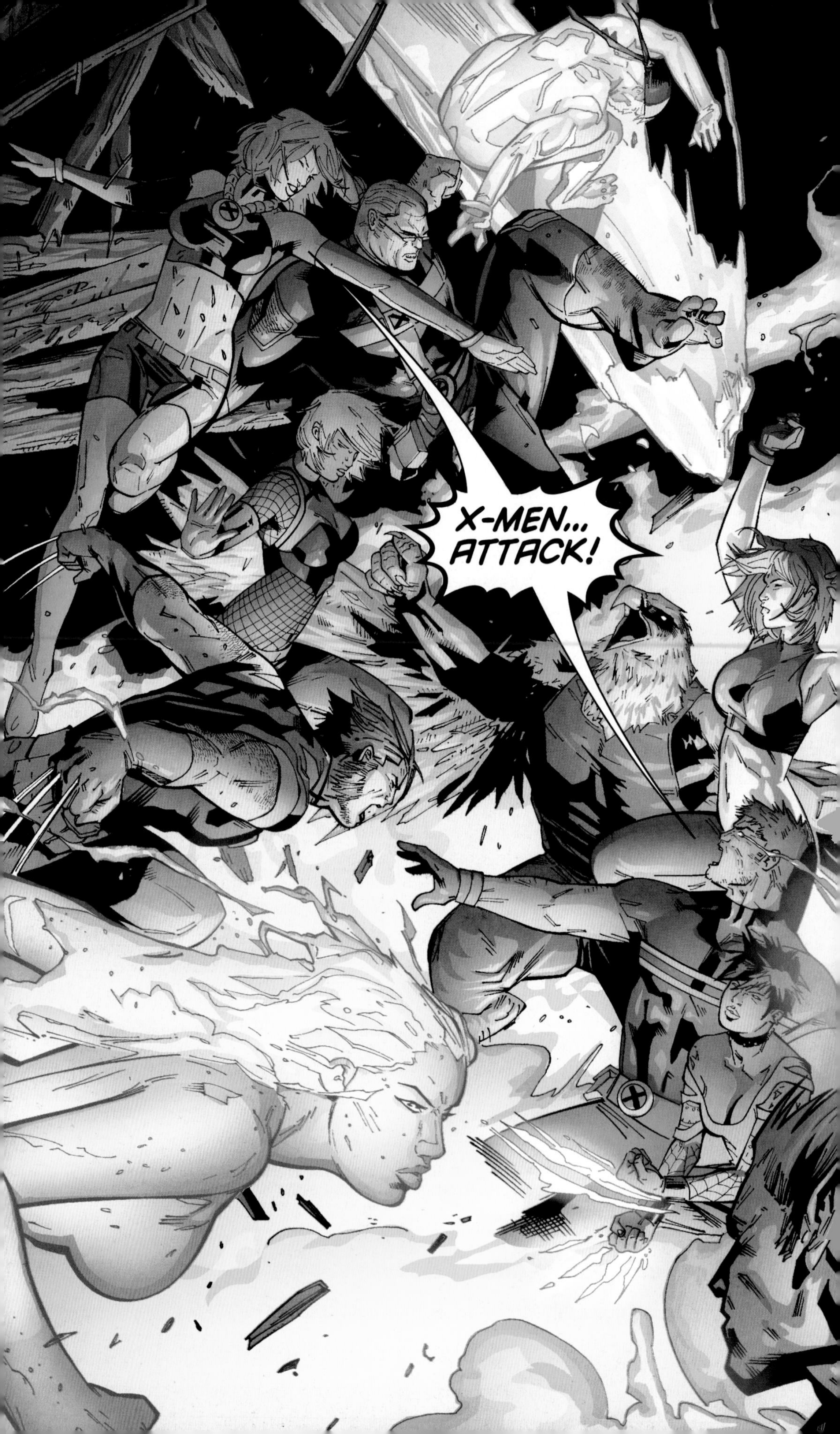
X-MEN... ATTACK!

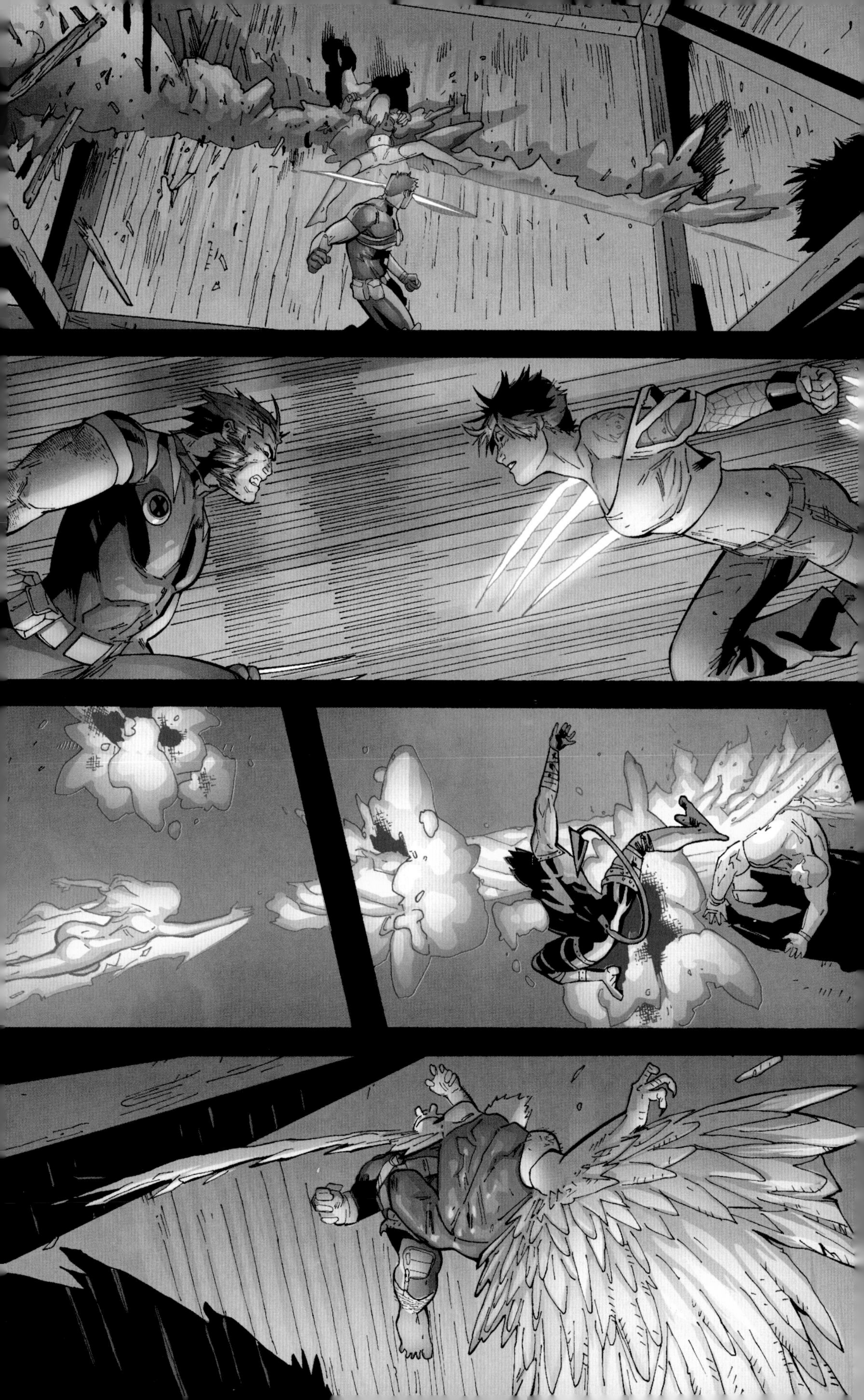

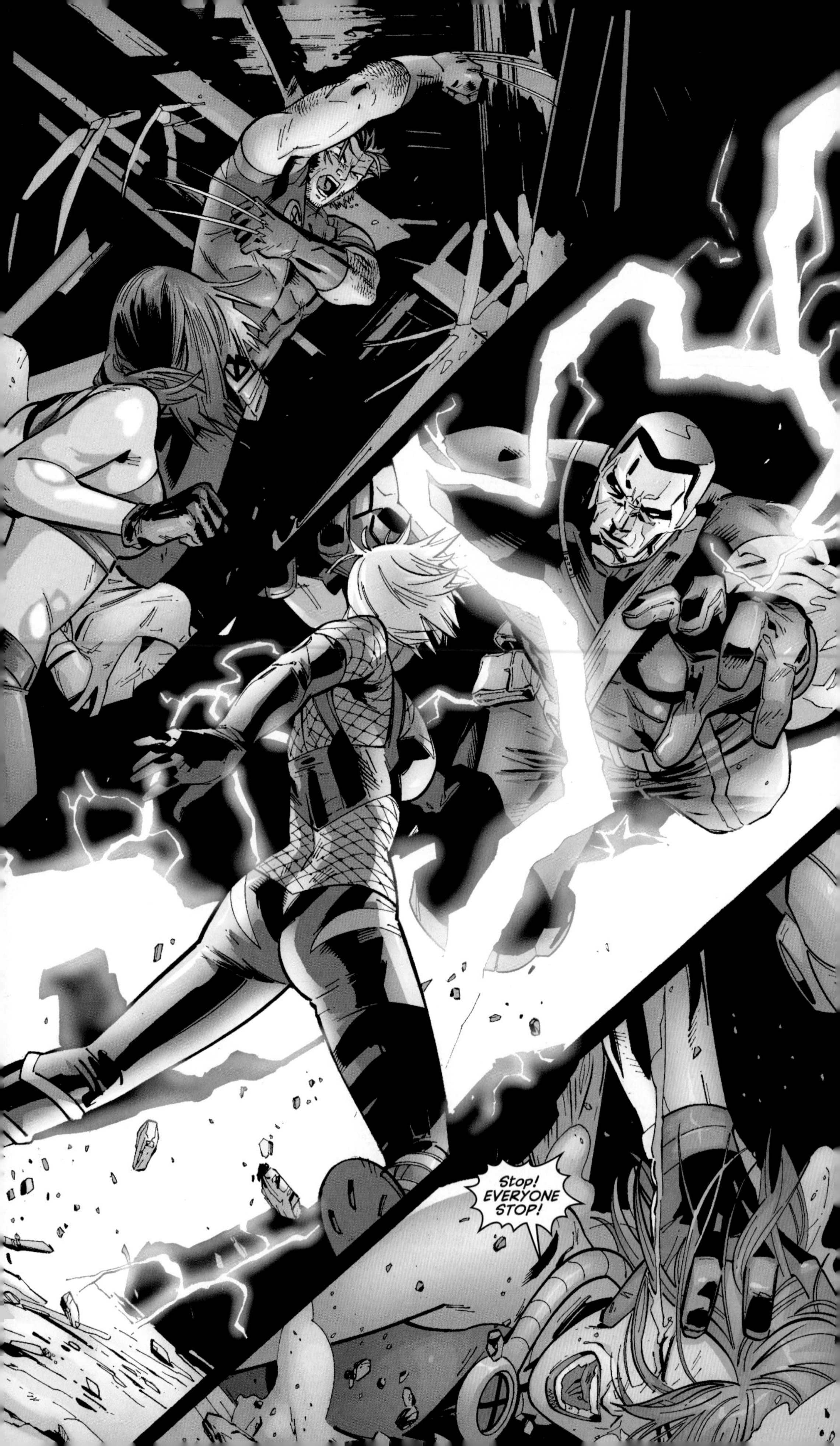

Stop! EVERYONE STOP!

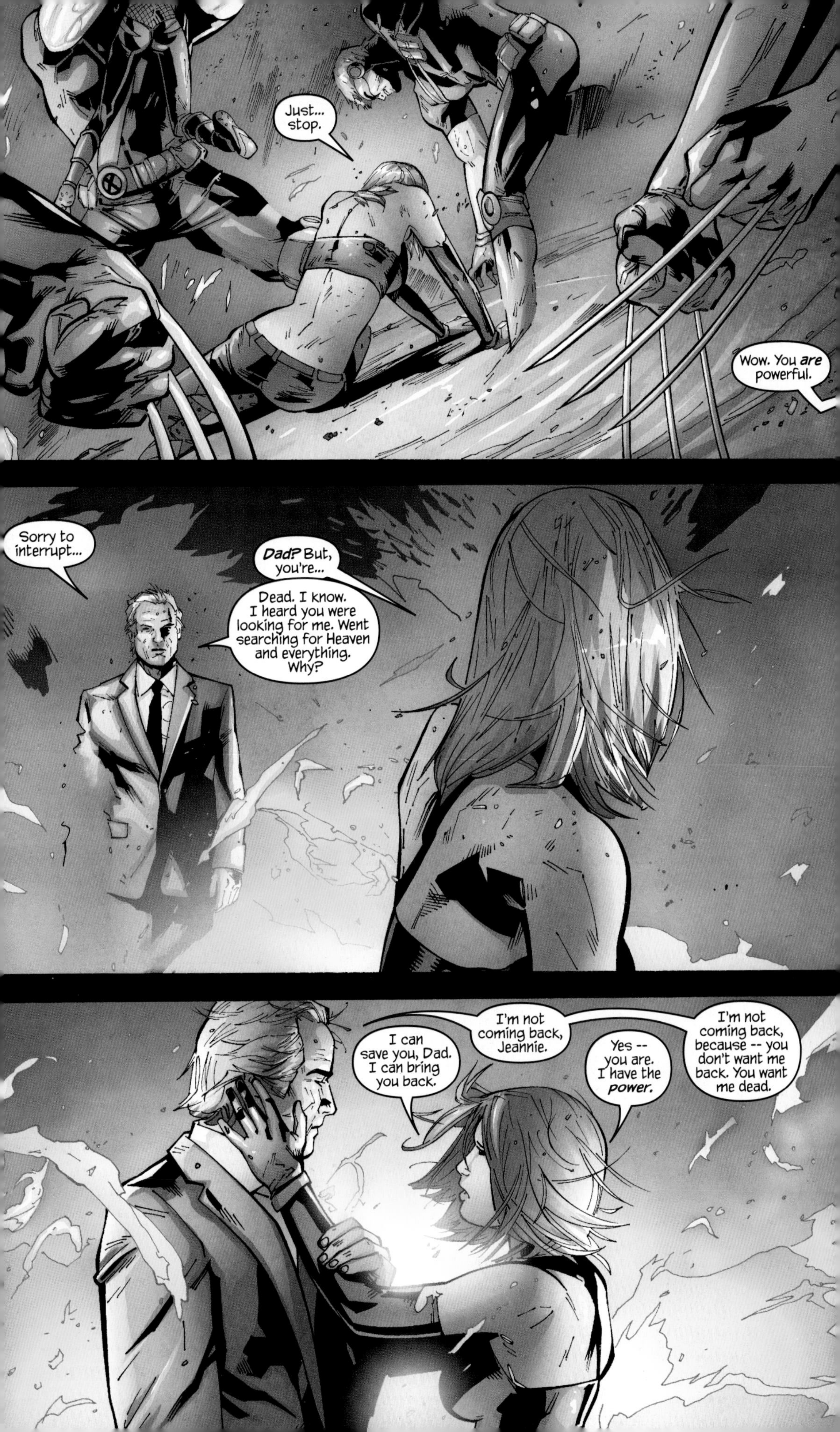
Just... stop.
Wow. You *are* powerful.
Sorry to interrupt...
Dad? But, you're...
Dead. I know. I heard you were looking for me. Went searching for Heaven and everything. Why?
I can save you, Dad. I can bring you back.
I'm not coming back, Jeannie.
Yes -- you are. I have the *power.*
I'm not coming back, because -- you don't want me back. You want me dead.

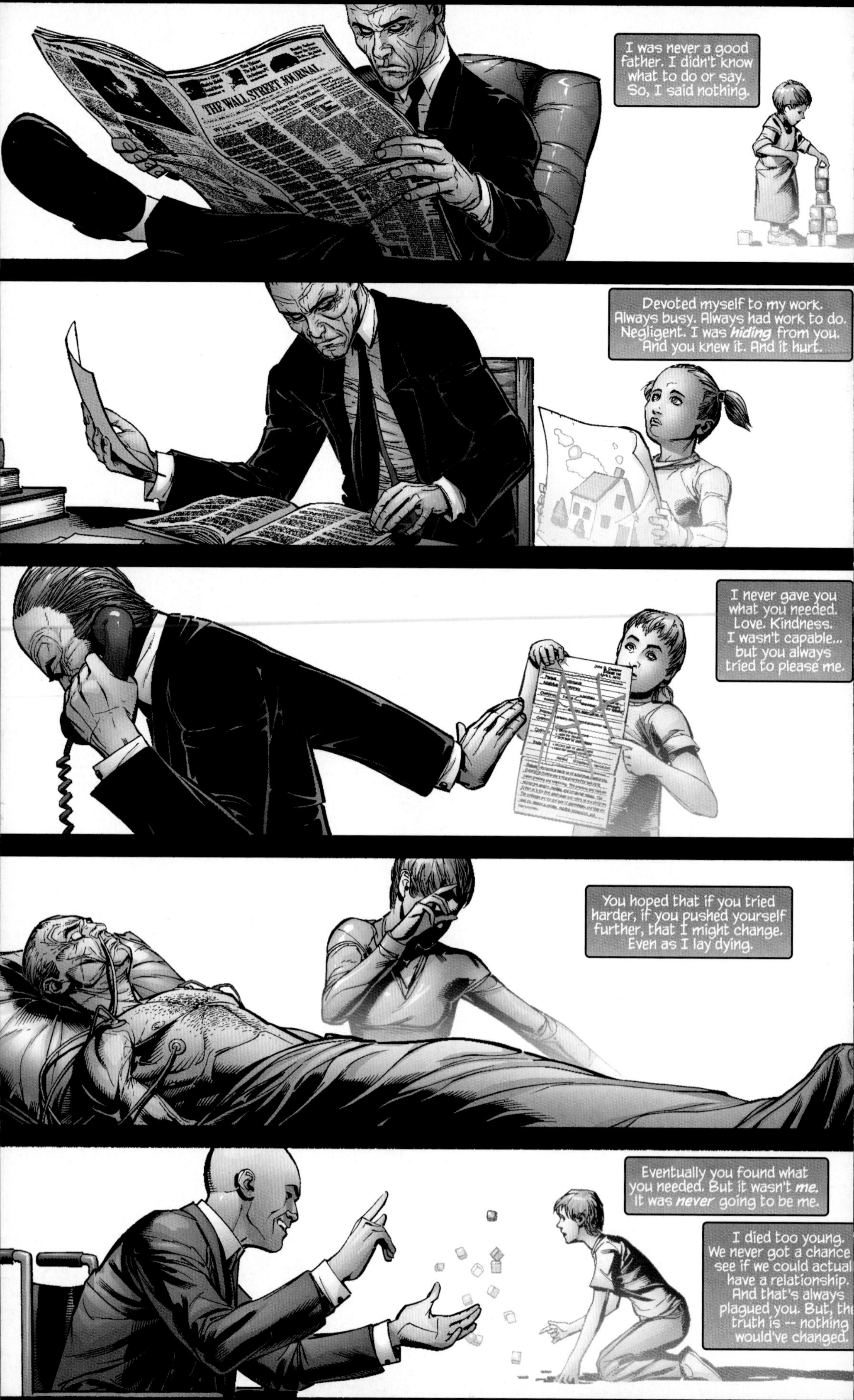
THE WALL STREET JOURNAL
I was never a good father. I didn't know what to do or say. So, I said nothing.
Devoted myself to my work. Always busy. Always had work to do. Negligent. I was *hiding* from you. And you knew it. And it hurt.
I never gave you what you needed. Love. Kindness. I wasn't capable... but you always tried to please me.
You hoped that if you tried harder, if you pushed yourself further, that I might change. Even as I lay dying.
Eventually you found what you needed. But it wasn't *me.* It was *never* going to be me.
I died too young. We never got a chance see if we could actual have a relationship. And that's always plagued you. But, th truth is -- nothing would've changed.

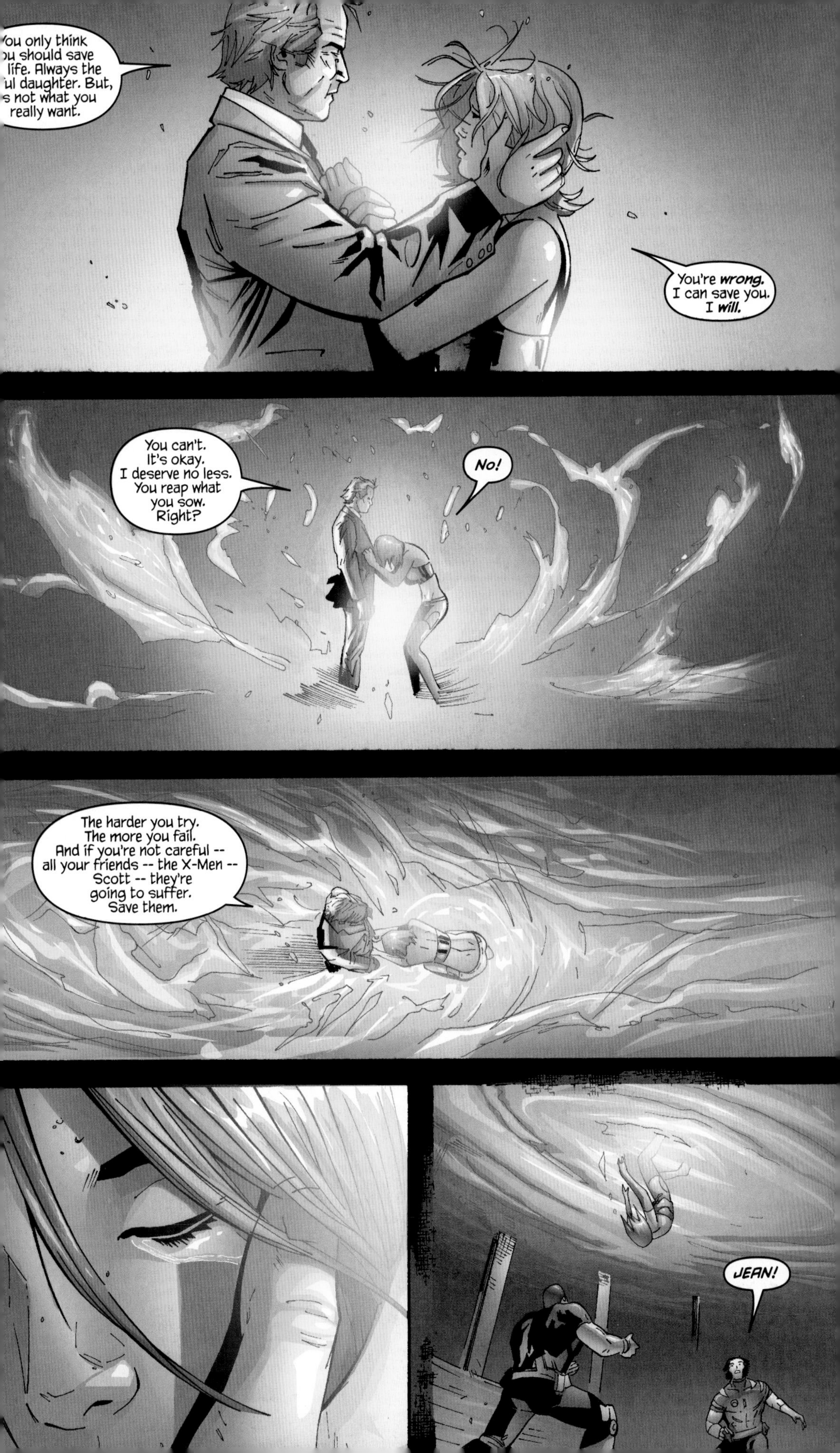
ou only think
u should save
life. Always the
ul daughter. But,
s not what you
really want.
You're wrong. I can save you. I will.
You can't. It's okay. I deserve no less. You reap what you sow. Right?
No!
The harder you try. The more you fail. And if you're not careful -- all your friends -- the X-Men -- Scott -- they're going to suffer. Save them.
JEAN!

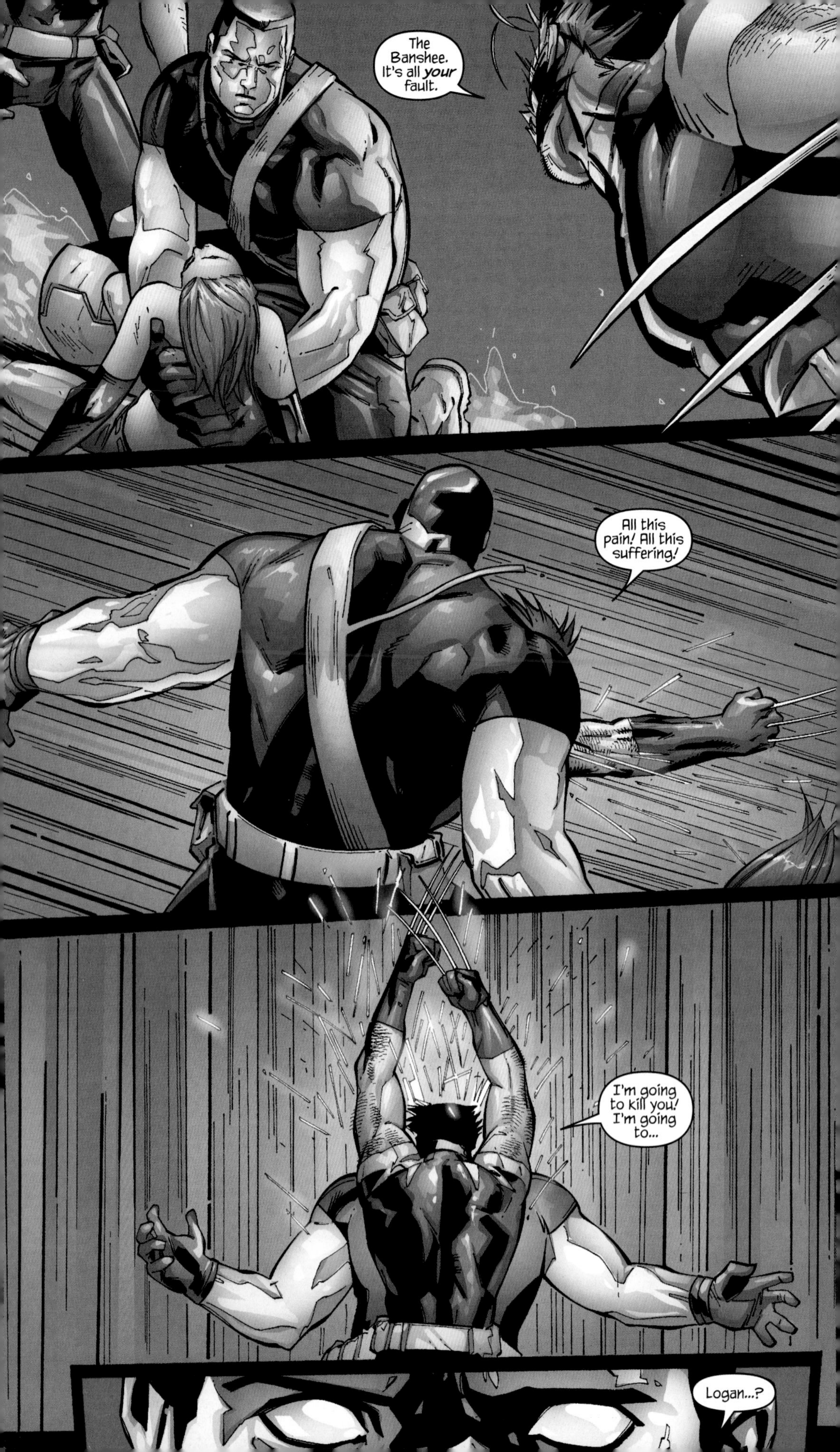
The Banshee. It's all *your* fault.
All this pain! All this suffering!
I'm going to kill you! I'm going to...
Logan...?

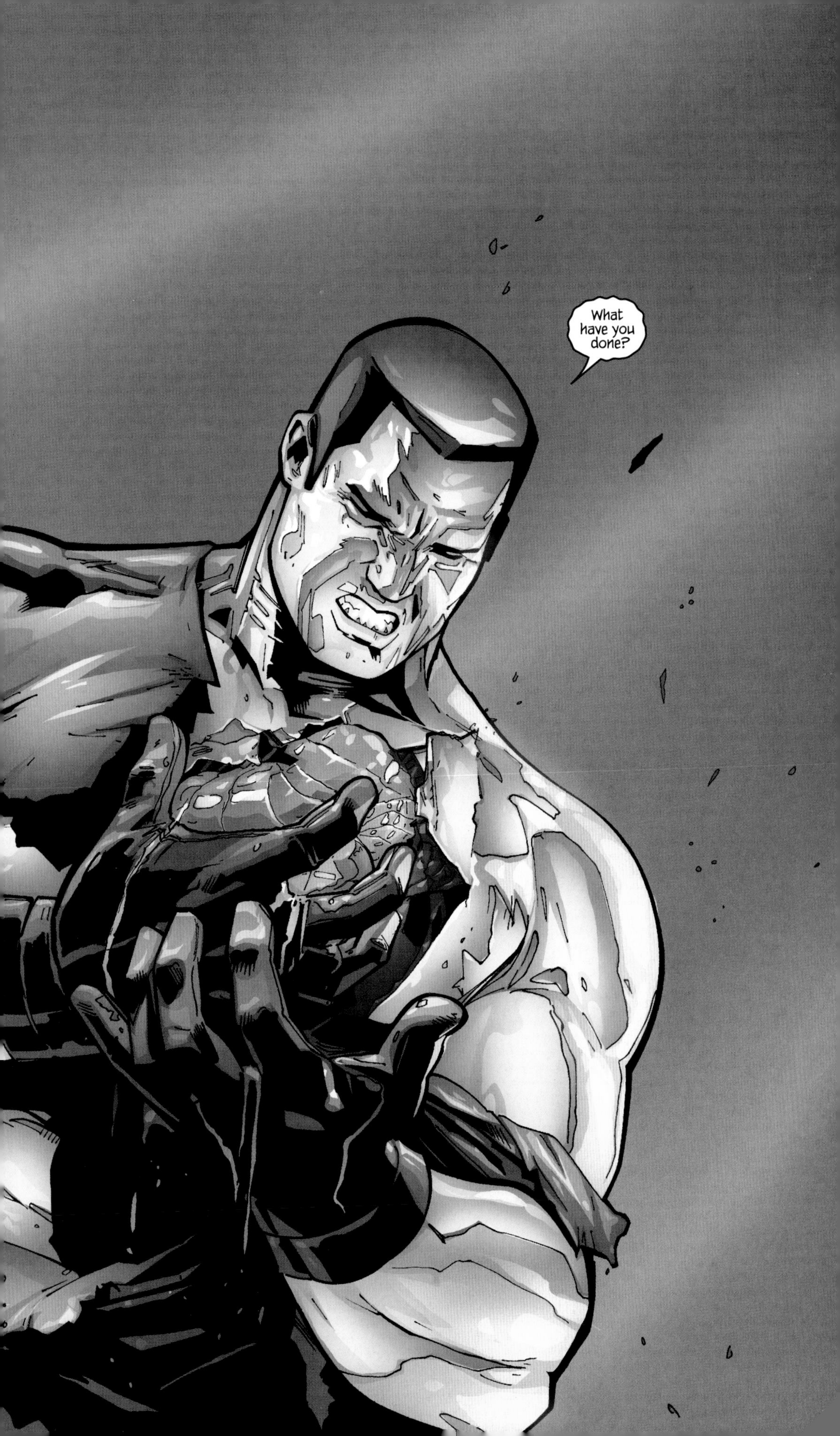
What have you done?

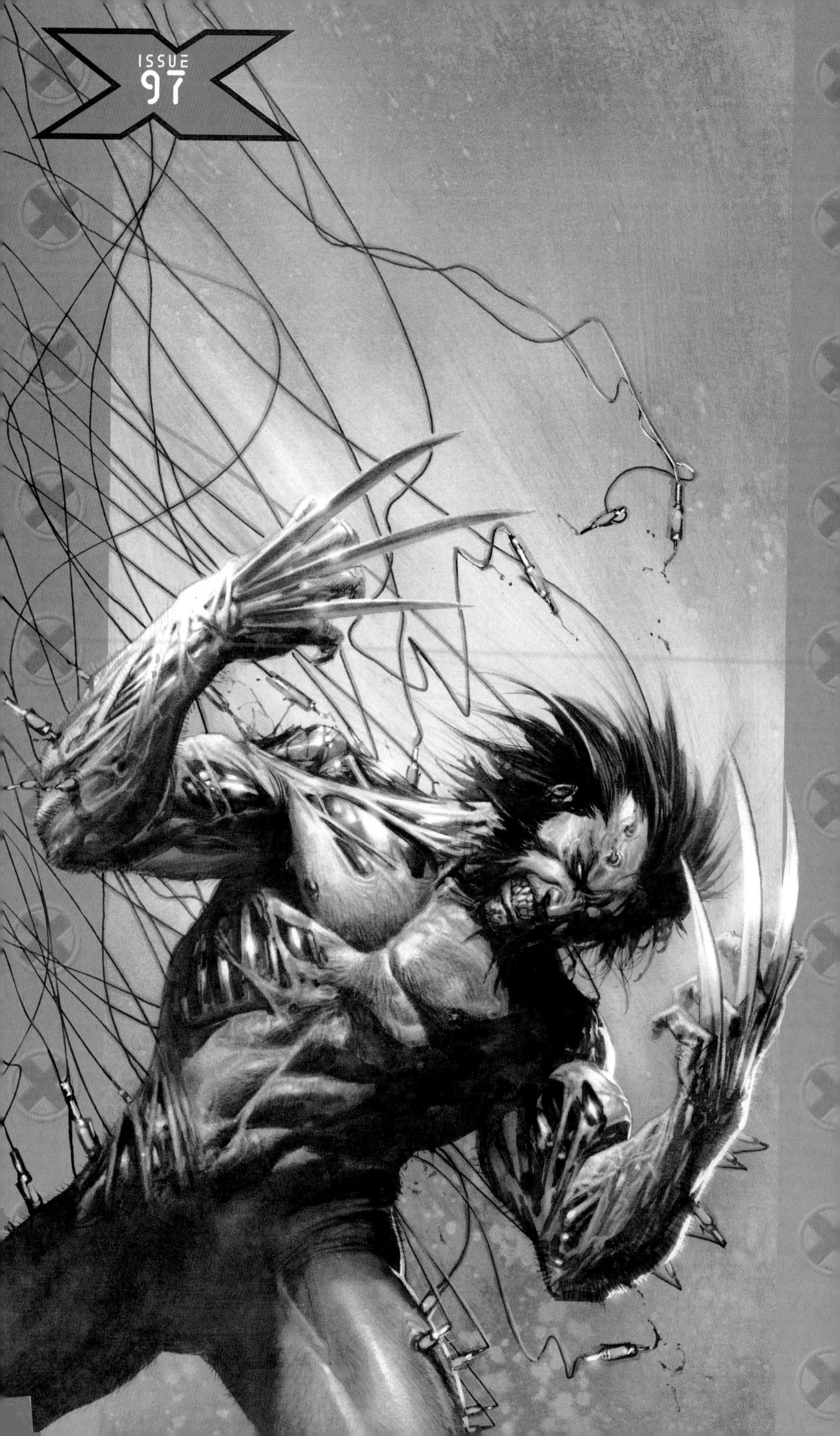
ISSUE
97

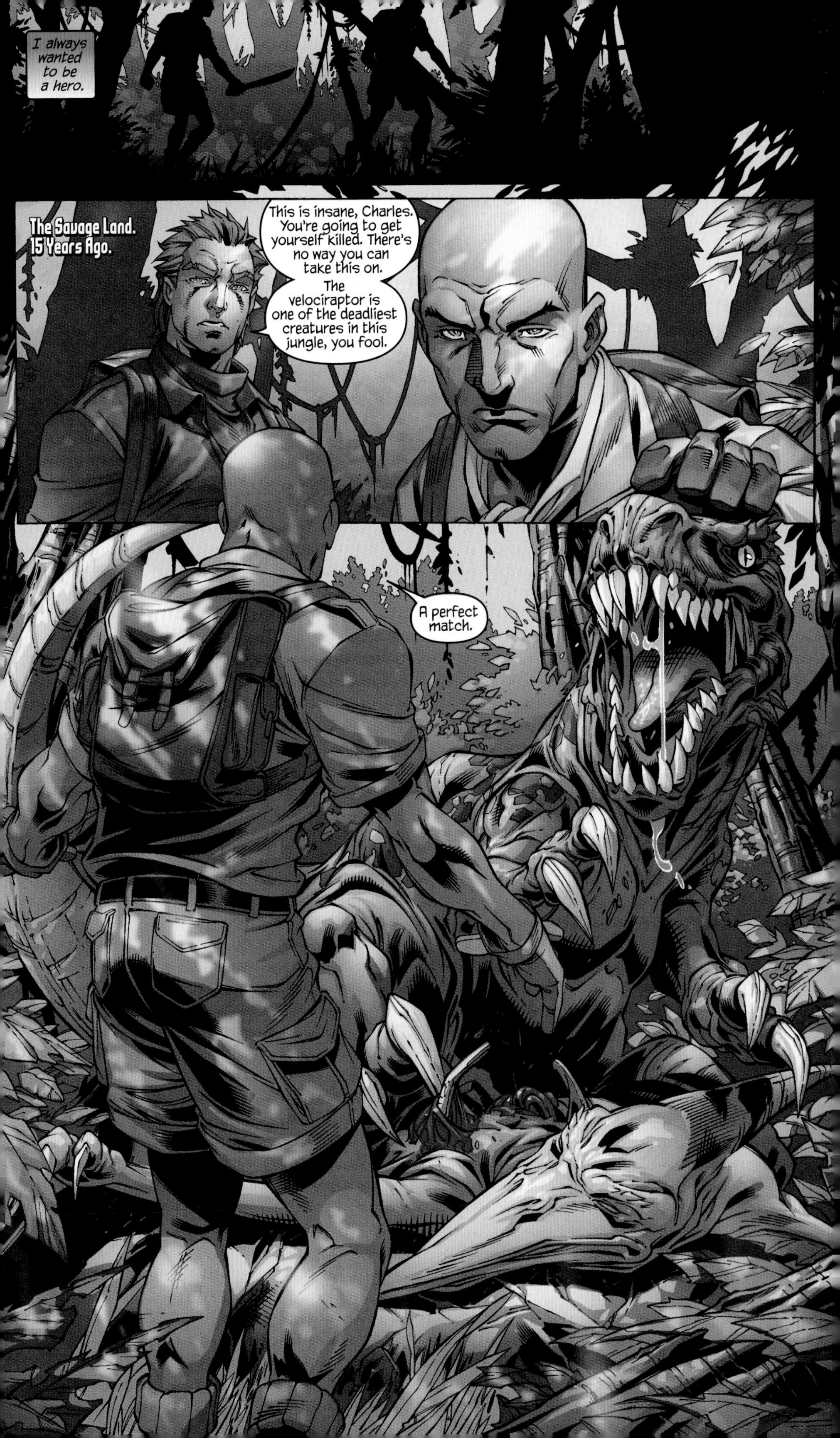
I always wanted to be a hero.
The Savage Land. 15 Years Ago.
This is insane, Charles. You're going to get yourself killed. There's no way you can take this on.
The velociraptor is one of the deadliest creatures in this jungle, you fool.
A perfect match.

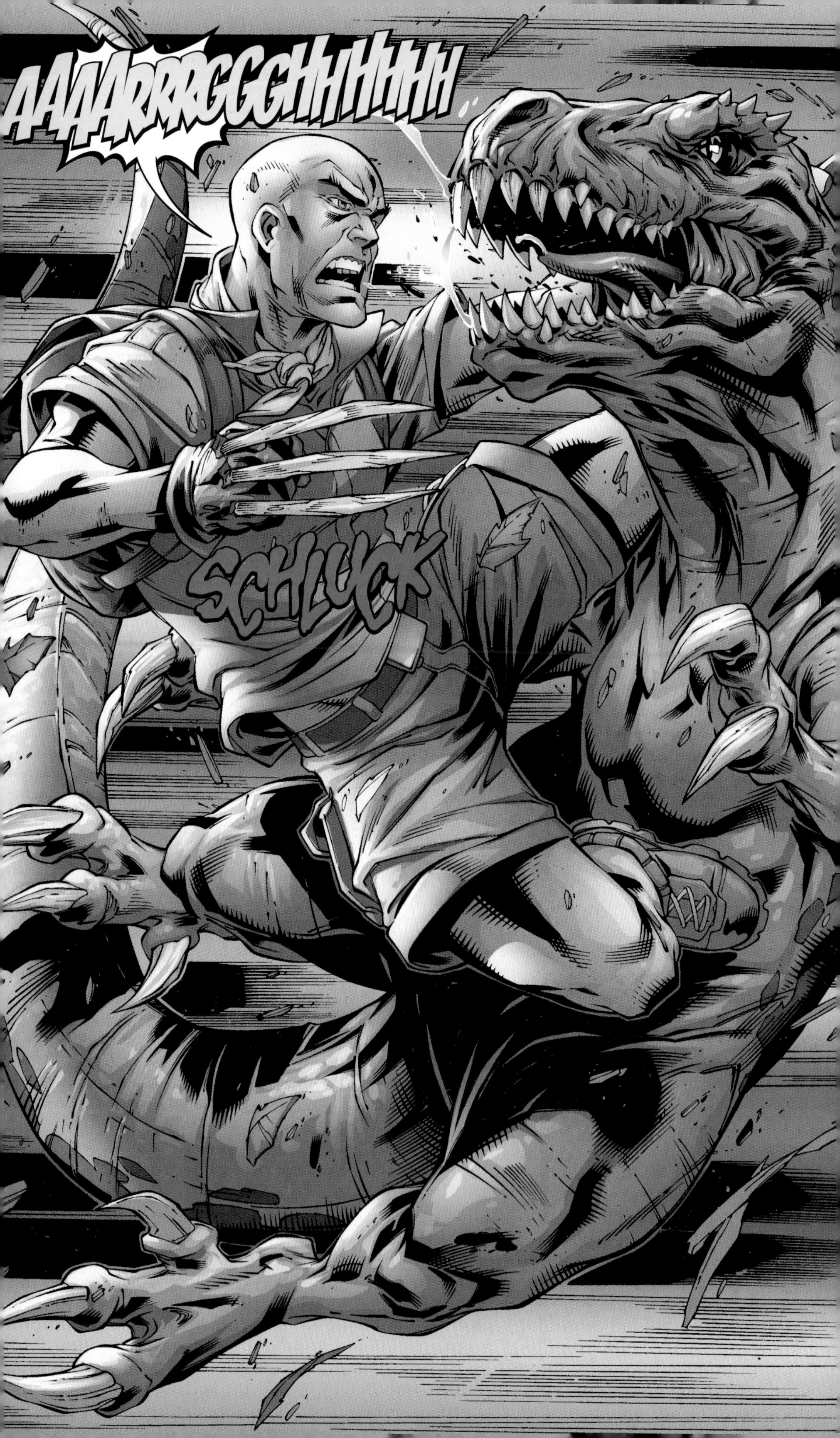
AAAARRRGGGHHHHHH
SCHLUCK

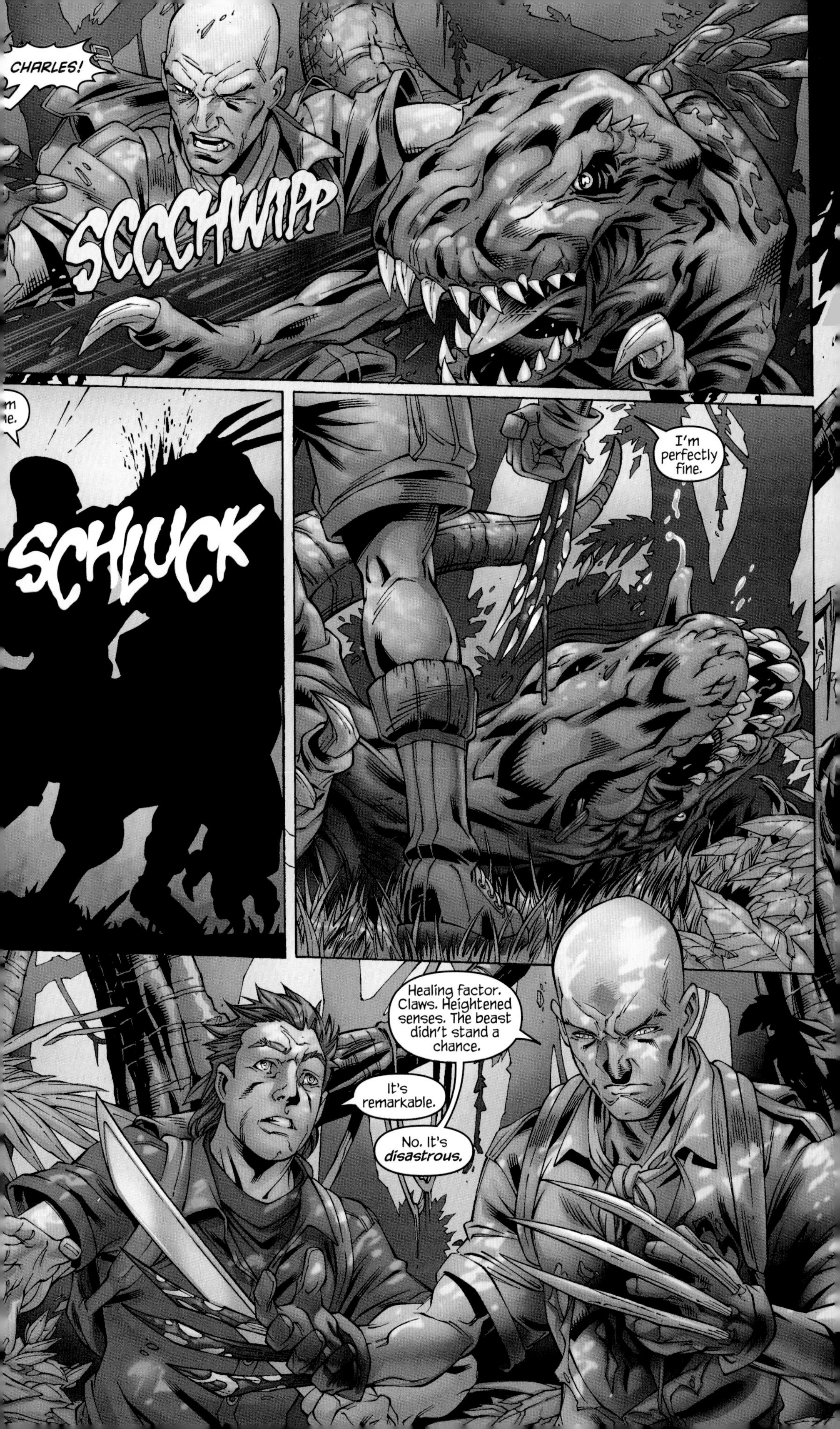
CHARLES!
SCCCHWIPP
SCHLUCK
I'm perfectly fine.
Healing factor. Claws. Heightened senses. The beast didn't stand a chance.
It's remarkable.
No. It's *disastrous.*

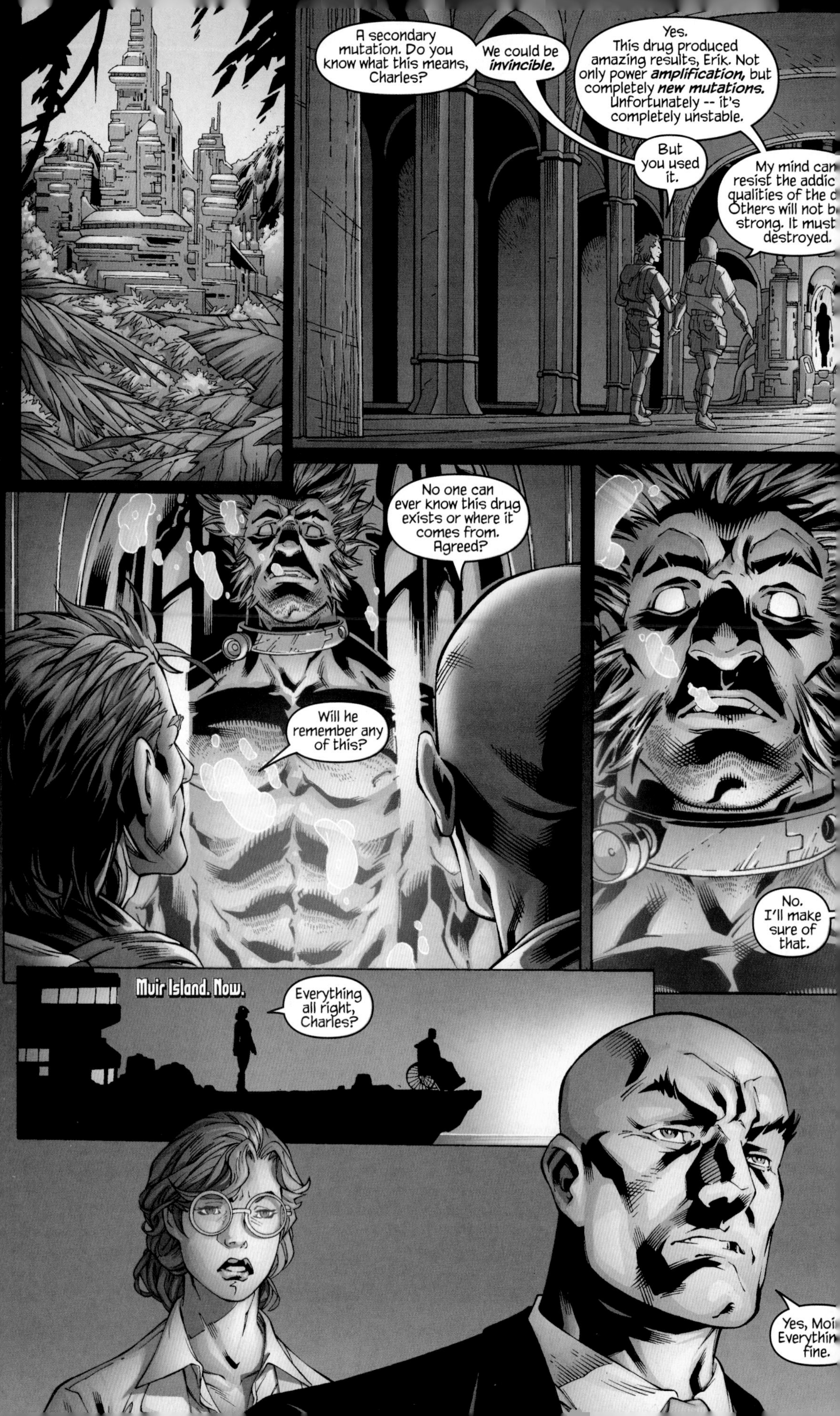
A secondary mutation. Do you know what this means, Charles?
We could be *invincible.*
Yes. This drug produced amazing results, Erik. Not only power ***amplification,*** but completely ***new mutations.*** Unfortunately -- it's completely unstable.
But you used it.
My mind can resist the addic qualities of the d Others will not b strong. It must destroyed.
No one can ever know this drug exists or where it comes from. Agreed?
Will he remember any of this?
No. I'll make sure of that.
Muir Island. Now.
Everything all right, Charles?
Yes, Moi Everythin fine.

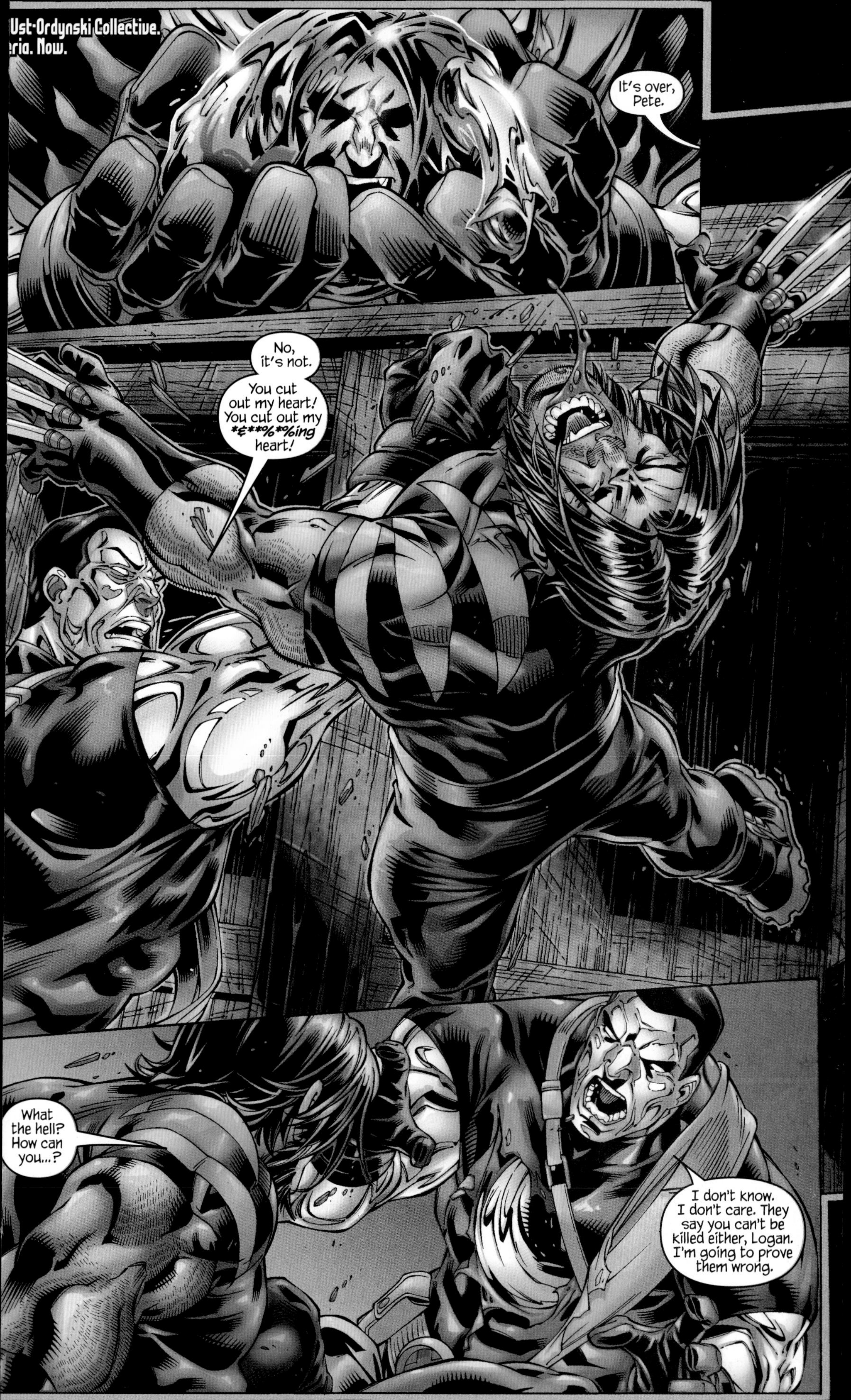

Ust-Ordynski Collective.
eria. Now.
It's over, Pete.
No, it's not.
You cut out my heart! You cut out my *€**%*%ing heart!
What the hell? How can you...?
I don't know. I don't care. They say you can't be killed either, Logan. I'm going to prove them wrong.

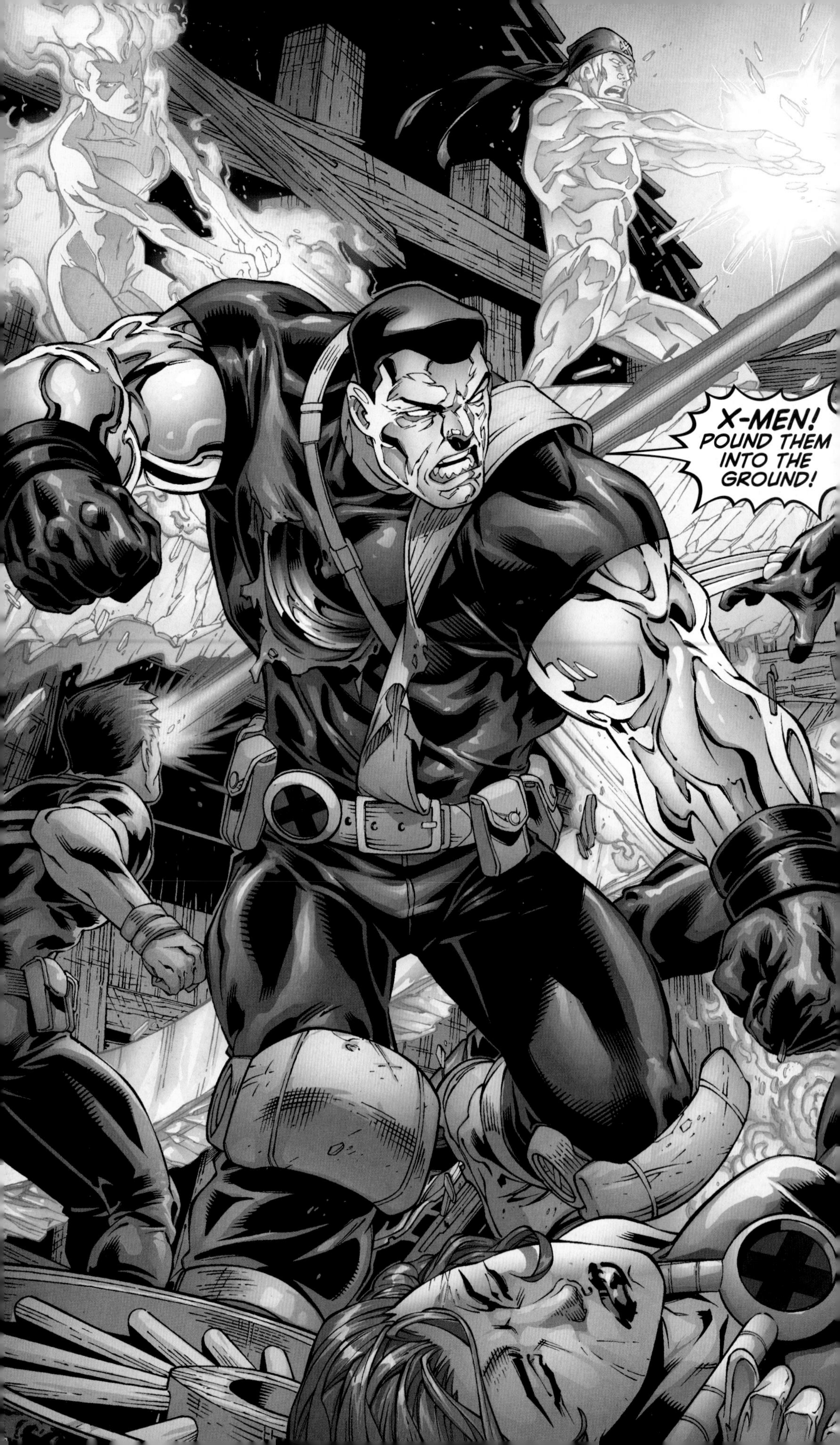
X-MEN! POUND THEM INTO THE GROUND!

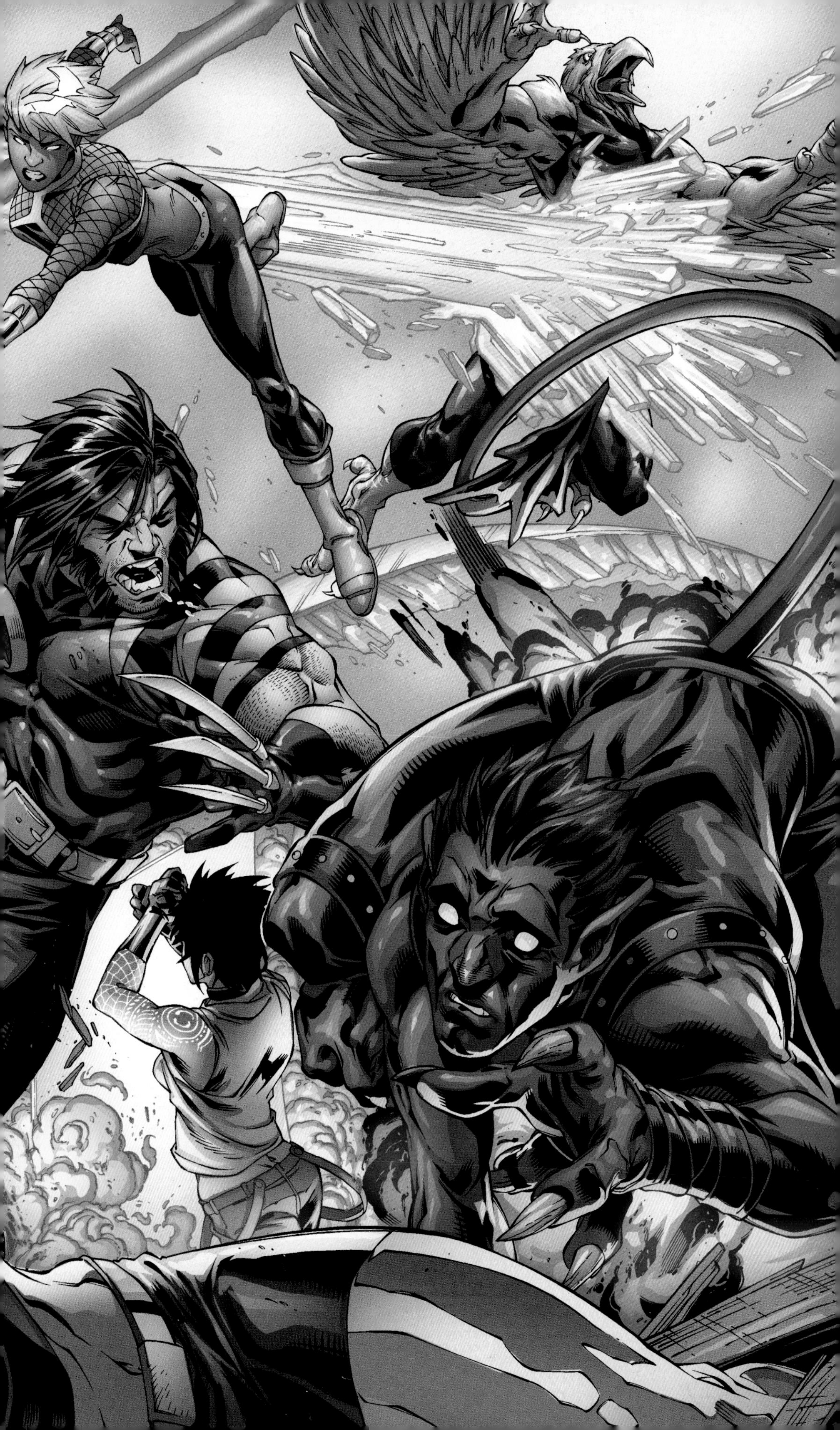

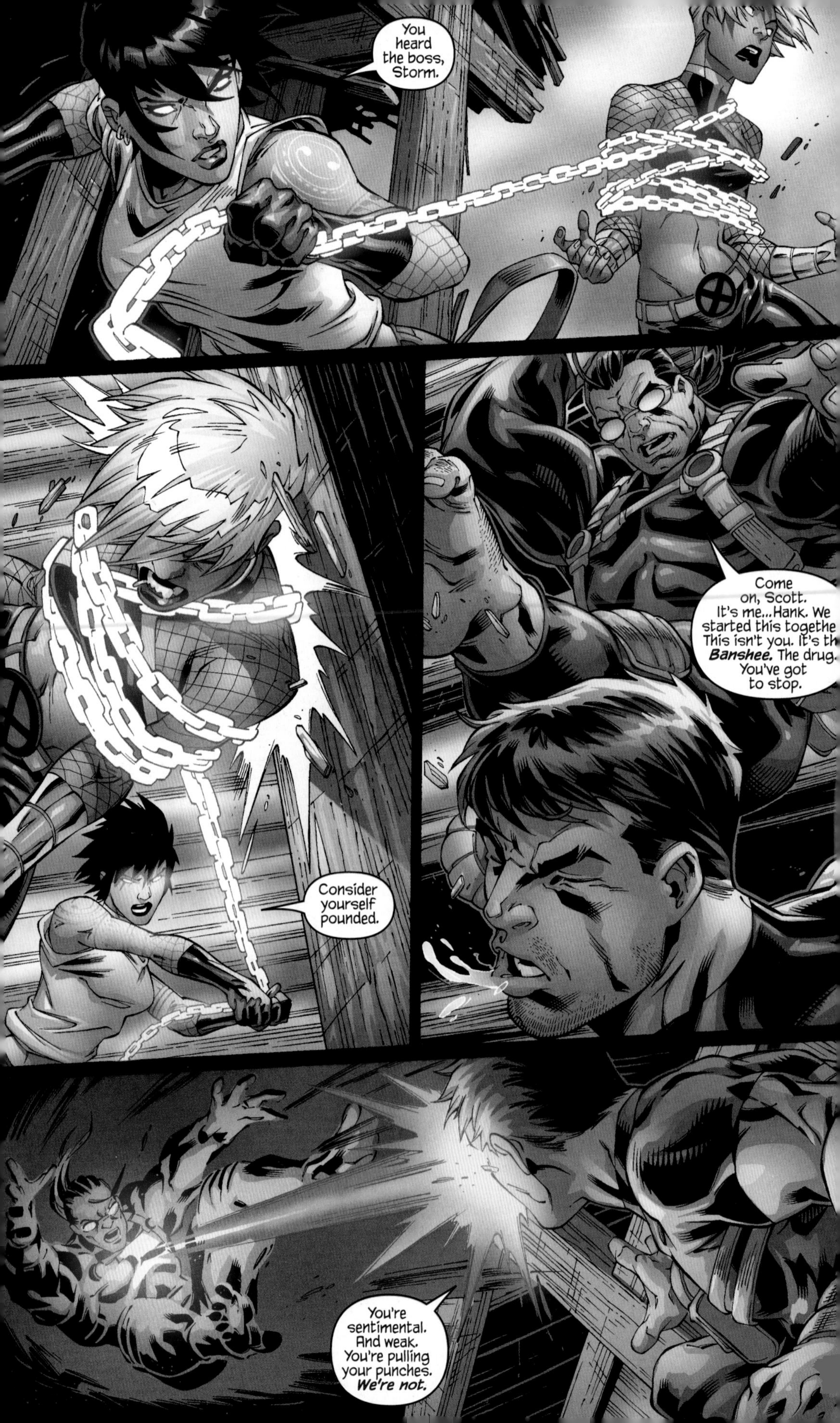
You heard the boss, Storm.
Consider yourself pounded.
Come on, Scott. It's me...Hank. We started this togethe This isn't you. It's th Banshee. The drug. You've got to stop.
You're sentimental. And weak. You're pulling your punches. We're not.

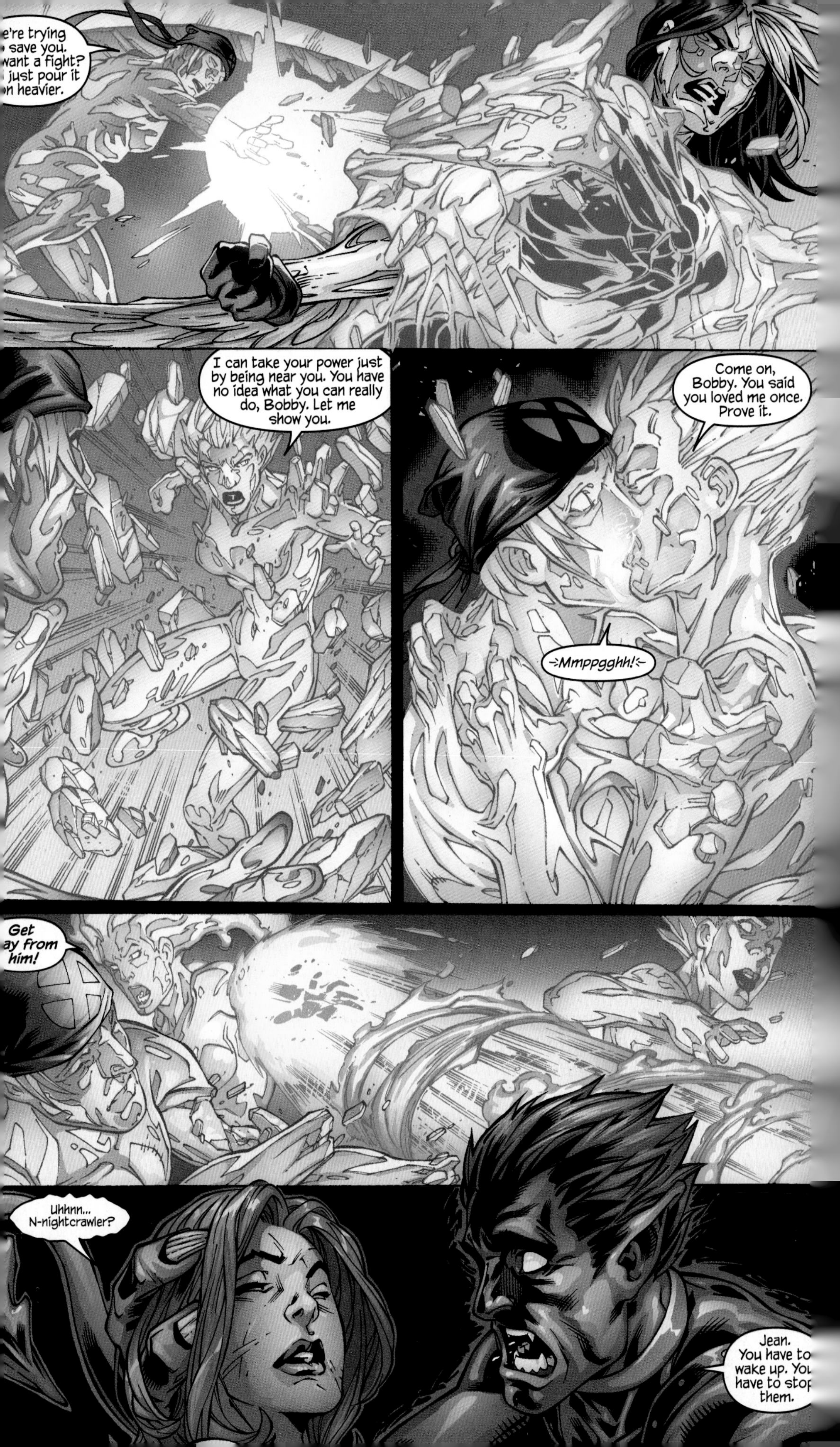
e're trying
save you.
want a fight?
just pour it
n heavier.
I can take your power just by being near you. You have no idea what you can really do, Bobby. Let me show you.
Come on, Bobby. You said you loved me once. Prove it.
Mmppgghh!
Get
ay from
him!
Uhhnn... N-nightcrawler?
Jean. You have to wake up. You have to stop them.

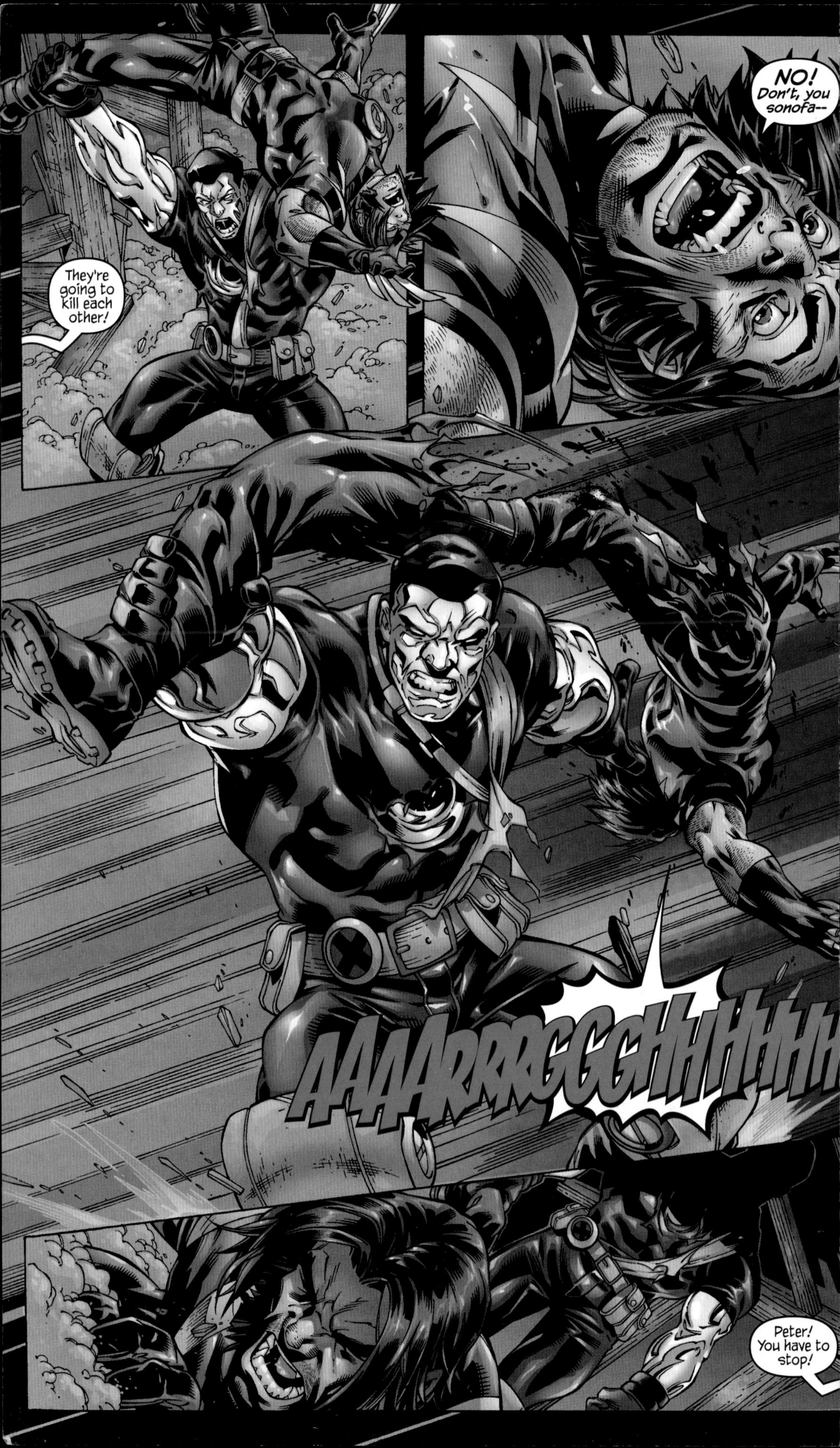
NO! Don't, you sonofa--
They're going to kill each other!
AAAARRRGGGHHHHHH
Peter! You have to stop!

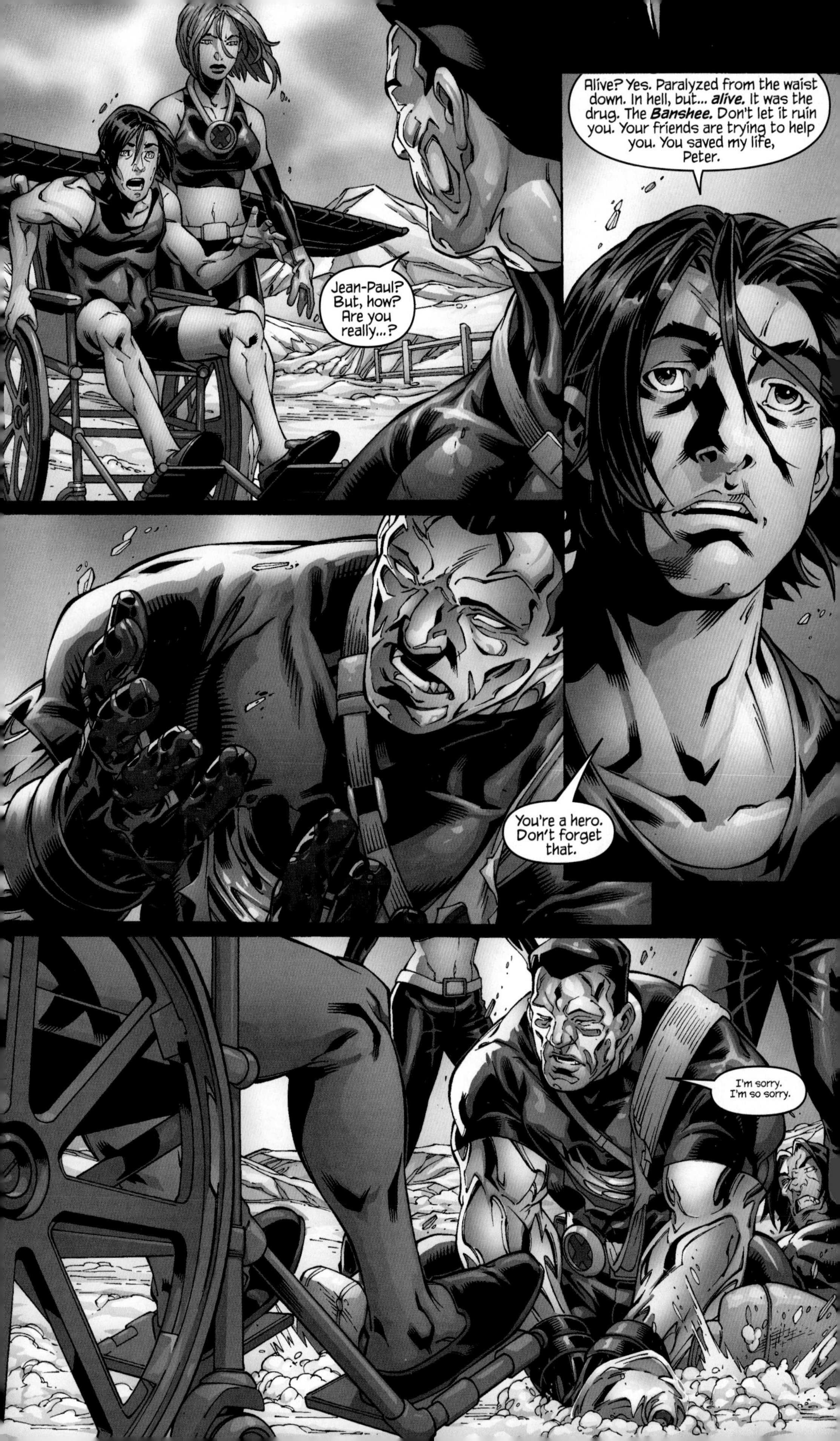
Jean-Paul? But, how? Are you really...?
Alive? Yes. Paralyzed from the waist down. In hell, but... *alive.* It was the drug. The ***Banshee.*** Don't let it ruin you. Your friends are trying to help you. You saved my life, Peter.
You're a hero. Don't forget that.
I'm sorry. I'm so sorry.

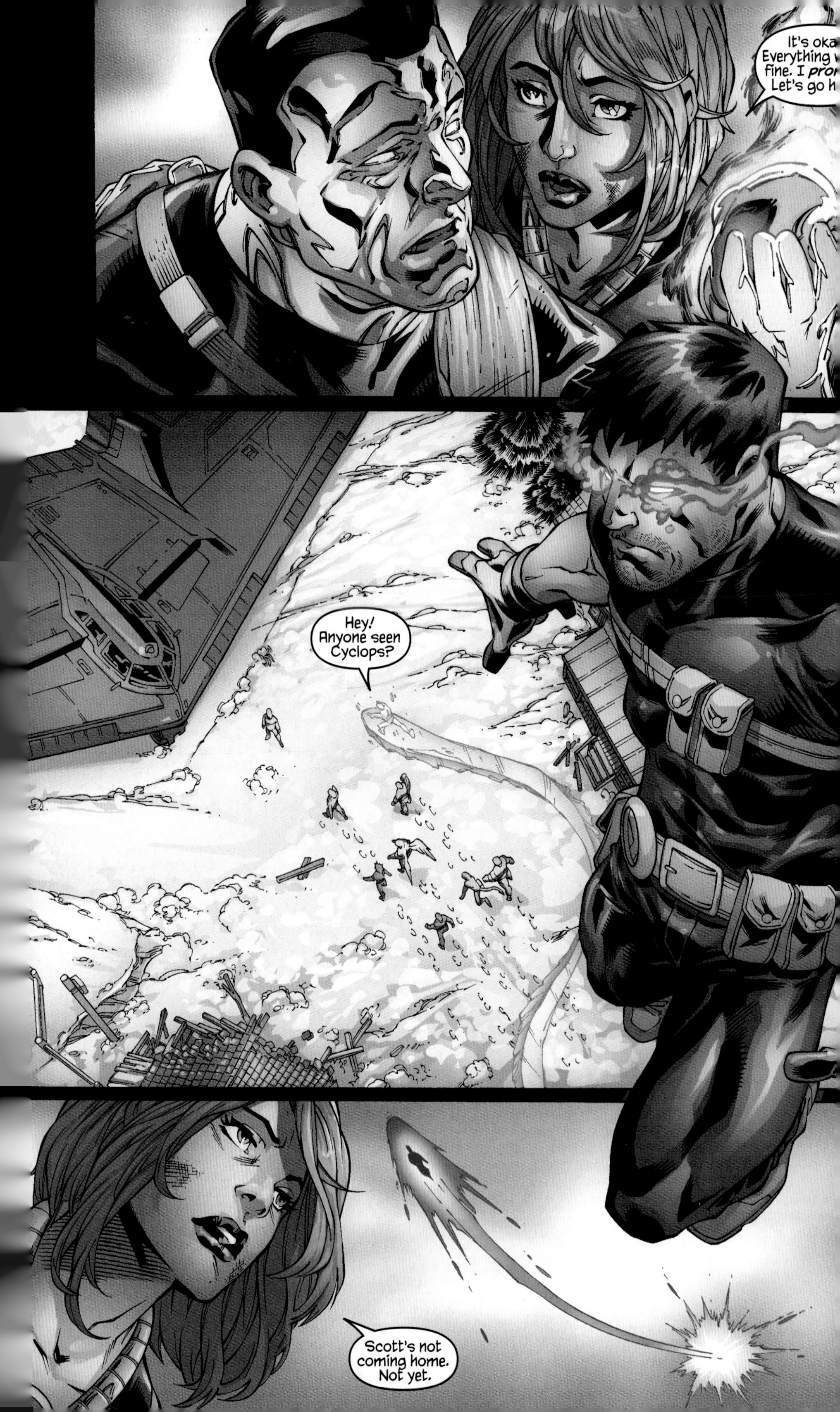
It's oka Everything fine. I pro Let's go h
Hey! Anyone seen Cyclops?
Scott's not coming home. Not yet.

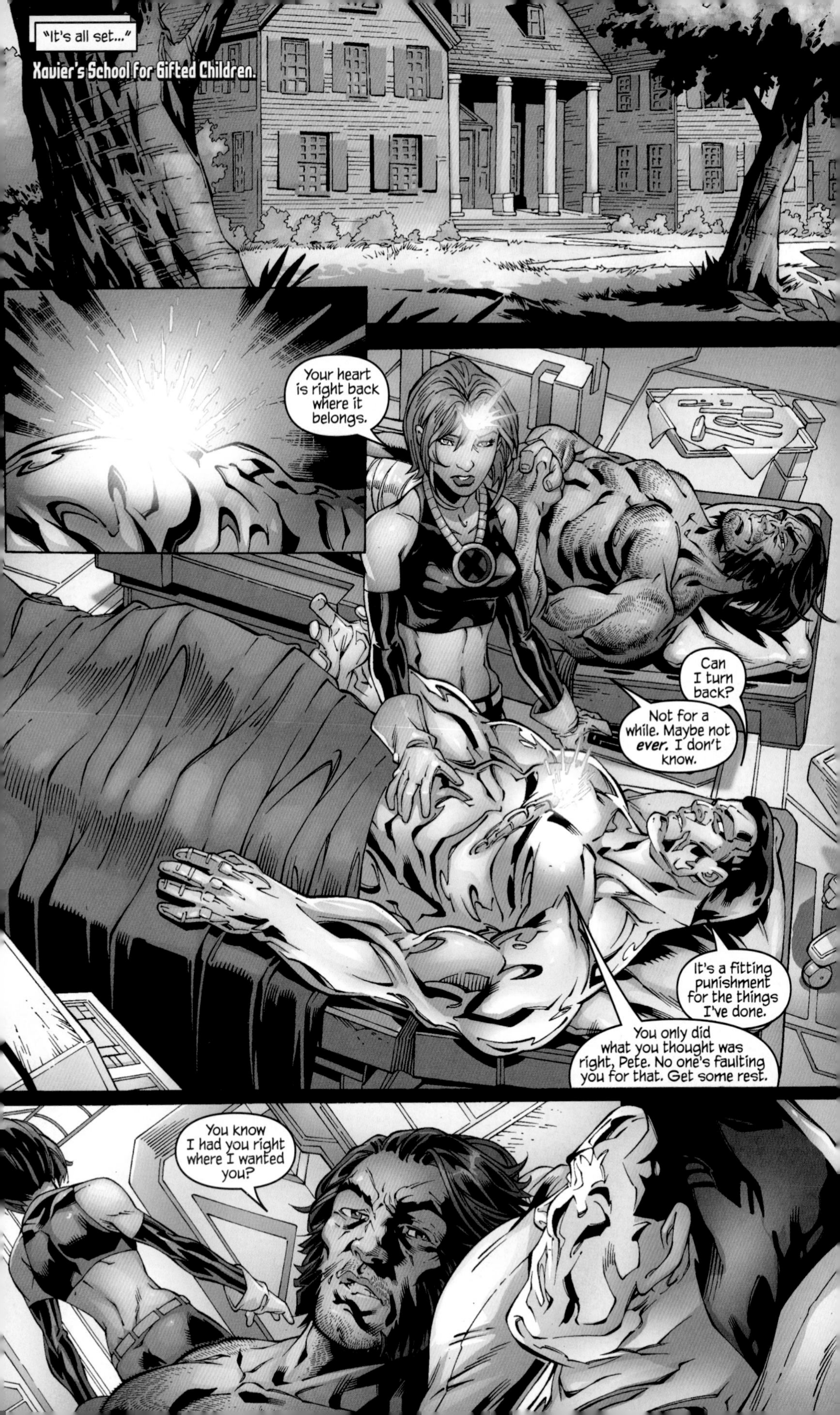
"It's all set..."
Xavier's School for Gifted Children.
Your heart is right back where it belongs.
Can I turn back?
Not for a while. Maybe not *ever.* I don't know.
It's a fitting punishment for the things I've done.
You only did what you thought was right, Pete. No one's faulting you for that. Get some rest.
You know I had you right where I wanted you?

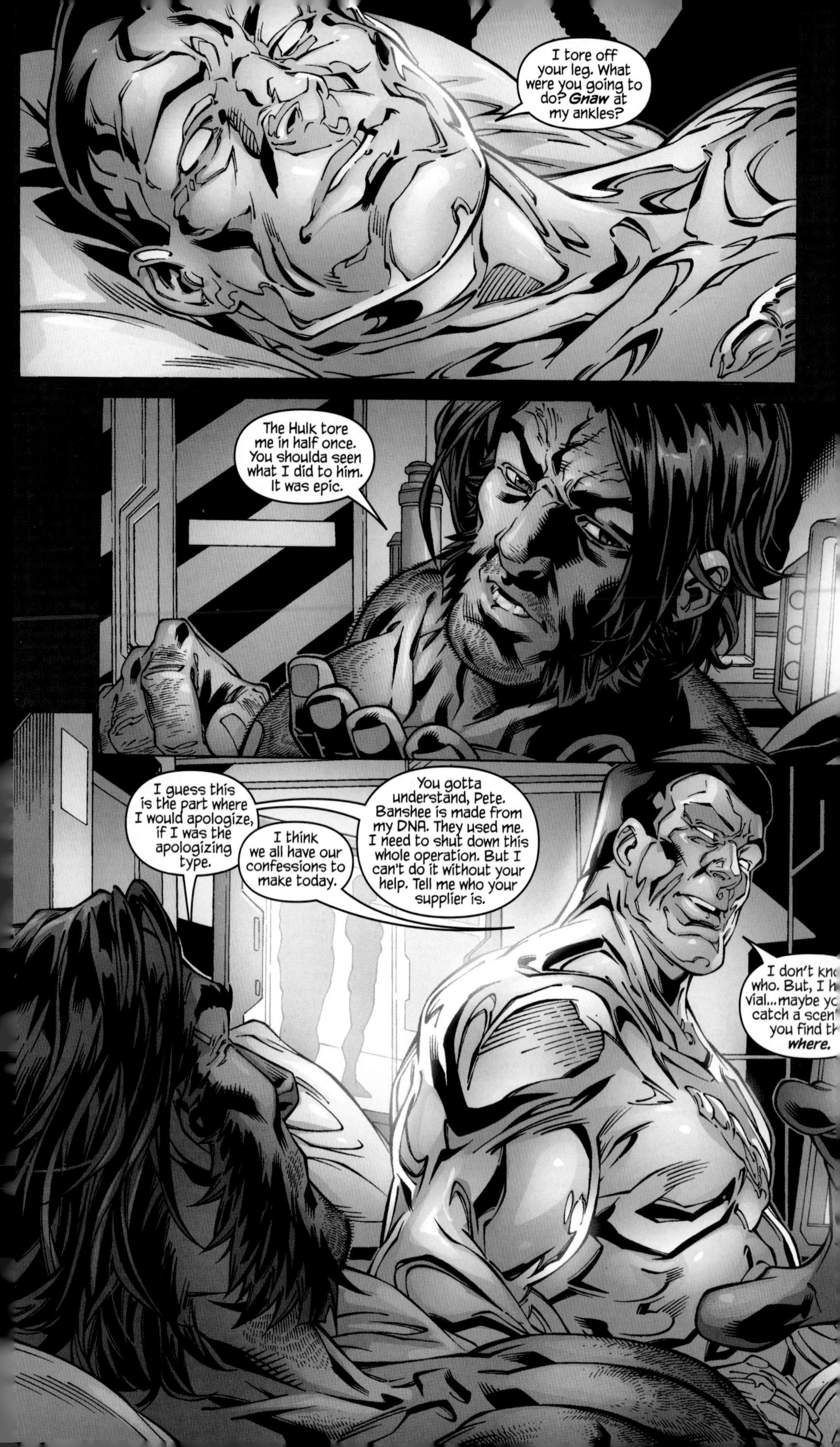
I tore off your leg. What were you going to do? *Gnaw* at my ankles?
The Hulk tore me in half once. You shoulda seen what I did to him. It was epic.
I guess this is the part where I would apologize, if I was the apologizing type.
I think we all have our confessions to make today.
You gotta understand, Pete. Banshee is made from my DNA. They used me. I need to shut down this whole operation. But I can't do it without your help. Tell me who your supplier is.
I don't kn who. But, I h vial...maybe yo catch a scen you find th *where.*

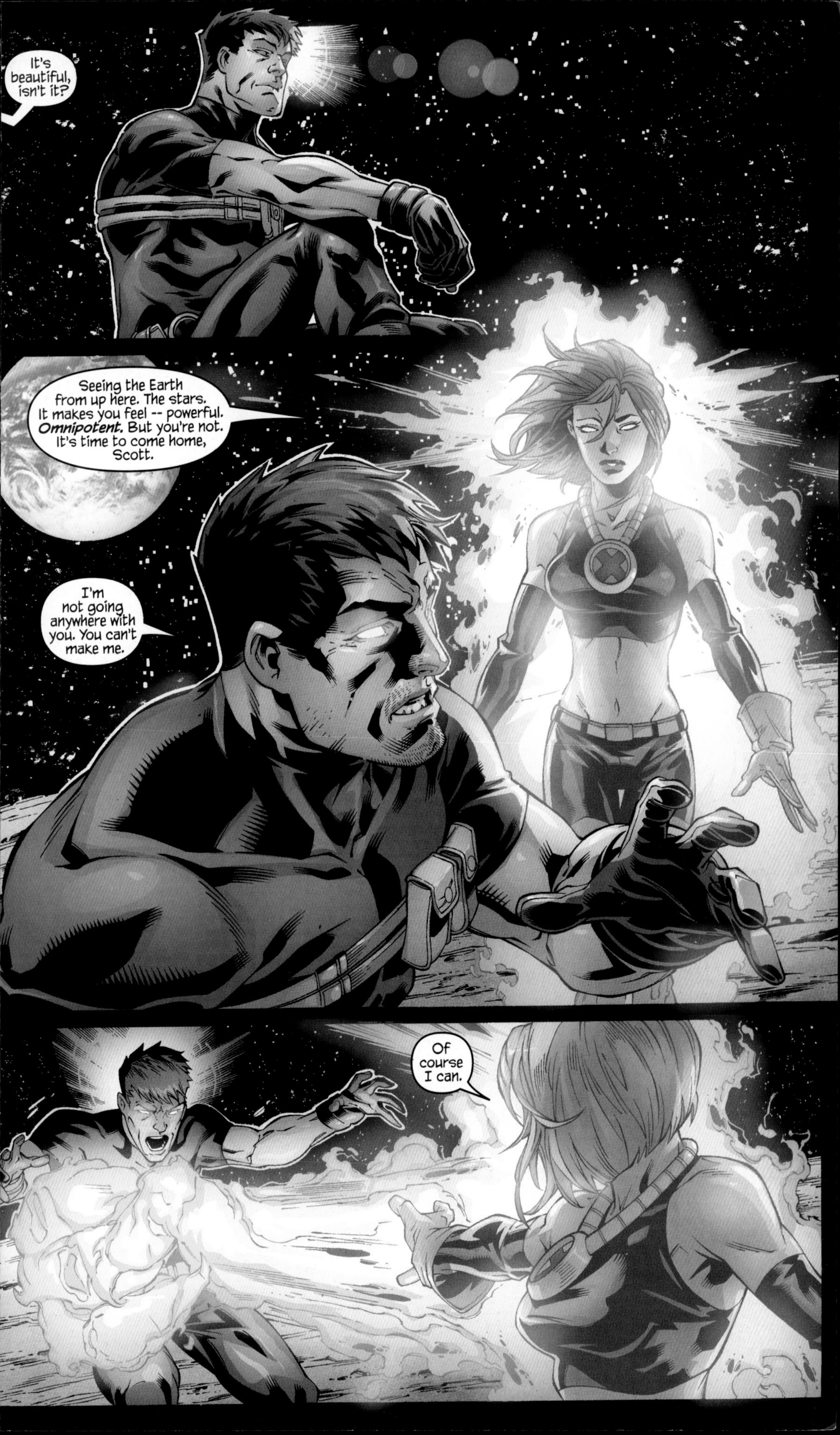
It's beautiful, isn't it?
Seeing the Earth from up here. The stars. It makes you feel -- powerful. *Omnipotent.* But you're not. It's time to come home, Scott.
I'm not going anywhere with you. You can't make me.
Of course I can.

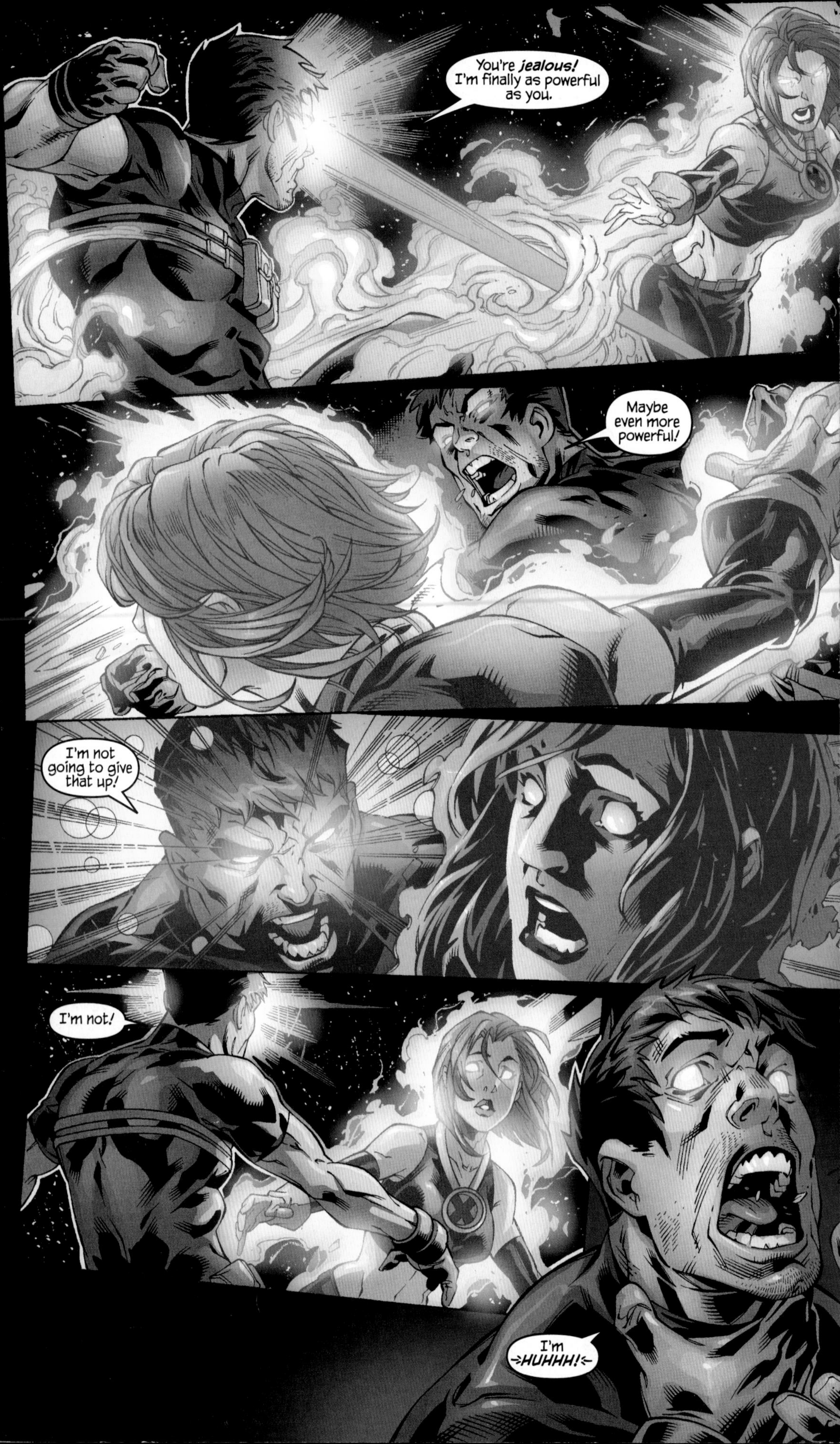

You're *jealous!* I'm finally as powerful as you.
Maybe even more powerful!
I'm not going to give that up!
I'm not!
I'm —HUHHH!—

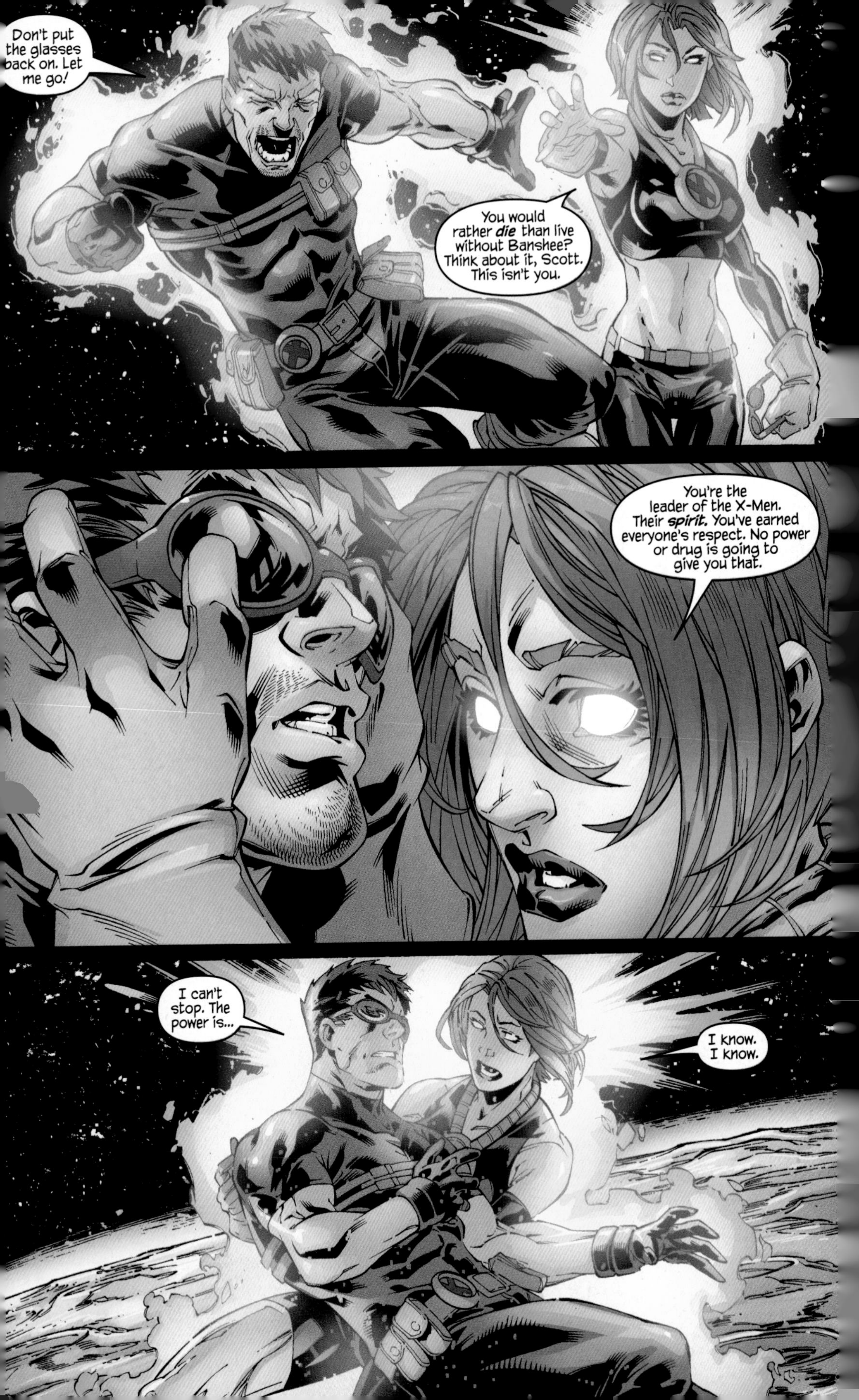

Don't put the glasses back on. Let me go!
You would rather *die* than live without Banshee? Think about it, Scott. This isn't you.
You're the leader of the X-Men. Their *spirit.* You've earned everyone's respect. No power or drug is going to give you that.
I can't stop. The power is...
I know. I know.

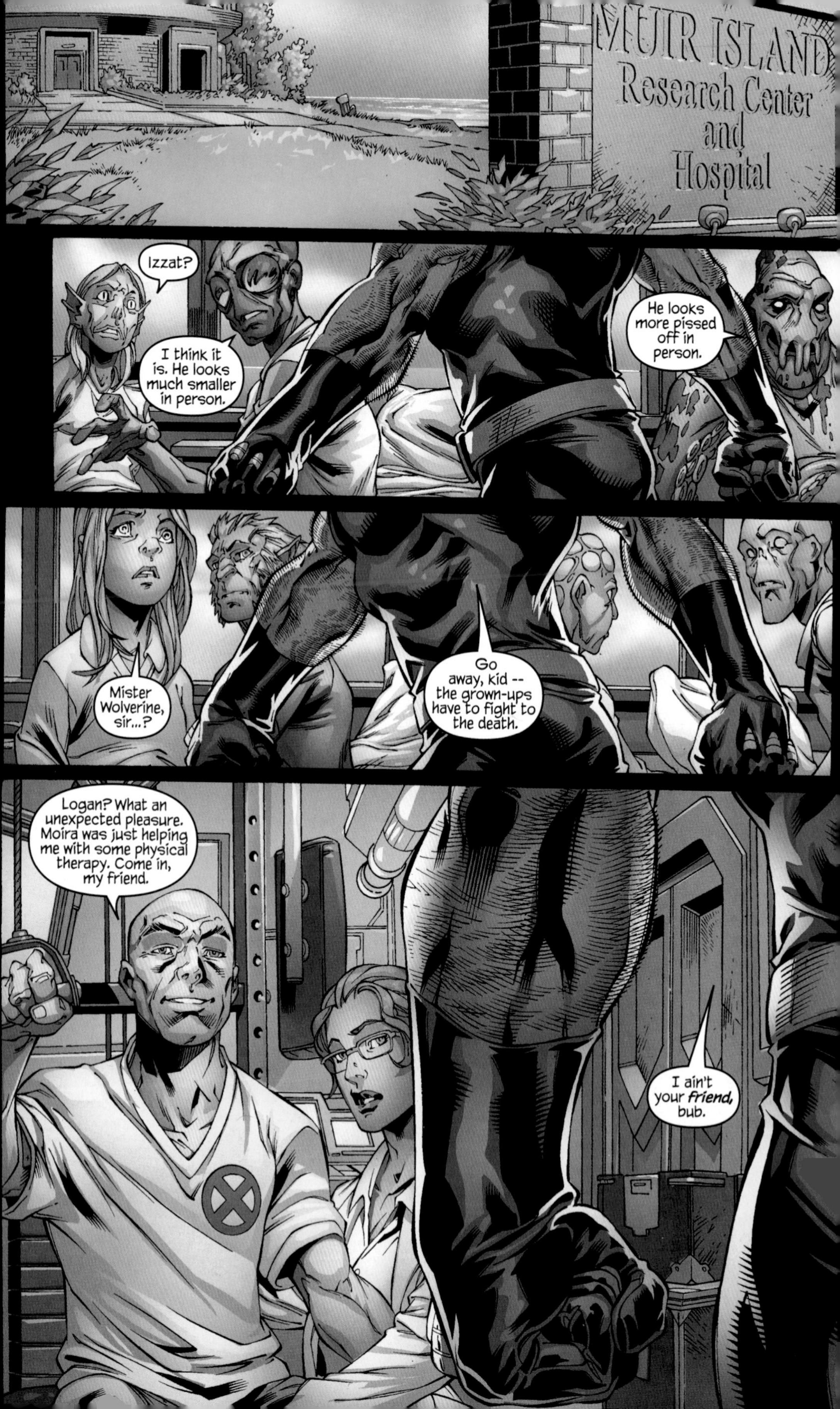

MUIR ISLAND
Research Center
and
Hospital
Izzat?
I think it is. He looks much smaller in person.
He looks more pissed off in person.
Mister Wolverine, sir...?
Go away, kid -- the grown-ups have to fight to the death.
Logan? What an unexpected pleasure. Moira was just helping me with some physical therapy. Come in, my friend.
I ain't your *friend,* bub.

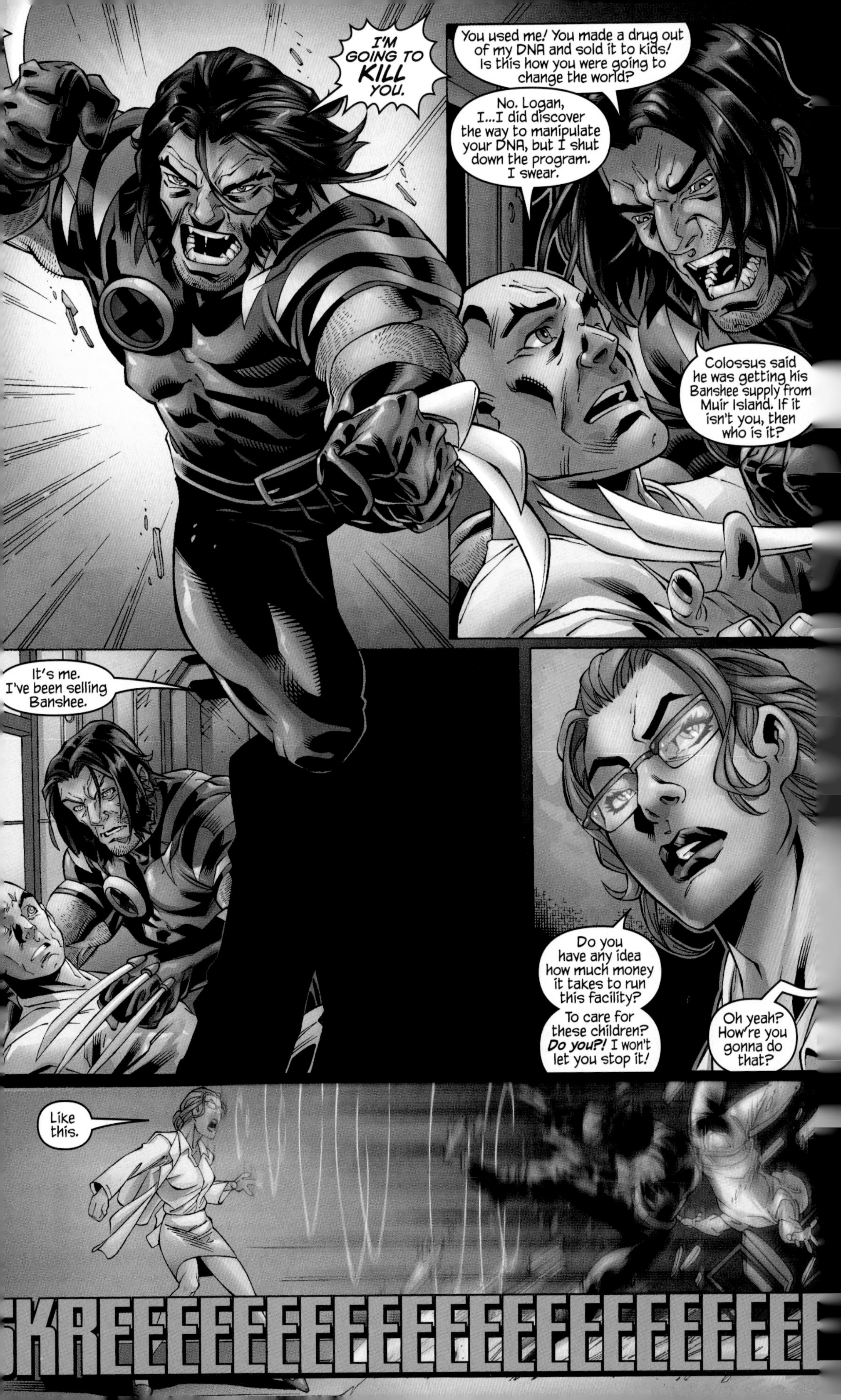
I'M GOING TO KILL YOU.
You used me! You made a drug out of my DNA and sold it to kids! Is this how you were going to change the world?
No. Logan, I...I did discover the way to manipulate your DNA, but I shut down the program. I swear.
Colossus said he was getting his Banshee supply from Muir Island. If it isn't you, then who is it?
It's me. I've been selling Banshee.
Do you have any idea how much money it takes to run this facility?
To care for these children? Do you?! I won't let you stop it!
Oh yeah? How're you gonna do that?
Like this.
SKREEEEEEEEEEEEEEEEEEEEEEEE

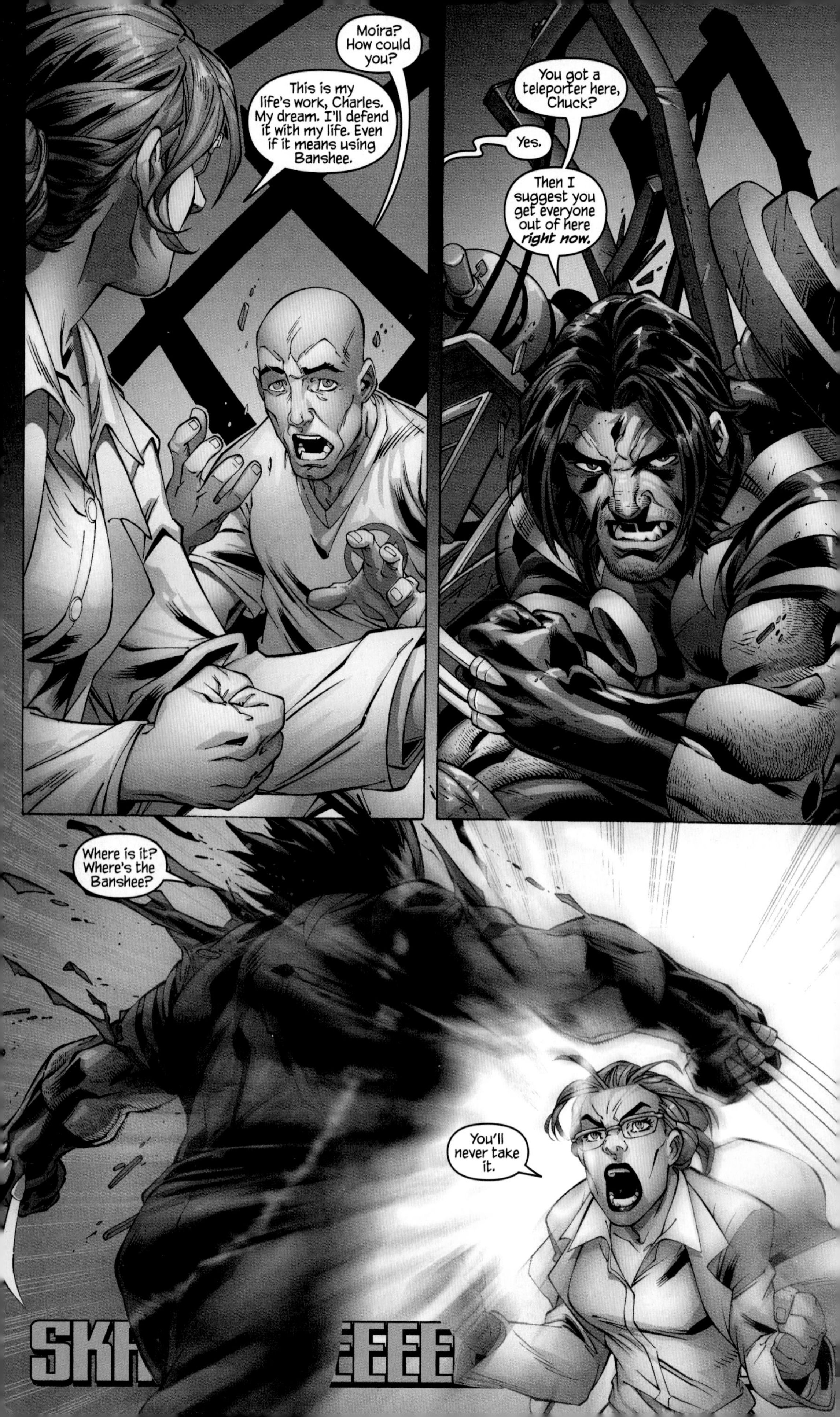
Moira? How could you?
This is my life's work, Charles. My dream. I'll defend it with my life. Even if it means using Banshee.
You got a teleporter here, Chuck?
Yes.
Then I suggest you get everyone out of here *right now.*
Where is it? Where's the Banshee?
You'll never take it.
SKH EEEE

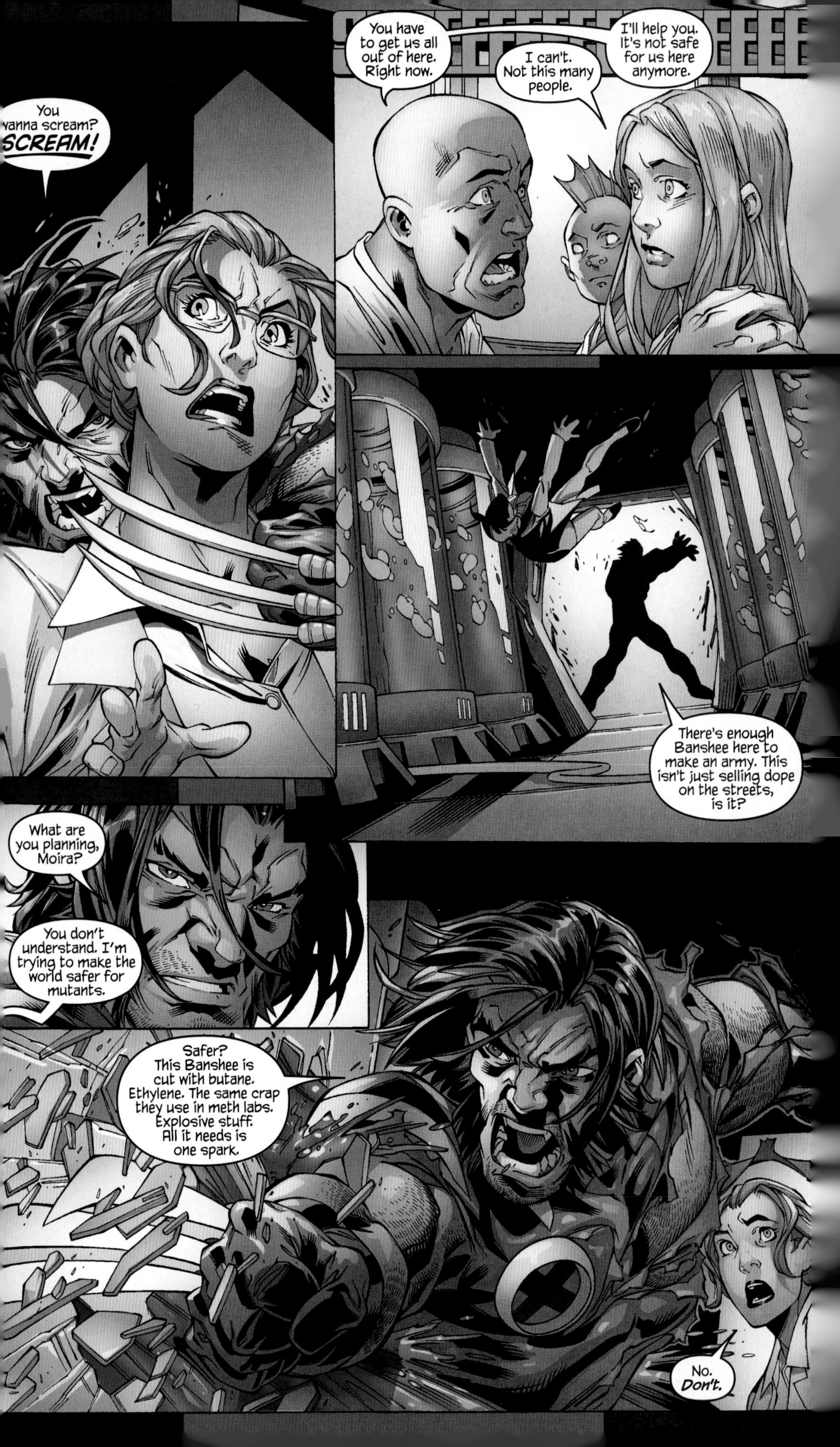

You wanna scream? SCREAM!
You have to get us all out of here. Right now.
I can't. Not this many people.
I'll help you. It's not safe for us here anymore.
There's enough Banshee here to make an army. This isn't just selling dope on the streets, is it?
What are you planning, Moira?
You don't understand. I'm trying to make the world safer for mutants.
Safer? This Banshee is cut with butane. Ethylene. The same crap they use in meth labs. Explosive stuff. All it needs is one spark.
No. Don't.

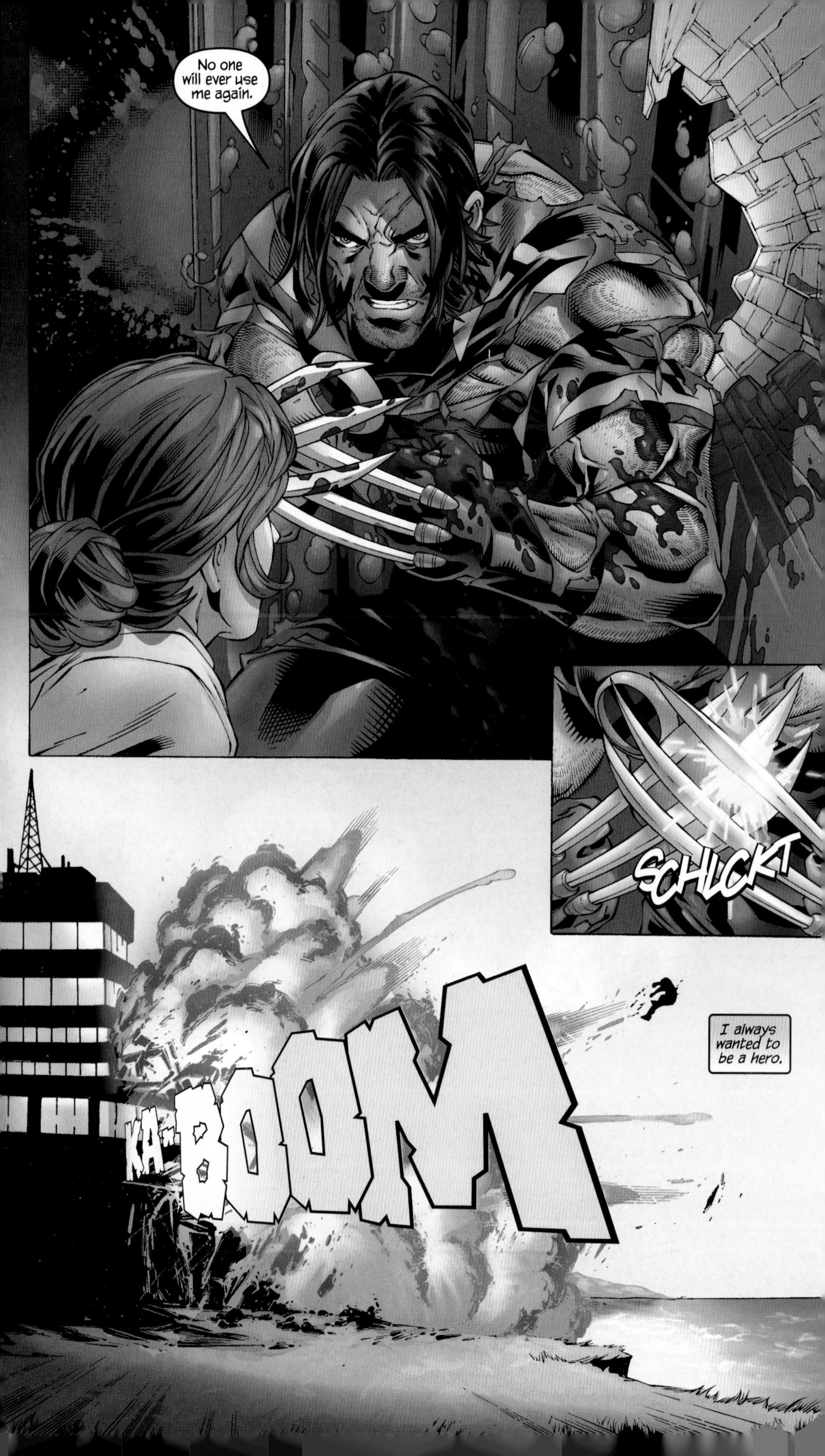

No one will ever use me again.
SCHLICKT
KA-BOOM
I always wanted to be a hero.

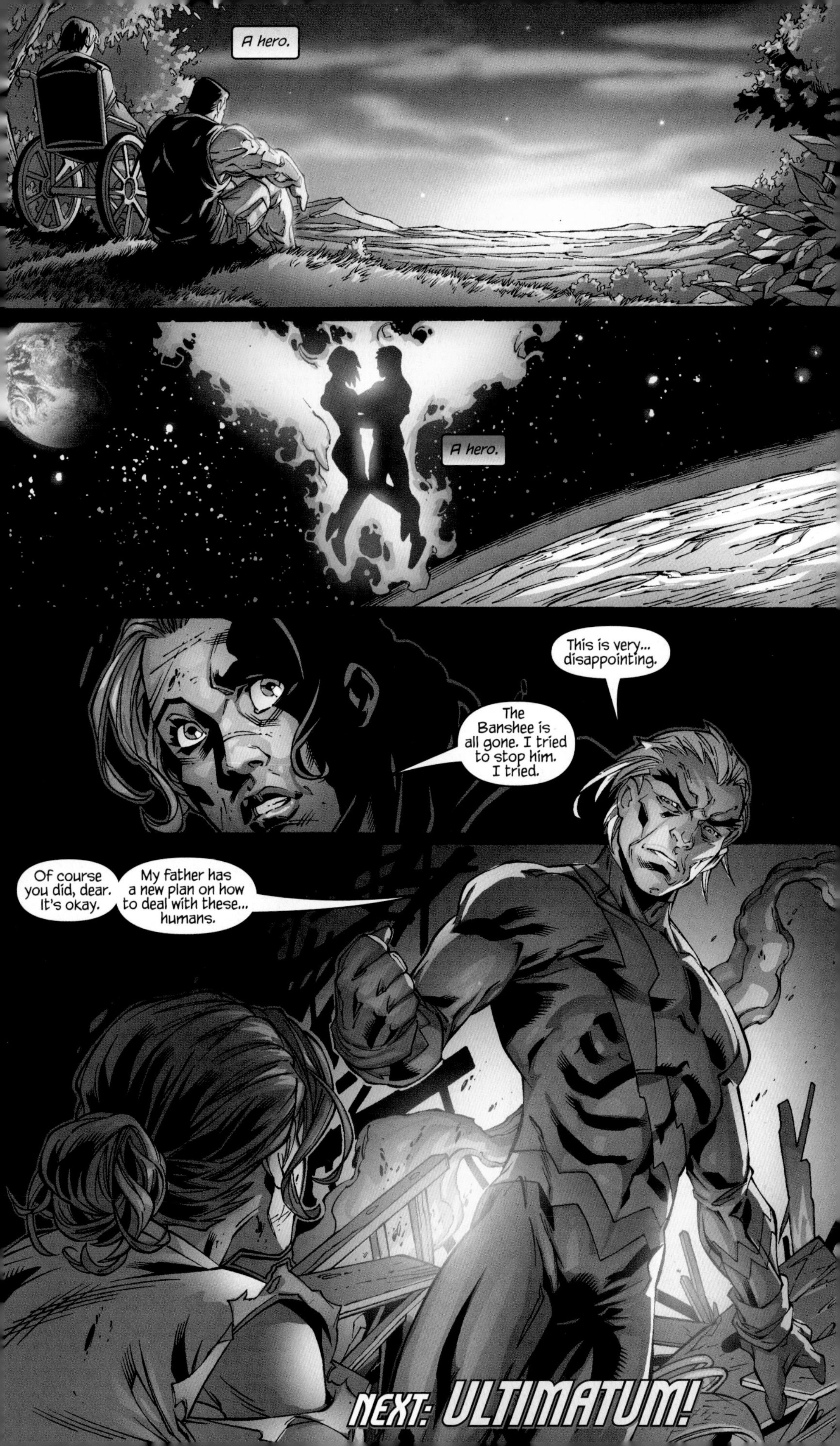
A hero.
A hero.
This is very... disappointing.
The Banshee is all gone. I tried to stop him. I tried.
Of course you did, dear. It's okay.
My father has a new plan on how to deal with these... humans.
NEXT: ULTIMATUM!

ULTIMATE X-MEN # 94

by

Aron E. Coleite

PAGE ONE

PANEL ONE - A COLD-WAR RUSSIAN PROPAGANDA FLYER OF CAPTAIN AMERICA. Like thos awesome JUAN DOE covers from 198. CAP leaps into ACTION. Face clenched i a mighty WAR CRY.

Russian WRITING covers the poster - reading, "ONE SOLDIER DOES NOT MAKE A ARMY." A PAIR OF HANDS holds the flier.

1 PIOTR'S CAPTION

All I ever wanted was to be a *hero*.

2 NIKOLAI RASPUTIN

(off-panel)

Piotr Rasputin! Those cows aren't going to milk themselves!

PANEL TWO - A simple bedroom. Bed. Dresser. Nothing fancy.

A 12-YEAR-OLD PIOTR (PETER) RASPUTIN stashes the CAPTAIN AMERICA flier unde his bed - you know - the place where you would stash porn.

Piotr doesn't look like the COLOSSUS we've come to know. He's skinny. A LANK BEAN-POLE of a kid, yet to grow into his body.

3 PIOTR

Be right there.

4 FLOATING TEXT

The Ust-Ordynski Collective. Siberia. 10 Years Ago.

PANEL THREE - Outside. The porch of the Rasputin Farmhouse. Simple. I could be Kansas.

Piotr, in a HEAVY COAT, is greeted by his father, NIKOLAI RASPUTIN. Nikola hands Piotr TWO BUCKETS. NIKOLAI is big, robust. He looks like an older ver sion of Colossus. His eyes are commanding, but there's a sensitivity to hi smile.

5 NIKOLAI RASPUTIN

Miriam's been acting up. So be a gentleman. Understand?

6 PIOTR

Yessir.

7 NIKOLAI RASPUTIN

Everything okay?

8 PIOTR

Yessir.

9 NIKOLAI RASPUTIN

You wouldn't *lie* to me? Would you?

10 PIOTR

Nossir.

PANEL FOUR - It's early. The SUN RISES on the horizon. Amazing oranges an pinks are starting to break through the blackness of night.

Piotr makes the long walk, BUCKETS IN HAND, across the beautiful snow cov ered fields of the Rasputin Family Farm. Each step leaves a footprint in th freshly fallen snow.

PANEL FIVE - The barn. Piotr sits amongst the CATTLE on a small work stool He's milking a COW, filling up his bucket.

11 ANATOL

(off-panel)

Piotr Rasputin?

12 PIOTR

Yes?

PAGE TWO

PANEL ONE - Large Panel. Standing just behind Piotr is:

ANATOL - a FAT, RUSSIAN MOBSTER. The GOONS standing with him are FATTER Dressed in heavy black overcoats and sporting SUB-MACHINE GUNS which SPIL OUT A HAIL OF GUNFIRE at:

Piotr. He turns his lanky body into ORGANIC STEEL. The BULLETS TEAR THROUG Piotr's CLOTHING and bounce off his SKIN. Piotr's scared out of his mind.

The COWS behind Piotr aren't so lucky - getting torn apart by the gunfire.

1 sfx: BDAM BDAM CHING B-DING ZING

EL TWO - Piotr falls to his knees amidst the carnage. The COW'S BLOOD stain hands. His face hangs - saddened - why the hell did they do this?

tol LOOMS over Piotr.

2 ANATOL

Dr. Zavadsky was right. You *are* one of those... Post-Humans. A *mutant*.

3 PIOTR

Please... *please* don't tell my father... he doesn't know... he wouldn't understand... he...

4 ANATOL

You're secret's safe with me.

EL THREE - On Anatol. Sinister.

5 ANATOL (CONT'D)

You know who I am?

6 PIOTR

(off-panel)
Anatol Spichkin. The Mobster.

7 ANATOL

Businessman. Russia's not a Communist farm anymore. When you want to *really* do something with your life, I have a job for you. Come see me at Pushkins.

NEL FOUR - Piotr watches Anatol head out the barn doors.

8 PIOTR

What...? What am I supposed to tell my father about these cows?

JEL FIVE - Tight on Piotr's SULLEN, STEEL FACE. We see Anatol reflected in otr's skin.

9 ANATOL

(off-panel)
You've lied to him about being a mutant. You'll figure something out.

GE THREE

NEL ONE - A beautiful, eagle-eye shot of the XAVIER estate. Mansion. untain. We can see a BASEBALL GAME in progress on the ball field.

1 FLOATING TEXT

Xavier's School for Gifted Children. Westchester County. Today.

NEL TWO - CYCLOPS is on the PITCHER'S MOUND -- staring down MARVEL GIRL - playing CATCHER. NIGHTCRAWLER stands ready at the plate. HAVOK's calling LLS AND STRIKES. Cyclops and Marvel Girl communicate telepathically.

2 MARVEL GIRL

(thought bubble)
Get your head in the game, Slim.

3 CYCLOPS

(thought bubble)
After everything with Xavier. And Apocalypse. And *you*. Jean, you come back here like nothing happened. Are we going to talk or...

4 MARVEL GIRL

(thought bubble)
No. Not today. Right now all I want is a fastball - outside corner. Nightcrawler has no reach.

NEL THREE - REVERSE SHOT ON: Wolverine and Firestar -- WATCHING the game rom the bleachers. (Baseball game in the BG) Wolvie's got a beer in hand. it, he seems particularly interested in the newbie - Firestar. Firestar eans back, totally bored out of her friggin' skull.
n the BG game, Nightcrawler gets a HIT. ROGUE steps into the batter's box.

5 FIRESTAR

So, Logan, the X-Men play baseball for fun? What do the Ultimates do, *Book Club*?

6 WOLVERINE

I know something else we could do, Firestar. You know… *fun*.

7 FIRESTAR

So... I'll pretend you never said that and... if you hit on me again I'll burn the hair off your nipples.

fx = CRACK

ANEL FOUR - Nightcrawler stands at first base, being held on by COLOSSUS. here's a tension between them. Colossus refuses to look at Nightcrawler.

8 NIGHTCRAWLER

Peter.

9 COLOSSUS

Kurt.

...this is awkward...

11 COLOSSUS

Why? Because the last time you saw me, you told me I was going to He
for being gay?

12 NIGHTCRAWLER

Yeah… *that*.

PAGE FOUR

PANEL ONE - Colossus looks away from Nightcrawler - focusing on his boyfr
NORTHSTAR - playing third base -- SUNSPOT takes a lead off the third
bag.

1 NIGHTCRAWLER (CONT'D)

Are you still... with Northstar?

2 COLOSSUS

Are you still King of the Morlocks?

3 NIGHTCRAWLER

It's more of a benevolent dictatorship. Listen, Peter...

PANEL TWO - On Nightcrawler. He looks somber. Trying to say the right t
here...

4 NIGHTCRAWLER (CONT'D)

I've been thinking. Seems it's the only thing I can do down in the
sewers and... you treated me like a *brother*. Like *family*. I'm sorry.
I was...

PANEL THREE - Cyclops THROWS the BASEBALL to Colossus who easily picks c
STUNNED Nightcrawler. Colossus is SMILING from ear to ear. Overjoyed.

5 COLOSSUS

(off-panel)
You're *out*!

6 NIGHTCRAWLER (CONT'D)

Vas? You *cheater*!

7 COLOSSUS

You should've been paying attention to the game.

8 ANGEL

(off-panel)
Hey! *HEY!* HELP!

PANEL FOUR - ICEMAN stands at the edge of the outfield. Angel and Daz
move to help.

Iceman looks like he's been through hell. CRACKS all over his ICY
and get this -- HIS ARM is BROKEN OFF. OFF! All that remains is an
STUMP.

9 ANGEL (CONT'D)

Bobby?! What the hell happened to you? Your *arm*...?

10 ICEMAN

(whispers, faded print)
Run.

11 DAZZLER

What?

PANEL FIVE - Dazzler and Angel can only watch as:

Iceman CRASHES on the GROUND - BREAKING into a HUNDRED pieces. Three CHU
of HIS FACE are large in the FOREGROUND - FROZEN in a SILENT SCREAM.
12 SFX: KREESH

PAGE FIVE

SPLASH PAGE - Large Panel. We finally get to meet ULTIMATE ALPHA FLIC
They're on the move. Pumped and ready to throw down. They are:

VINDICATOR. Same basic idea as the original. The Captain America for Cana
Maple Leaf and all. He's the icon, so I think he should stay close to
original, but maybe, reverse the colors or something. The only thing
portant is that Vindicator has RED VIALS OF LIQUID attached to his unifo
Somewhere. Arms. Belt.

SHAMAN. We will learn that this isn't Michael Twoyoungmen, but actually J
PROUDSTAR (the X-Men's THUNDERBIRD.) Native American. Muscular. I think i
be awesome if his uniform was a combination - Shaman's colors or GREEN

STRANGE - but designed with Proudstar's Thunderbird Logo and DOMINO MASK. It'd
be awesome if his hands were in some sort of cool DR. STRANGE pose - powering
up with SUPERNATURAL POWER.

SASQUATCH. You know, Sasquatch. (Although this isn't going to be Walter
Langkowski, so...you can mess with it if you want to.)

AURORA. I'm a fan of the longhaired, sexy as hell, seductress Aurora (and not
the short haired '80s Duran Duran version.) I think she should be in the same
uniform as the original to help longtime readers help identify her.

SNOWBIRD. The ethereal goddess. Except maybe, let's make her an actual
ESKIMO or INUIT. All in WHITE polar-bear fur and leather - her CAPE BILLOWING
as she flies in the AIR. She looks like the ANTI-STORM.

SUNFIRE. That's right. SHIRO YOSHIDA. I'm a big fan of the CONTAINMENT SUIT
version of Sunfire from Age of Apocalypse - so I think a riff on that would
be appropriate. A FULL-BODY BLACK containment suit, that can barely hold in
his NUCLEAR POWERED FIRE.

JUBILEE. Punk rock. No uniform. Pierced. She's wearing a plaid school-girl
skirt and an open white button down shirt - underneath which we can see a
DAZZLER T-SHIRT (she's a fan.) Her eyes are GLOWING with energy as she CLENCHES
TWO MASSIVE FIREWORKS in her hand - ready to kick some ass.

1 VINDICATOR
I think he said, *"run."*

PAGE SIX

PANEL ONE - Firestar and Wolverine. She FLAMES up. Ready for the fight.
Itching for it. Wolverine holds her back - some of his own fire in his
eyes.

1 FIRESTAR
Bobby! Ohmygod. They... they *broke* Iceman!
2 WOLVERINE
Flame off. This isn't your fight -- it's *mine*.

PANEL TWO - Wolverine walks past Cyclops - handing him his beer - as if Cyke
is the team mascot.

3 WOLVERINE (CONT'D)
They call themselves *Alpha Flight*.
4 CYCLOPS
What's *that* supposed to mean?
5 WOLVERINE
Don't know. Don't care. They're rip-off Ultimates at best.
6 CYCLOPS
What's their beef with you?
7 WOLVERINE
Same as everyone else. We had a *past*. I betrayed them. They want re-
venge. Isn't that right, Mac?

PANEL THREE - On Vindicator. Energy is just crackling from his eyes.

8 VINDICATOR
I don't know who you *think* I am, but I don't have any fight with you.
9 WOLVERINE
    (off-panel)
You broke Bobby into a million pieces--

PANEL FOUR - Wolverine LEAPS - ARMS extended - CLAWS OUT. Just ABOUT to rip
the hell out of Vindicator. One of Wolverine's CLAWS is touching the RED VIAL
on Vindicator's Uniform.

10 WOLVERINE (CONT'D)
--my turn to break *you*!
  sfx: SKREESH

PANEL FIVE - Vindicator BLASTS Wolverine a MILE into the AIR - launching him
into the STRATOSPHERE.

  sfx: BA-WHOOOM

PANEL SIX - On Firestar. Looking up in the sky. How far did they launch
Wolverine?

13 FIRESTAR

Oy.

14 CYCLOPS
    (off-panel)
X-Men...

SPLASH PAGE - X-Men versus Alpha Flight. The start of a massive, epic ba
tle.

1 CYCLOPS (CONT'D)

...ATTACK!

2 VINDICATOR

I've got the telepath. Secure the target and take down the rest.

Vindicator FLIES INTO THE AIR and releases a DEVASTATING BLAST OF ENERGY th;
takes out MARVEL GIRL.

Cyclops and Havok team up - managing to get off BLASTS that SPLIT Alpha Fligl
-- but, it's not enough as --

SASQUATCH and SNOWBIRD run into action. SASQUATCH SHOVES SUNSPOT down int
the MUD -- his mouth is OPEN, FANGS GLISTENING in a ROAR about to lock horr
with ROGUE.

JUBILEE fires off BLASTS of her "FIREWORKS" - but now they're more lil
GRENADES. BOOM! BOOM! BOOM! She takes out Nightcrawler, Angel, Dazzler ar
others with her devastating BLASTS.

THIS IS WAR!

PANEL ONE - In the sky. The newbie Firestar goes head-to-head with Sunfir«
They're FIRE-JETS hit each other. A stalemate. (Like the duel between Harr
Potter and Voldemort at the end of Goblet of Fire.)

Firestar is obviously outmatched. Sunfire's FLAME is much stronger. Firestar
going to lose.

1 FIRESTAR

Little help. Anyone. *Hello*?

PANEL TWO - STORM flies up to help Firestar, but she runs smack into SNOWBII
- who NAILS Storm with an AVALANCHE OF SNOW.

2 STORM

I'm com-aaahhhHHHH!

3 SNOWBIRD

Call yourself a *Goddess*? You're nothing but a *golden cow*.

PANEL THREE - Sasquatch has ROGUE pinned to the ground with one hand - whil
holding a BOULDER in the other - about to smash it down on Rogue's head.

4 SASQUATCH

I'm not letting you touch me. I remember the last time.

5 ROGUE

Do I know you?

6 SASQUATCH

Tsk, tsk. Now that would be giving it all away.

PANEL FOUR - Cyclops and Havok fire their respective ENERGY BLASTS at SHAMAl
Shaman hovers above the ground, his legs crossed in the LOTUS position, a
if this was the easiest thing ever. Shaman holds his HANDS in DR. STRANC
incantation position, creating MYSTIC SHIELDS (see John Romita JR's version c
this - it rocks) which easily deflect Cyclops and Havok's assault.

7 CYCLOPS

Keep concentrating, Alex.

8 HAVOK

I'm pouring everything I have and -- and it's still not enough. What
the hell do these guys want?

9 VINDICATOR

(off-panel)
Northstar...

PANEL ONE - On Aurora and Vindicator - floating menacingly in the sky - look
ing downward.

1 VINDICATOR (CONT'D)

You are *property* of the Canadian Government and will return to duty at
Department H. Immediately.

2 AURORA

Come now, brother. There's no need for this to get uglier.

PANEL TWO - Colossus, STEEL, stands in front of Northstar - guarding his bo;
friend.

3 COLOSSUS

Jean-Paul...?

                    4 NORTHSTAR
Peter. Please. I ran away from these monsters. You... you don't know
what they're capable of.

                    5 COLOSSUS
Don't worry. They won't lay a hand on you.

NEL THREE - Same shot as 1. Except Aurora, speed streaks coming off her
dy, holds an UNCONSCIOUS NORTHSTAR over her shoulder and VINDICATOR let's
f an ENORMOUS BLAST OF ENERGY

                    6 AURORA
You were saying?

                    7 VINDICATOR
Get him back to the jet. Playtime's over everyone. It's time to bolt.

NEL FOUR - Colossus pulls himself out of a deep crater. Pissed as all hell.
 only see his EYES as he emerges.

    sfx: CHOOM

GE TEN

NEL ONE - Shaman FLIPS OVER Cyclops EYE-BLAST.

                    1 CYCLOPS
How'd you avoid my...?

                    2 SHAMAN
I'm not a magician...

NEL TWO - Shaman LANDS - PIVOTS AND BASHES Cyclops in the face with the
CK OF HIS FIST -- SUPER STRONG -- CRUSHING his VISOR and knocking Cyclops
nconscious.

                    3 SHAMAN (CONT'D)
…I'm a *mutant*!

NEL THREE - In the FG, Cyclops falls to the ground with a THUD. In the BG,
lpha Flight -- silhouetted -- walk away from the battle.

                    4 SHAMAN (CONT'D)
And Alpha Flight is gonna make that name *mean* something again.

NEL FOUR - The cockpit of Alpha Flight's jet. Alpha Flight take their seats
s they return from the battle. Northstar is unconscious. Aurora is just
inishing restraining him. Snowbird's in the driver's seat. Jubilee's rid-
ng shotgun.

                    5 SNOWBIRD
Jubilee, I can't believe you wore that shirt. We're supposed to be
professionals.

                    6 JUBILEE
I wanted to get Dazzler's autograph, Snowbird. I didn't know I'd be
blowing her up.

                    7 VINDICATOR
How's your brother, Aurora?

                    8 AURORA
Ready for the trip north.

NEL FIVE - Vindicator looms over Snowbird's shoulder.

                    9 VINDICATOR
Why aren't we off the ground?

                    10 JUBILEE
    (off-panel)
Something's holding us back.

                    11 SNOWBIRD
Not something…

GE ELEVEN

NEL ONE - Splash-esque. Large. Colossus GRASPING onto the tail of the JET
 as the FLAME from the ENGINE pours out all over him. Drenching him in FIRE.
urning off his clothes.

hen, three smaller panels along the bottom of the page.

                    1 SNOWBIRD
"…Some*one*."

NEL TWO - AURORA floats - UPSIDE DOWN - near Colossus. Smiling. The taunt-
ng witch.

                    2 AURORA
Fight's over, *mon abruti*. Let go.

Never.

                              4 AURORA
You're truly in love? It would almost be romantic if it wasn't so *des-perate*. You have no idea what you're up against.

PANEL THREE - SUDDENLY: Colossus is covered in darkness. He's shocked.
Jet. Aurora. It's all gone. Where did everything go?
                              5 AURORA (CONT'D)
        (tail-less balloon)
I move faster than light - and I can steal it away from you.
PANEL FOUR - Colossus can only watch -- Defeated -- smoke rising off his me
frame -- as Aurora and Alpha Flight disappear into the distance.
                              6 AURORA (CONT'D)
    Au Revoir, Homme de Bidon!

PAGE TWELVE

PANEL ONE - Later. The Infirmary. ICEMAN'S in the FOREGROUND. STILL I
but REASSEMBLED. Monitors attached to him.
                              1 BEAST
        (off-panel)
Rogue and Bobby are going to be fine. Turns out you *can* put Humpty
Dumpty together again.
PANEL TWO - Widen to find -- Beast, Marvel Girl, Cyclops, Dazzler and Ang
Colossus sits away from the group - armored - smoke still coming from
body.

                         2 BEAST (CONT'D)
The implications of Iceman's abilities are incredible. We need to con-
tact Professor X -- immediately.
                              3 MARVEL GIRL
No. Xavier needs to rest. Recover. We can handle this ourselves.
                              4 COLOSSUS
We're wasting time. We have to find Northstar.
                              5 CYCLOPS
I know you're worried about your boyfriend, but...
PANEL THREE - Colossus gets right up in Cyclops face. Angry as all hell,
trying to control his rage.
                              6 COLOSSUS
But, *what*...? If it was Jean we'd already be on the Blackbird. They
abducted him!
                              7 CYCLOPS
And kicked our collective ass in the process. There were only five of
them.
                              8 COLOSSUS
We were caught off guard!
                              9 CYCLOPS
Five, Pete. Five against Twenty-Five. If we're going to war -- we
need more information.
                              10 WOLVERINE
        (off-panel)
I think I have something.
PANEL FOUR - Beast and Marvel Girl turn to see Wolverine standing in the doc
way. He still has the BLAST HOLE on his shirt where Vindicator nailed hi
                              11 MARVEL GIRL
Logan. Are you okay? Where the hell did you land?
                              12 WOLVERINE
Maine.
                              13 MARVEL GIRL
You're kidding.
                              14 WOLVERINE
Nope. Good local beer up there. Had a helluva time hitching a ride
back. But, I knew you'd all wanna see this...
PANEL FIVE - Tight on Wolverine's hand -- he's holding a VIAL filled with
RED LIQUID (the one he snatched from Vindicator earlier.)
                              15 WOLVERINE (CONT'D)
Nabbed it offa Vindicator. Alpha Flight's secret weapon. A *drug*.
Power-enhancer. They call it *Banshee*.

GE THIRTEEN

NEL ONE - Marvel Girl takes the vial from Wolverine. Dazzler looks on.

1 WOLVERINE (CONT'D)

Fentanyl. *Mutant-Growth-Hormone*. Testosterone. Dopamine. It's liquid *nightmare*. Addictive. *Lethal*.

2 MARVEL GIRL

I've never heard of it.

3 DAZZLER

No offense, but you're not exactly *street* -- living Upstate -- in a mansion. No offense.

4 MARVEL GIRL

None taken.

NEL TWO - On Dazzler. Keenly aware that her piercings and tattoos make her ry much an outsider.

5 MARVEL GIRL (CONT'D)

(off-panel)
So, what is it? How does it work?

6 DAZZLER

Gives normal humans temporary powers. Flight. Invisibility. Heard about one kid -- thought he was intangible and jumped in front of the F Train. Poor sap.

NEL THREE - On Beast -- thinking -- Marvel Girl in the BG.

7 MARVEL GIRL

And what would happen if a mutant took it? Hank?

8 BEAST

I think we just saw it, Jean. Secondary, even tertiary mutations.

9 MARVEL GIRL

In English.

10 BEAST

We're not fighting mutants here. These guys... They're *gods*.

NEL FOUR - Marvel Girl looks at Colossus. His face is cold. Stoic.

11 CYCLOPS

(off-panel)
I want everyone in the Danger Room. Now that we know what we're up against. We're gonna start running scenarios. We've gotta be smarter, better, faster.

NEL FIVE - Marvel Girl turns to Cyclops as the others exit the room. She's ncerned.

12 MARVEL GIRL

Something's wrong with Peter.

13 CYCLOPS

Yeah... *Northstar was kidnapped*.

14 MARVEL GIRL

This isn't about that. At least, I don't think it's about that. I don't know. I have to read Peter's mind.

GE FOURTEEN

NEL ONE - Cyclops grabs Jean's hand - as if that could stop her.

1 CYCLOPS

Wait, just-- Don't you remember how we all felt about Xavier?

2 MARVEL GIRL

So?

3 CYCLOPS

Everyone suspected he was reading our thoughts. *Manipulating* us. People don't know what to think since you came back. Don't give them a reason to fear you.

4 MARVEL GIRL

Oh, Scott. They already do.

NEL TWO - Marvel Girl makes a little Phoenix in her hand, cradling it - ke a pet.

5 MARVEL GIRL (CONT'D)

Why do you think Vindicator took me out first? I don't need Banshee to become a god. I already *am*.

NEL THREE - Marvel Girl is central. Cyclops behind her.

                    6 MARVEL GIRL (CONT'D)
    Peter's our friend. And he's hurting. I can find out why.
                    7 SCOTT
    Just because you *can*, doesn't mean you *should*.
                    8 MARVEL GIRL
    He won't even know I'm...

PANEL FOUR - Marvel Girl stays in the exact same part of the panel, as s
goes into COLOSSUS' MEMORY. Maybe she's colored differently - more ether
al. (Or maybe the memory is colored in Black and White and Marvel Girl's
color.)

Marvel Girl is back at Colossus' childhood farm (from page one and tw
Nikolai stands outside Piotr's BEDROOM DOOR.

                    9 MARVEL GIRL (CONT'D)
    ...there?

                    10 NIKOLAI RASPUTIN
    Piotr Rasputin. I've been calling you for ten minutes!

                    11 PIOTR
        (off-panel)
    Just a minute.

PANEL FIVE - But, Nikolai doesn't like the secrecy. He opens the door.
                    12 NIKOLAI RASPUTIN
    What're you doing in here?

                    13 PIOTR
        (off-panel)
    Dad! No!

PAGE FIFTEEN

PANEL ONE - Nikolai and Marvel Girl look down at Piotr in his bed, NAKE
with another BOY. Piotr and the Boy are embarrassed - trying to get out
bed. Trying to get out of this compromising position. But, the image is ve
clear. (Please make sure the bed sheet or blanket covers their crotches.)
                    1 PIOTR (CONT'D)
    Dad. I can *explain*! I...

PANEL TWO - Over Piotr's shoulder as he looks up at his father. Nikolai hea
off into the house -- his face, sad - disappointed. Not engaging his so
Marvel Girl watches Nikolai go. Saddened by Peter's pain.

PANEL THREE - Marvel Girl stands in the same place, as the scene around h
changes.

We're now in the back of a FANCY RUSSIAN RESTAURANT -- Piotr stands -- ha
literally in hand as he talks to Anatol -- sitting in his PRIVATE BOOTH. (
the table is a full spread. Caviar. Cornish game hen. Vodka. Vodka. A
Vodka.

                    2 ANATOL
    I'd love to offer you a job, Piotr -- however, I *can't*.
                    3 PIOTR
    But, you said...

                    4 ANATOL
    Turning your skin into steel might make you *bullet proof*, but Dr.
    Zavodsky says you can barely lift your own arms. Weak as a little
    girl. Totally *useless*.

PANEL FOUR - On Piotr. Hang dog. Rejected.
                    5 PIOTR
    The metal is heavy, it's...

                    6 ANATOL
        (off-panel)
    Go home.

                    7 PIOTR
        (whisper, faded text)
    I can't.

                    8 ANATOL
        (off-panel)
    What's that?

                    9 PIOTR
    I said I *can't*. Go home. Not *ever*.

PANEL FIVE - Anatol BITES into his CAVIAR - some of it dribbles down his chi
Pig.

                            10 ANATOL
Well... There is *one* solution -- if you're *willing*.   They call it
Banshee. It will make you -- *effective*.
                            11 PIOTR
     (off-panel)
Yes, of course -- *anything*.
                            12 ANATOL
That's my boy.
NEL SIX - Marvel Girl watches, horrified -- as Piotr ROLLS UP his sleeve,
atol procures a HYPODERMIC NEEDLE filled with a RED FLUID - BANSHEE.
                        13 MARVEL GIRL
Peter. Please. Please say you didn't... You're *not*.
                            14 PIOTR
Why...? Why do they call it Banshee?

GE SIXTEEN

NEL ONE - SPLASH-ESQUE - An amazing collage of images -- that all hit Marvel
rl in a barrage.

 the middle, dominant - Colossus and Marvel Girl's FACE - merged together
half and half - SCREAMING FOR DEAR LIFE. AGONY.

ound the perimeter we see various images from Colossus' life and the entire
n of the Ultimate X-Men series. Including:

atol INJECTING Young Piotr with the Banshee.

rvel Girl meeting Colossus for the first time - in BOOK ONE. Marvel Girl
gs Colossus.
                        1 MARVEL GIRL
You are not alone. Welcome to the X-Men, honey.

lossus THROWING a SENTINEL in the air (from BOOK SIX.)

 the Locker Room -- Colossus, in full X-Men costume, shooting up Banshee
 as Storm pokes her head around the corner.
                            2 STORM
Colossus, Pete -- we found Magneto. We gotta run.
                            3 COLOSSUS
I'll be right out. Just a minute.

lossus PUNCHING OUT Magneto.

lossus buying a suitcase filled with BANSHEE VIALS from a MYSTERIOUS SHADOW
GURE.

NEL TWO - Back in reality. The KITCHEN. Colossus, in flesh form, picks
mself up off the floor. The aftermath of Marvel Girl's psychic cry. His
se is bleeding. There's a BROKEN GLASS of ORANGE JUICE on the floor.
                    4 COLOSSUS (CONT'D)
Jean!

GE SEVENTEEN

NEL ONE - The Danger Room. The X-Men (Wolverine, Nightcrawler, Angel,
azzler, Storm, Beast, Firestar) spar against ROBOTS -- that vaguely resemble
e shape of Alpha Flight. Wolverine's distracted.
                         1 WOLVERINE
Did'ja just hear something?

d then --

NEL TWO - SPLASH-ESQUE - Marvel Girl, all TK'd up, CRASHES BACKWARD right
rough the DANGER ROOM'S CEILING -blasting apart metal and flooring and
ires and insulation and stuff.

t on her trail, leaping through the hole is COLOSSUS. Pissed as hell. He's
st PUNCHED Marvel Girl. And he's looking to inflict more pain.

 sfx: BA-DOOM

GE EIGHTEEN

NEL ONE - Colossus LANDS, in the most kick-butt pose possible -- All piss
d vinegar. Furious. Ready to throw down.
                         1 COLOSSUS
You had no *right*!

NEL TWO - Storm sends Colossus HURTLING to the wall in a SUDDEN and FURIOUS
st of wind. Marvel Girl lying at her feet.

Peter! What the hell's going on here?

                    3 MARVEL GIRL
Colossus is *using* Banshee. He's lied to us. He's an *addict*.

PANEL THREE - On Colossus, pinned to the wall.

                    4 COLOSSUS
It's a *necessity*. Just because I turn to steel, doesn't make me super
strong. Banshee makes me --

                    5 MARVEL GIRL
(off-panel)
Effective.

PANEL FOUR - On Marvel Girl, picking herself up off the floor. Her
bloody. Practically crying.

                    6 MARVEL GIRL
Peter. This... You're *killing* yourself. You know that. Right?

PANEL FIVE - On Angel and Firestar. Angel, ever looking to be the voi
reason.

                    7 ANGEL
Isn't this...Isn't this the same thing the Ultimates do? Power-enhanc
ing drugs? Like Giant-Man?

                    8 FIRESTAR
I heard Giant Man's a *junkie*.

PANEL SIX - On Colossus getting pissed - defensive - argumentative. Get
up in Wolverine's face.

                    9 COLOSSUS
And what about Captain America? He used the super-soldier serum to
become a better warrior.

                    10 WOLVERINE
There's nothing you can say that's gonna make this okay, Pete.

                    11 COLOSSUS
There's no difference!

                    12 WOLVERINE
I *know* Cap. You're no Cap.

PAGE NINETEEN

PANEL ONE - On Nightcrawler, pissed -- Cyclops entering behind him.

                    1 NIGHTCRAWLER
That's *bull*! How many lives has Peter saved? Our lives?

                    2 CYCLOPS
Ease up, Kurt.

                    3 NIGHTCRAWLER
No, Scott. It's easy to judge when you can heal from gunshot wounds c
stop bullets mid-air. But, the rest of us aren't as lucky.

PANEL TWO - Colossus picks up one of the Danger Room ROBOTS HEAD in his h
Like Hamlet holding Yorick's skull.

                    4 COLOSSUS
Villains are getting more dangerous. They'll do *anything* to get what
they want. We must be willing to do the same -- or we'll get *buried*.

                    5 MARVEL GIRL
(off-panel)
Are you suggesting we use Banshee?

                    6 COLOSSUS
Yes, Jean... I am.

PANEL THREE - Marvel Girl. Eyes fiery. Phoenix creeping out.

                    7 MARVEL GIRL
We are *not* having this discussion. This is a drug free institu-
tion. *Zero tolerance*. If anyone is using -- you will be *expelled*.
Understood?

PANEL FOUR - TIGHT ON COLOSSUS - We only see his CHEST and THE BOTTOM OF
FACE. Marvel Girl is reflected against his metallic skin. The reflectio
distorted. Monstrous. She offers out her hand.

                    8 MARVEL GIRL (CONT'D)
(off-panel)
Peter... You're addicted. You're addicted and you don't even realize
it. Let me... I can *help* you.

9 COLOSSUS
And if I say no -- will you *force* me to quit? You have the power.
Will you *abuse* it? Does that make you any different than me?
NEL FIVE - Marvel Girl powers off. Turning her head away. Shamed.
10 COLOSSUS (CONT'D)
    (off-panel)
I'm going to get Northstar back. Consider me expelled.

GE TWENTY
NEL ONE - AN X-MEN TEAM PHOTO. The original team from Millar's inception.
ast. Storm. Colossus. Cyclops. Marvel Girl. Two hands hold the frame.
NEL TWO - In the foreground the picture is now in a TRASH CAN -- as Colossus,
g slung over his shoulder, heads out the door.
NEL THREE - Colossus walks alone across the Xavier estate. It's early. The
n rises in the distance. (Similar to pg. 2, panel 4)
NEL FOUR - In the HANGAR. The BLACKBIRD looms over Colossus - his ticket
t of Xavier's. Colossus looks up at the Blackbird.
1 CYCLOPS
    (off-panel)
You know how to fly that thing?
NEL FIVE - Colossus turns to see Cyclops.
2 COLOSSUS
If you've come to stop me…Don't bother.
3 CYCLOPS
Actually... I want to *help*.

GE TWENTY ONE
NEL ONE - Colossus walks past Cyclops.
1 COLOSSUS
And why would you ever think that I would actually trust you?
NEL TWO - Cyclops grabs Colossus by the shoulder, stopping him.
2 CYCLOPS
Because of Jean.
NEL THREE - On Cyclops.
3 CYCLOPS (CONT'D)
I love her. But she scares me. What if she ever turned against
us? None of us could stop her. Not one of us. We need -- *plans*.
Strategies.
NEL FOUR - On Colossus.
4 CYCLOPS (CONT'D)
    (off-panel)
We all need each other. Now more than ever. You can't do this alone.
NEL FIVE - Colossus looks away from Cyclops. Smiling.
5 COLOSSUS
I'm not alone…

GE TWENTY TWO
LASH PAGE - Colossus stands with his X-Men - all juiced up on BANSHEE - we've
ver seen the X-Men quite like this before!
ZZLER - her TATTOOS glowing with power, she's able to control HARD-LIGHT
NSTERS based on her TATTOOS. Maybe she has a couple of the BEASTS on GLOWING
ASHES.
GEL - who's mutated further, becoming more like an EAGLE (think of BEAK from
ant Morrison/Marc Silvestri's future X-Men.) Muscular. Wings for arms.
rd head.
GHTCRAWLER - turning his teleportation power into an offense weapon. He
elds BRIMSTONE BOLTS in his hands. And just wait'll you see what else he
n do.
GUE - now able to ABSORB MULTIPLE ABILITIES just by being in proximity -
ke Mimic. She's sporting STEEL SKIN, BLUE HAIR (with a LIGHT-BLUE STREAK,
OWING YELLOW EYES and WINGS.
1 COLOSSUS (CONT'D)
…Welcome to the X-Men.
2 FLOATING TEXT
TO BE CONTINUED!

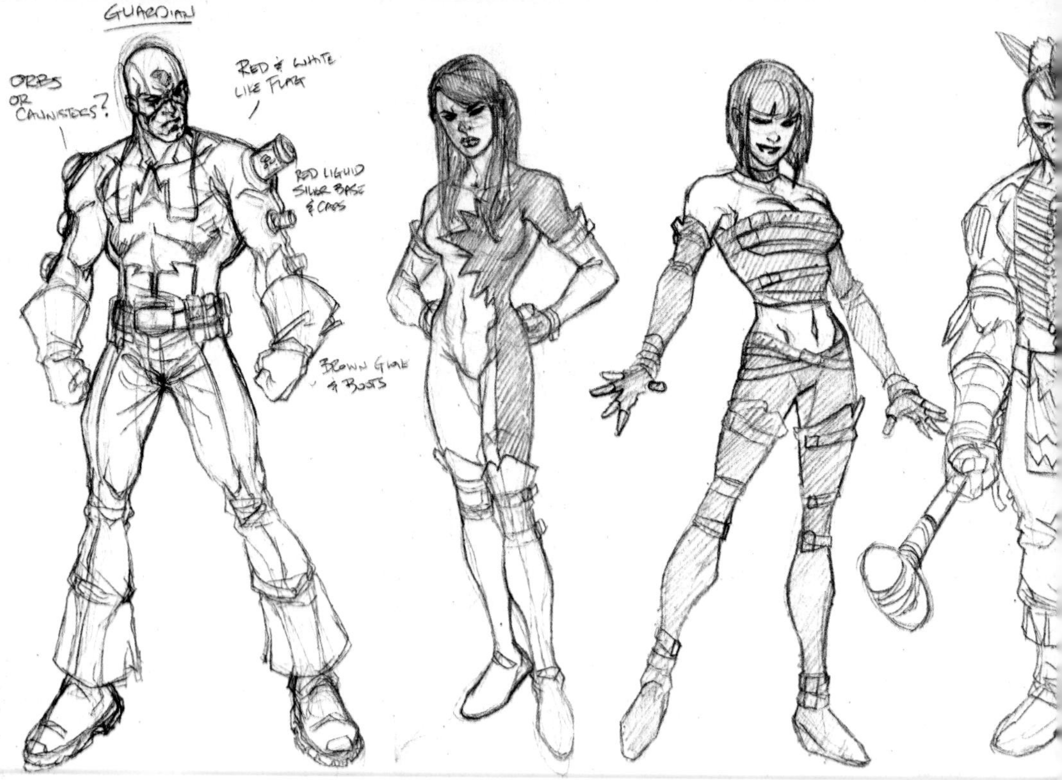
GUARDIAN
ORBS OR CANNISTERS?
RED & WHITE LIKE FLAG
RED LIQUID SILVER BASE & CAPS
BROWN GLOVE & BOOTS

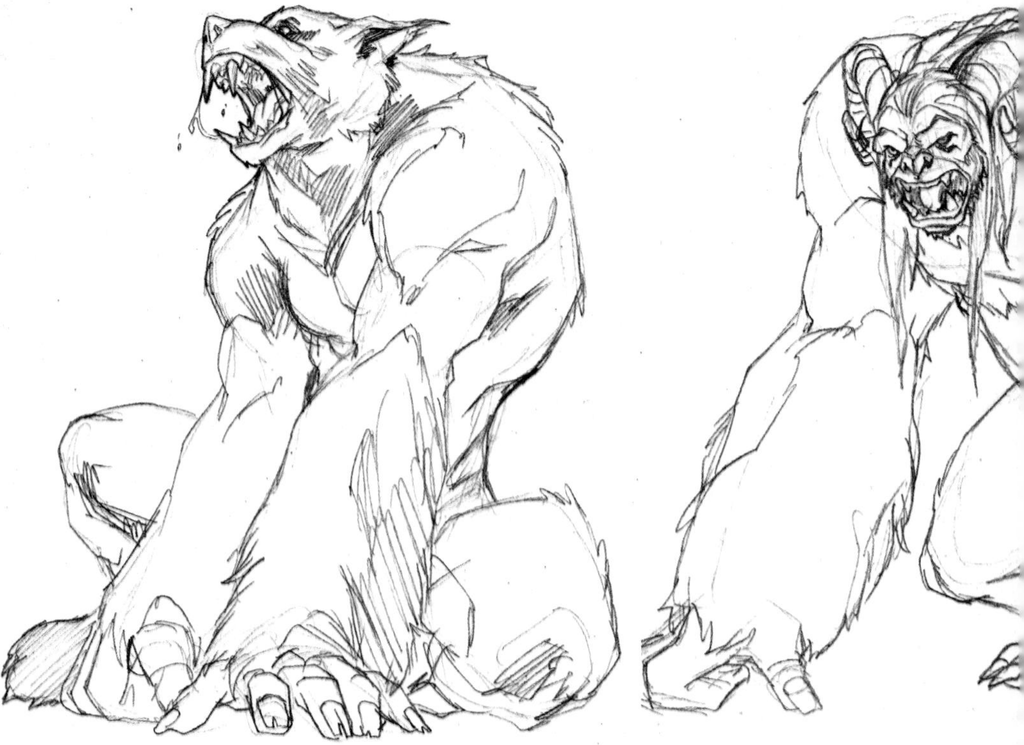

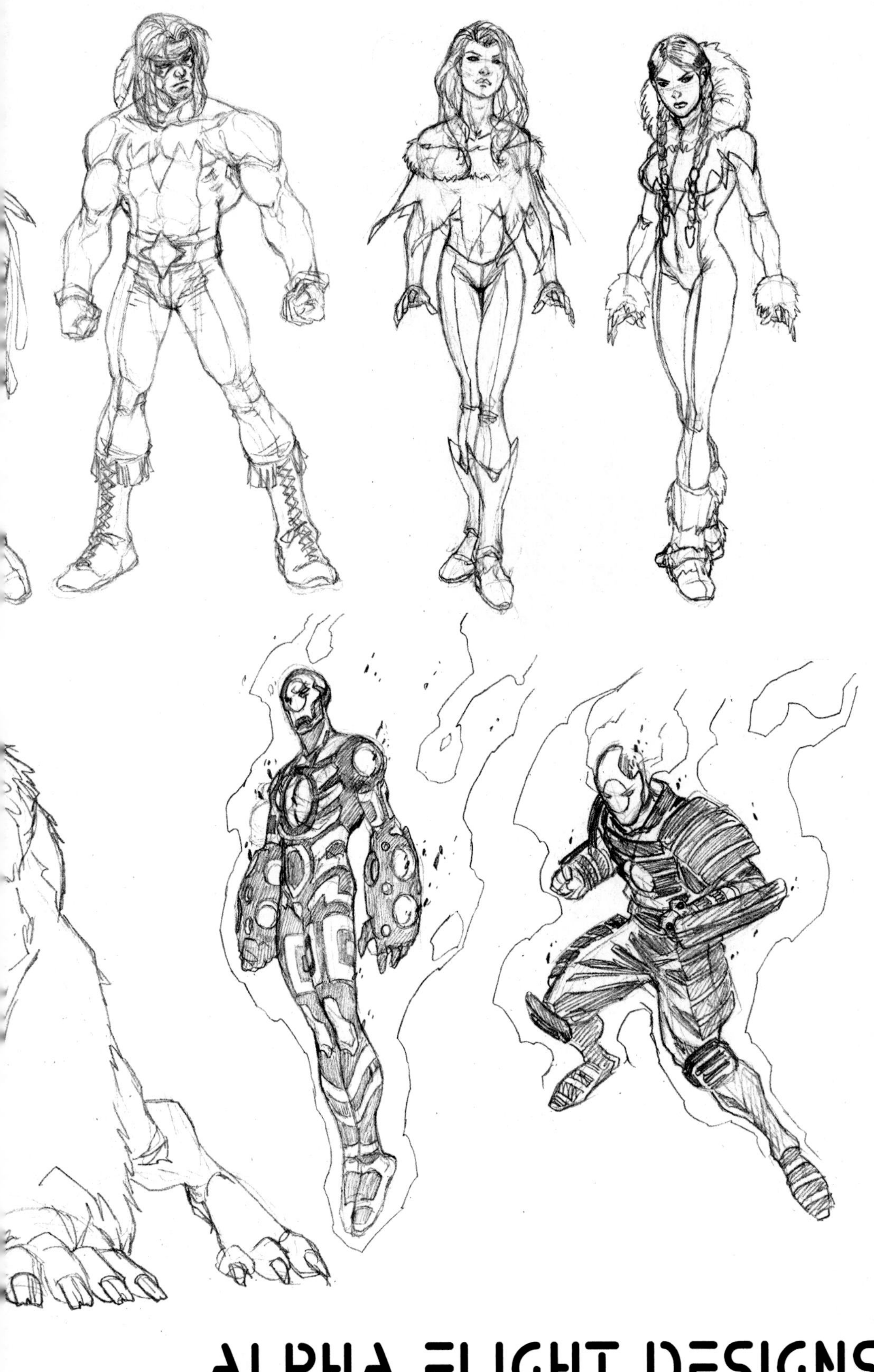

ALPHA FLIGHT DESIGNS

by Mark Brooks

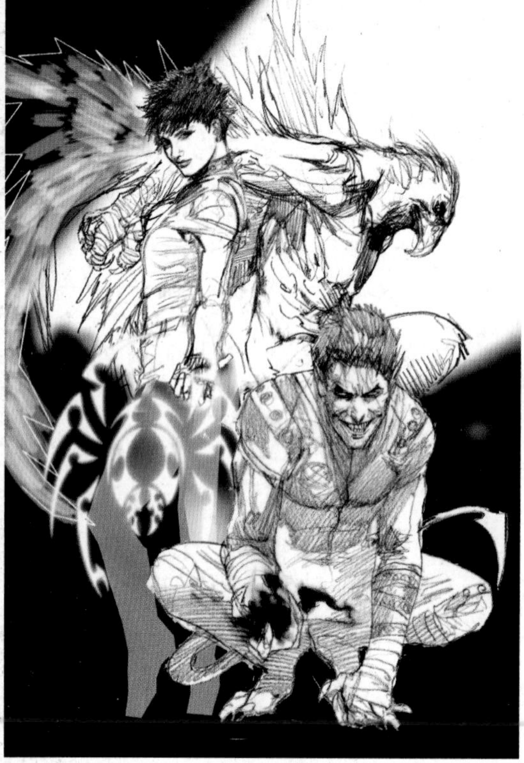
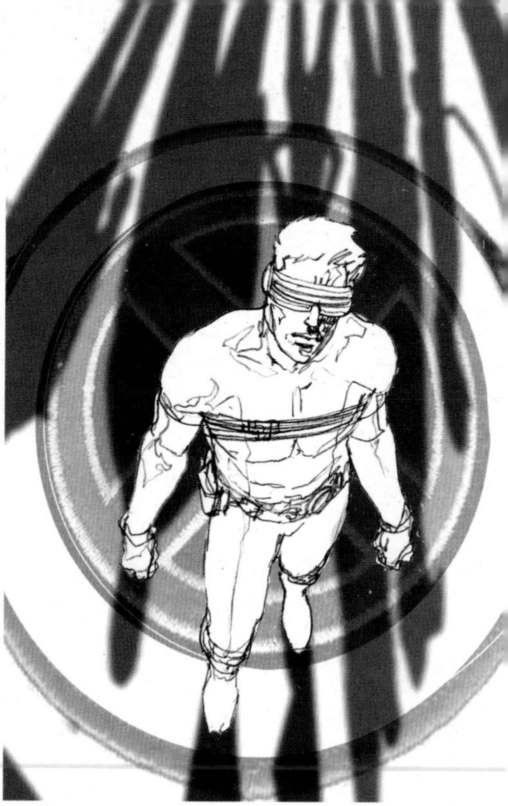
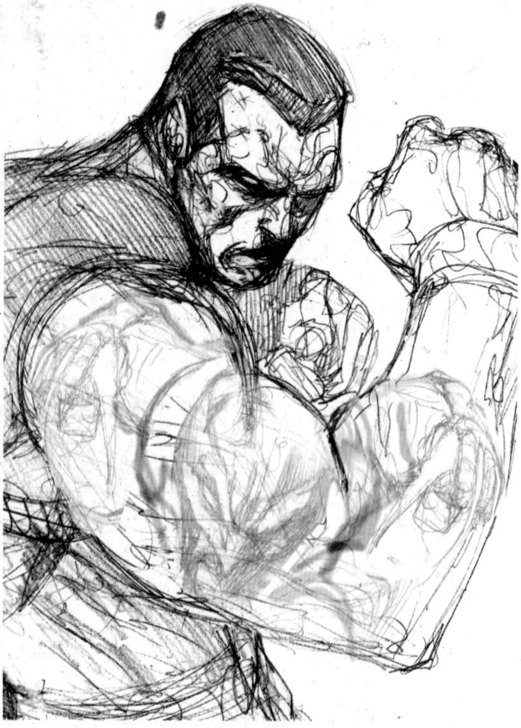
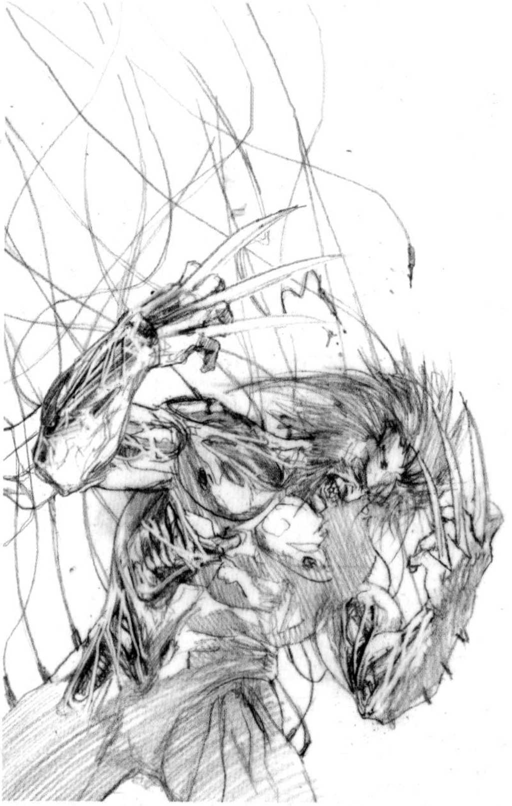

COVER SKETCHES

by Gabriele Dell'Ott